Just War
A Wadsworth
Casebook in Argument

Sharon K. Walsh

Loyola University Chicago

Evelyn D. Asch

Northwestern University

THOMSON
™
WADSWORTH

Australia • Canada • Mexico • Singapore • Spain
United Kingdom • United States

THOMSON

WADSWORTH

Just War: A Wadsworth Casebook in Argument
Sharon Walsh / Evelyn Asch

Publisher: *Michael Rosenberg*
Acquisitions Editor: *Dickson Musslewhite*
Editorial Assistant: *Steve Marsi*
Production Editor: *Samantha Ross*
Director of Marketing: *Lisa Kimball*
Executive Marketing Manager: *Carrie Brandon*
Manufacturing Manager: *Marcia Locke*
Compositor/Production Manager: *Shepherd, Inc.*
Cover Designer: *Joseph Sherman*
Printer: *Webcom Ltd.*

Cover Image: © The Museum of Modern Art/Licensed by SCALA/Art Resource NY. Rivera, Diego (1866–1957) © Banco de Mexico Trust. Agrarian Leader Zapata. 1931. Fresco, 7'9¾" × 6'2". Abby Aldrich Rockefeller Fund. (1631.1940)

Printed in Canada.
1 2 3 4 5 6 7 8 9 10 07 06 05 04 03

For more information contact Wadsworth, 25 Thomson Place, Boston, MA 02210 USA, or you can visit our internet site at http://www.wadsworth.com

ISBN 1-4130-0014-2

Library of Congress Control Number: 2003112831

Credits appear on Page 299, which constitutes an extension of the copyright page.

Contents

Preface

We have focused this book, both Part One on Argument and the Casebook on Just War and Peace, on the relationship between reading and writing and readers and writers. Our philosophy of teaching and our classroom practice have convinced us that good writing is stimulated by the challenges that meaty texts present. The readings you will find here come from the fields of religion and ethics, of political science and scripture. They center on the crucial issues of war and peace that have always concerned us humans but confront us even more starkly in these years after September 11, during which we have gone to war twice. The writers of these texts are some of the great thinkers of the past as well as thinkers of the present day, who struggle to deal with the horrors of war and see beyond them to the possibilities of peace. Augustine, Gandhi, Luther, the Catholic bishops, Aquinas, Walzer, and many others will create a conversation, a debate, an argument they invite us to join. Just as they engage passionately with ideas, they provide us the opportunity to do so. They demand that we understand what they have to say, respond to it, and go further to construct our own conversations, debates, and arguments.

The two parts of the book move from reading to writing. In Part I, Chapters 1 and 2 focus on understanding argument and its failures, with emphasis on analyzing exemplary texts. Chapter 3 presents a method for writing argumentative essays that are based on reading and research. Part II, the Casebook on Just War and Peace, also moves from reading to writing. Each chapter supplies background for each writer, includes questions about the texts and their argument, raises issues worth exploring, and provides ideas for writing as both conversation and argument. We have designed these features of the text to make challenging readings accessible to students. Chapter 4 traces the development of Just War traditions. Chapter 5 shows changes to and adaptations of these traditions. Chapter 6 explores peace positions, and Chapter 7 considers the Just War notion in practice during earlier American wars, the war in Afghanistan, and the war in Iraq.

There is also another relationship between readers and writers that we would like to explore: between your the readers of this book and us the authors. We imagine that your instructors are like us, enjoying the give and take of the classroom, sometimes snowed under by the papers we assign, but convinced that our students can learn to write well. We want our students to learn to write well by observing good writers in action, engaging in worthwhile discussion, and experiencing the urge to have their say. We imagine that you are like our students: lively, bright, often engaged with the class; but sometimes not, sometimes unsure of what you think, sometimes unwilling to say what you think, often lacking confidence in your writing skills.

We write this book for you, hoping that you will discover, as we did, that it is satisfying to chew on the ideas, engaging to enter a conversation with the writers and each other, and—even—fun to make one's own voice heard through argument.

Sharon K. Walsh
Evelyn D. Asch

Acknowledgments

This casebook on Just War grew out of our work with the Loyola University Chicago English Department Shared-Text Project. We are grateful to our colleagues who shared with us their philosophy of teaching and their recommendations for worthwhile texts and effective assignments. Their commitment to developing new course materials and to challenging their students has inspired us. We thank past and present members of the Shared-Text Committee, Angela Adams, Jennifer Ash, Claudia Becker, Joyce Fleming, Danielle Glassmeyer, Nancy Hostetter, Margaret Loweth, Carol Martin, and Sandra Urban. Margaret reminded us of the needs of all levels of students when creating questions and assignments. Carol, and her husband Dennis, helped us by suggesting sources and listening to ideas. Sandy generously shared some of the thoughtful writing assignments for which she is known. Frank Fennell, chair of the English Department, has been a strong supporter of the Shared-Text Project and of this casebook, and we thank him.

Our writing students continue to make our teaching challenging and rewarding. Our English 106 students in particular have contributed to this casebook by their stimulating discussions of the casebook readings and by their unexpected and insightful responses. Special thanks to Frances Ryder and Emily Fitzgerald, whose work appears in Part I and in the Appendix.

We would also like to thank Janise Hurtig for her comments on the manuscript, Carrie Eder for suggesting cartoons, and Rabbi Lewis Barth for suggesting passages from Maimonides and the Hebrew Bible. Dawn Lynn, of the Loyola Libraries, kindly assisted us with research assignments.

This casebook would not exist without the encouragement and enthusiasm of Jain Simmons of Thomson Learning. Special thanks to our editor, Dickson Musslewhite, who helped us to define the project and has answered our many questions. We appreciate his belief in us and his support of our work. Karen Judd and Samantha Ross at Wadsworth have ensured the smooth passage of our manuscript through production. We are grateful for their expertise and tolerance of our ignorance of the publishing process.

There would be no need of these acknowledgments without the support of our families. Dick Hartenstein, Sharon's husband, hotly debated the Iraq War with her, pushing her to see multiple sides of the issue, and provided unfailing encouragement. Evelyn's husband, John Tingley, not only made it possible for her to spend the many hours necessary for the project, but also drew upon his wide reading to suggest sources and ideas, and upon his editorial expertise to recommend revisions. Rachel and Nathaniel Tingley put up with a preoccupied and busy mother, finally inquiring if Sharon were moving in. We thank them all for their love and patience.

Is There Such a Thing
as a Just War?

On a bright blue day in September, our view of ourselves as Americans and our view of the world changed drastically. September 11, 2001, not only meant a terrorist attack that left thousands dead, but it also meant terrible images burnt into our consciousness: the collapse of the twin towers of the World Trade Center, a gaping hole in the Pentagon, and the remains of a jetliner scattered in a Pennsylvania field. The September 11 attack not only meant the end of our sense of invulnerability, our immunity from the kinds of wars that had wracked other continents during the twentieth century; but it also meant that all at once we were plunged into a new kind of war, the War on Terrorism. With this new war came the call of President George W. Bush to root out terrorist organizations like al Qaeda wherever they existed. Should a country harboring such an organization not have the will or the means to do so, the United States would supply both the will and the means. This is an assertion that needs to be questioned because it has led to war in Afghanistan and Iraq. One way of framing the necessary questions is to examine Just War thinking as it has developed over time.

The urgent and ongoing debate arising from these questions is not only about how we should respond to actual aggression by terrorists or states supporting them, but it is also about how we should respond to the threat of aggression. Some believe that attacking the Taliban in Afghanistan and, later, waging war against Saddam Hussein in Iraq

1

were appropriate actions according to Just War theory, the longstanding tradition that has formulated the criteria by which wars may be judged. Others would say that war is never justified. Still others argue that these conflicts do not constitute a just war.

To understand this debate, we will examine some of the classic texts defining the Just War tradition; texts that modify or expand this tradition; texts presenting peace positions; and applications of these positions to earlier wars. Then we will look at how these arguments have been applied to the post–September 11 actions of the United States.

Admittedly, the debate we have framed in this casebook is couched in academic terms, but its relevance to our real world lives should be clear to us, citizens and residents of the United States alike. The decisions our leaders make may cost many their lives. The choices we make when we elect our representatives will have a great impact on both how safe we will be and what kind of country we will have. The conversations, debates, and arguments we will have concerning Just War do matter, for they will affect the way we, readers and writers together, think about this crucial and unavoidable concern of our new century.

PART ONE

Analyzing and Writing Arguments

1

Analyzing Arguments

Recognizing Arguments

Imagine this scene: Two adults are screaming at each other, hurling insults and accusations back and forth. Or this: Children trying to decide on which game to play engage in a shouting match. Because we describe these activities by the term "argument," we often think of argument as a negative activity. We might ask our children or our friends not to argue, as if arguing were only the equivalent of fighting or disagreeing. For our purpose though, argument refers to a very common and widespread process by which we draw conclusions from evidence that has been laid out or make decisions based on reasons provided. Argument is not so much about winning or losing, though we do talk about debate in those terms; it is more about concluding, deciding, solving or resolving, persuading, all very positive and practical human activities.

Where Is Argument Found?

Argument pervades our private and public discourse. We make arguments, whether in speech or in writing, when we raise questions and answer them; demonstrate problems and solve them; or outline issues or alternatives and delineate the ways to address or decide them. Through argument we weigh evidence, alternatives, and competing claims. Through argument we may come to theoretical answers and solutions, but we also make decisions or choices that will lead to action in the real world.

The Private Sphere

Argument is a large component of our private thoughts, our stream-of-consciousness. A writer debates internally how she should organize her text; she sketches out possibilities, evaluates them, and then chooses. A student lays out problem-solving strategies and selects the one most likely to succeed. We argue with ourselves: I should major in business because I'll be able to get a job. We engage imaginary opponents: Dad, you should help me with grad school since I received a scholarship for college tuition.

Important also to family life, argument ranges from the trivial to the serious as a way to negotiate differences: Who will sit in the front seat? What movie shall we see? Where shall we go on our vacation? How shall we budget our money? What values shall we teach our children?

The Professional and Business Domain

Argument is central to contemporary medical practice as doctors can no longer rely on their patients' unquestioning acceptance of the doctors' dictates. Rather, canny doctors list the reasons pro and con of a medical procedure or treatment, weigh them, and offer a medical opinion.

Underpinning business and commercial life, argument appears in business plans, proposals, loan applications, marketing strategies, ad campaigns, and stock recommendations. From team decision making to the deliberations of the board, both employees and managers use argumentative strategies to arrive at decisions.

The Public Forum

Intrinsic to making a case in our law courts, argument structures a trial as the prosecutor opens with what is to be proved, provides the requisite evidence to support this claim, and makes a closing statement demonstrating what has been proved. The defense's role is to undermine or rebut the prosecutor's argument. Demonstrating that the prosecutor's evidence is flawed, countering it with other evidence, or constructing an alternative theory of the case are all ways defense attorneys strive to attack the prosecutor's case.

Argument is crucial to our democratic deliberations, particularly in the debate format where the reasons for or against an issue or proposition are weighed. We see it in speeches given in Congress to argue for the passage of a bill or by the president to the American people to lay out the reasons for going to war.

The Academic Classroom and Symposium

Finally, argument is fundamental to our academic discourse. Every time we formulate a thesis and prove it, or establish criteria and weigh the value of a work of art against them, or provide statistics or other evidence to support an assertion, we engage in argument. Students write essays, professors write articles, and scholars give papers. Faculties debate curricula and policy, departments argue for appointments and tenure, and students debate issues. These argumentative strategies have a long history, begun by Aristotle in his *Rhetoric.* More recent discussions of argument include the Toulmin and Rogerian methods. Toulmin argument is rooted in Aristotelian logic, but replaces the syllogism with a **claim** and **warrants** for that claim. The **Rogerian** method (explained very fully in Robert Miller and Robert Yagelski's *The Informed Argument* [Wadsworth]) focuses on locating a common ground between arguers or arriving at consensus.

What Are the Components of Aristotelian or Classical Argumentative Strategy?

Argument is closely allied to **rhetoric,** the study of how language may be used to achieve a desired effect. Those who follow Aristotle's guidance utilize or respond to three elements of argument: **ethos,** the persona that speakers or writers project to their audience; **logos,** the type of reasoning on which the argument is based as well as the content of the argument; and **pathos,** the emotional appeals speakers and writers make to their audience. Each of these strategies may be used legitimately or validly, or they may be used fallaciously.

Notice that both speakers and **audience,** the listeners to or readers of the argument, have reciprocal roles in each element of this triad. Speakers and writers must always keep the audience in mind when trying out an argumentative strategy. Unless the audience responds as expected to this strategy, the argument cannot be called truly successful.

Ethos: Evaluating the Writer's Assumptions, Credentials, Reputation, and Use of Authority

Discussions of argument based on the Aristotelian model generally begin with ethos because we intuitively give much weight to the trustworthiness of the speaker or writer. If we do not trust the speaker or believe the writer to be qualified, we are likely to dismiss the argument no matter how good the logic. We can determine the persona writers project to their audience by asking questions like the following: What kind of person is the speaker or writer? What does he or she believe? How do those beliefs underlie the argument? Is this someone with appropriate credentials? How do we know from evidence within the text? Are there sources outside the text that will help us find out? How do other experts and the writer's peers esteem this writer? What sources or authorities does the writer rely on? Given the answers to the preceding questions, how can we judge the writer's credibility?

Assumptions

What are the speaker's assumptions, premises, beliefs, and values that underlie or stand behind the argument? Does the speaker or writer make them explicit, presume the readers share them, or hide them?

Thomas Jefferson's *Declaration of Independence* (see p. 182 in Casebook) makes explicit a set of beliefs or convictions from which his premises follow. His thinking is grounded in eighteenth-century political philosophy. He spells out his assumptions, so all his readers can make the connections between his assumptions and premises. Probably few of Jefferson's readers could have enunciated the basis for the claim that "whenever any Form of Government becomes destructive of these ends, it is the right of the People to alter and abolish it," so Jefferson does it for them, making an interlocking chain of assumptions: Men are created equal and are also given inalienable rights by their creator to "Life, Liberty, and the pursuit of Happiness"—the divine rights of humans rather than the Divine Right of kings! And wonder of wonders: "to secure these rights, Governments are instituted among Men"! Governments are not put in place merely to perpetuate power or to ensure the prosperity of the rulers, nor should they be imposed upon the governed through might; rather, they derive their power from the consent of the governed. When all these preconditions are in place, then and only then can Jefferson state his first premise with some possibility that it will be accepted.

In his September 2002 speech to the United Nations (U.N.), American President George W. Bush has a different challenge (see p. 223 in Casebook). His primary audience, members of the U.N., knows what its mission is, but he must recall the delegates to that ideal and urge them to take action against Iraq, lest the U.N. be found lacking the will to back up its resolutions with consequences. To this end, he states his assumptions when he recalls the hope for peace and the means of resolving conflict that the U.N. represents: "The United Nations was born in the hope that survived a world war—the hope of a world moving toward justice, escaping old patterns of conflict and fear." He also reminds the members that the U.N. developed the Security Council so that, unlike the League of Nations, "our deliberations would be more than talk, our resolutions would be more than wishes." Later when Bush proceeds to enumerate the resolutions the Security Council passed and the demands it made vis-à-vis Iraq, the implication that the U.N. risks becoming a toothless giant if it does not enforce its resolutions hangs in the air.

Credentials

What education, training, experience, knowledge, and expertise does the speaker or writer have? What evidence of the speaker's credentials is there within the text? What outside sources can help us determine these credentials? We suggest consulting such biographical and bibliographical sources as the *Encyclopedia Britannica, Who's Who, Contemporary Authors,* university/department Web sites and library listings.

Even if we did not know that Jefferson had a wide-ranging intelligence and would serve his country as ambassador to France and as president, we can discern from *The Declaration of Independence* his skills as a logician and rhetorician.

Whatever one thinks of President Bush's mediocre college performance, he has both an MBA from Harvard and business experience, and was a two-term governor of Texas. Most important, though, his position as President of the United States provides him with the credentials to make policy and speak for the United States. As commander in chief of the military, he can send troops to enforce the resolutions of the United Nations.

Reputation

How do peers and colleagues review the work? Do they value its contributions to the field? What is the quality of the forum in which the writer is published? Is it a major newspaper or a respected press? How has the response to a writer or speaker changed over time? Has the reputation increased or diminished? To find book reviews, good sources are the London *Times Literary Supplement* (TLS), *New York Times, New York Review of Books, Book Review Digest, Chicago Tribune,* journals of opinion, and professional and scholarly journals. *Contemporary Authors* and the *Dictionary of Literary Biography* provide assessments of authors' reputations.

To illustrate the importance of evaluating both the credentials and reputation of a writer, let us examine the credentials of Charles Colson, author of "Just War in Iraq" (see p. 234 in Casebook). Colson's academic background includes a B.A. from Brown University and a J.D. from George Washington University, both respectable credentials for writing about Just War theory. His inclusion in *Christian Century,* a reputable conservative publication, confirms Colson's qualifications as a worthy proponent of the prowar position. However, Colson's involvement with the Watergate scandal, subsequent felony conviction, and imprisonment raise red flags. For some readers, his conversion prior to going to prison and the prison ministry he established mitigate his offense. Other readers may question the sincerity of that conversion or determine that the felony conviction is sufficient to undermine his credibility.

Use of Authority

We use the word *authority* in various ways: The CEO has the authority (from the board or the stockholders) to make a decision. Here the CEO derives his power from those who employ him. I have the authority to sign checks for my aunt who signed a legal power of attorney permitting me to act in her name. The writer speaks with the authority earned by credentials and position. The words writers choose and the rhetorical and argumentative strategies they employ most certainly help create ethos. But authors can also add weight to their words by appealing to the authority of someone higher, more expert, more experienced, or more credible. Important questions to ask about credentials include the following: How does the writer use other authorities? Whom does the writer enlist or cite as an authority? Is it someone with better credentials than the writer's, ones pertinent to the topic, ones that readers will understand and appreciate?

Thomas Jefferson has authority to speak for the colonists, having been designated by the Continental Congress to draft *The Declaration.* He also uses God as his ultimate authority. In the introduction, he claims that "Nature's God" entitles a people, having found it necessary to dissolve its "political bands," to have a "separate and equal station." He assumes that "all men are created equal," and "that they are endowed by their Creator with certain unalienable rights." In his conclusion he also calls upon God as "Supreme Judge of the world" to witness their right intentions and expresses their "firm reliance on the protection of divine Providence." Calling on God as Creator, Providence, and Judge reminds his readers of their commonly held beliefs that God is all-encompassing and all-powerful and reassures them that the colonists' cause is just, binding them together in a series of morally necessary actions. For those among the British or the colonists who are frightened by the revolutionary nature of *The Declaration,* calling upon God strengthens the case.

President Bush uses two types of authority to validate his claims that Iraq is not abiding by the U.N. resolutions and that Iraq must be held accountable. He supports his assertion that Iraq has failed to fulfill Security Council Resolution 688 by citing a 2001 finding by the U.N. Commission on Human Rights. He refers several times to the findings of U.N. weapons inspectors. In addition, he states that the Secretary General's coordinator for the return of prisoners reported that more than 600 prisoners from the Gulf War remain unaccounted for, a breach of Resolution 686 and 687. U.N. members skeptical of the United States are likely to accept U.N. authorities where they might not accept U.S. intelligence agencies as an authority.

The more forceful appeal to authority comes from Bush's assertion that the United States will exercise its authority to act unilaterally if need be to achieve the righteous end of defending our peace and security, if the U.N. does not support its own resolutions. One might infer that Bush is referring not only to the peace and security of the United States, but also to that of the whole world. He does this twice. First he asserts that "the purposes of the United States should not be doubted. The Security Council resolutions will be enforced—the just demands of peace and security will be met—or action will be unavoidable." His final words reiterate that position: "By heritage and by choice, the United States of America will make that stand. And, delegates to the United Nations, you have the power to make that stand, as well."

Audience: Considering the Reader's Needs

The writer usually has a specific initial audience in mind, and the greater the writer's knowledge of those who comprise this audience, their values and assumptions, their desires, their knowledge, and their mental capacity, the more likely the argument is to succeed. Crucial questions for the writer are: Who is the intended audience? Does this differ from the actual audience? Is the audience likely to agree with the writer's assumptions? If not, what strategies might be used to find some common ground, to get the audience on the writer's side? What are the tone and language appropriate for the intended audience? In addition to the intended audience, we can think of the actual audience as a series of concentric circles radiating from the original audience. For a speech, the actual audience is people in the room, people who see it on television or the Web, people who hear it on the radio, people who read it the next day, and so on.

The audience must also assess the choices the writer has made. Has the writer kept the needs and desires of the various audiences in mind? Has the writer given them the information they need to understand the argument and done so without talking down to them or talking over their heads?

Jefferson, for example, must have had the colonists first and foremost in mind since he wishes to convince them that action to overturn the government is justified. The lengthy list of grievances must be intended to persuade them as well to pay "decent respect" to the views of the world. King George and Parliament are unlikely to be convinced by this argument, so Jefferson can expect only to declare that the American colonies are independent, not that Britain will accept this action. As for their British brethren, Jefferson hopes for some sympathy and, from other countries like France sympathetic to the desire to overturn a tyrannous king, more concrete forms of support like money and troops. Of course, Jefferson, well aware of the momentous nature of *The Declaration,* must also have been writing for the ages as well.

President Bush can assume that his audience of U.N. delegates takes the work of the United Nations seriously and does not want its power undercut by unilateral action by the United States, so he cautions the delegates to ask: "Are Security Council resolutions to be honored and enforced, or cast aside without consequence? Will the United Nations serve the purpose of its founding, or will it be irrelevant?" He has decided to gain the backing of the United Nations, so he uses language to establish common ground with it: "We owe it to all our nations to prevent that day [the Iraqis getting nuclear weapons] from happening" and "My nation will work with the U.N. Security Council to meet our common challenge."

Given the instant, worldwide communications available today, he must also keep this larger audience in mind. To his domestic audience for whom it is important that he gain U.N. support, he demonstrates that he is trying to do so. To those nations and people who are not convinced that Iraq has failed to comply with U.N. resolutions, he reiterates both Iraq's multiple breaches of these resolutions and the proof of these breaches. He defines his target audience in Iraq when he says, "If the Iraqi regime wishes peace, it will . . ." He repeats this refrain four times, underscoring both what specific demands he is making and that he speaks to the regime, not the Iraqi people.

Rogerian Argument: Finding Common Ground with Readers

Anyone who has worked on committees, boards, or councils understands the importance of finding common ground on which to base a decision; otherwise, decisions may be delayed or, if reached, so displease some members of the group that the group cannot function effectively. Here is where listening techniques derived from the field of psychology, especially from the work of Carl Rogers, are very valuable. If listeners can restate positions of the other group members clearly and fairly, acknowledge the strengths of a position they disagree with, recognize the weaknesses of their own position, and remind themselves of their common goals, the group will have a much better chance of reaching the consensus needed to make a decision. The outcome is less likely to be a narrowly-won victory and more likely to be a satisfactory determination.

While it is certainly possible to construct a written Rogerian argument using the process indicated above, argumentative essays are less likely to follow the Rogerian pathway, especially with hotly debated issues. Effective arguers do, however, borrow elements from this approach, particularly in introductions intended to draw readers into a discussion.

Raising objections to their own arguments is another way writers acknowledge the importance of their readers' positions. The latter strategy fails, however, if writers see readers' objections only as impediments to be removed from the argumentative ground. Rather, they must sincerely explore the strengths of a position contradictory to their own. Laurie Calhoun in "Violence and Hypocrisy" (see p. 114 in Casebook) undoubtedly senses that many readers will find her argument controversial, given that she accuses those that promote a war that will inevitably kill civilians of hypocrisy. Note how she uses an opening scenario to induce readers to come along with her by describing an experience that all readers should be able to see as wronging them:

> Imagine: You awaken in the middle of the night to the sound of piercing sirens. Suddenly the ceiling comes crashing down. You are trapped under rubble, bones broken, joints popped from sockets. Blood pours down your face from the gash on your head. Children are shrieking in the next room. The bombs continue to fall; your head begins to throb. You don't know how much longer you have to live or if you'll ever see your family again.

Because she uses powerful visual images and emotionally charged phrases like those in the last sentence of the quotation, Calhoun expects that readers will not only be engaged but also open to her case.

In the next six paragraphs, Calhoun adds controversy and complicates the issue, at each point probably losing the sympathy of some readers but hoping to bring other readers along with her to the end. This approach is more likely to gain a hearing for her argument than if she had started with "If you don't accept my position, you are hypocrites"!

The next two sections of Calhoun's essay, "The Just War Tradition" and "Noncombatant Immunity," illustrate how she listens to the other side by briefly enunciating the tenets of the tradition and by exploring fairly and at length how earlier thinkers have resolved problems associated with civilian casualties. At the same time, however, she provides linguistic signals that she does not "buy" these arguments to set up her own argument which will follow: "Whether 'collateral damage' victims have been wronged is supposed to be a function of the intentions of the people who dropped the bombs and the relative weight of devastation vis-à-vis the military objective achieved. Somewhat suspiciously, the answer given by military authorities always seems to be 'no.'"

Logos: Understanding the Writer's Reasoning

While logos suggests the English word logic, it goes beyond logic to consider the ways we think or proceed rationally. We think of logos as the heart of argument, for here we provide both the necessary information and the logical structure to convince our readers.

Induction

Inductive reasoning is the process by which we draw conclusions or generalizations based on a series of experiences or examples. It is the way much of our learning takes place. For example, if a child gets sick every time she drinks milk, we conclude that the milk has caused the illness. If a toddler burns himself by touching the lit burner of a stove and a lighted candle, he very quickly concludes that flames burn.

How Does Inductive Reasoning Translate to Argumentative Writing?

Induction can lead to very sophisticated and successful arguments. *The Declaration of Independence* relies heavily on a series of examples to prove its case. The body of the document is a lengthy list of the outrages perpetrated by the government of Great Britain against the American colonists. Jefferson lists eighteen categories of outrages that King George has perpetrated against the Colonies, what Jefferson calls "a history of repeated injuries and usurpations, all having in direct object the establishment of absolute Tyranny over these States." A short list of grievances would not have the same impact. He also builds his case by saving the most heinous offenses, assaults on life, for the last five positions in his list. At the end of these "Facts . . . submitted to a candid world," few could argue that his generalization is unfounded.

Induction also plays a significant role in President Bush's September 12, 2002, address to the United Nations, urging the group to enforce its sanctions against Iraq. The weight of his argument comes from the listing of the U.N. resolutions that Iraq has abrogated. First, Bush asserts that "by breaking every pledge . . . Saddam Hussein has made the case against himself." In subsequent paragraphs, Bush lists U.N. resolutions which were broken, years in which breaches occurred, and specific breaches that occurred (paragraphs 11–21). Howard Zinn in "A Good Cause, not a Just War," an essay published in *The Progressive* (see p. 214 in Casebook), also uses an inductive strategy when he argues against the morality of the War in Afghanistan, listing multiple instances of harm inflicted on civilians. Note that such a long list is logically persuasive, but it also has emotional impact.

Argument by Analogy

Argument by analogy is a legitimate form of inductive reasoning that uses similarities between examples to draw conclusions. When we draw on our experiences, we may reason by analogy. For example, a teacher might reason that students in class A are like those in class B and that the same lesson would therefore work as well in B as it did in A.

Many writers also seek out historical analogies to bolster a point. Susan Thistlethwaite does this in " 'Just War' or Is It Just a War?" (see p. 231 in Casebook) when she compares the prospect of Americans waging war on Iraq to the behavior of the barbarians sweeping from the north at the time of Augustine. Howard Zinn uses definition to create an analogy between war and terrorism. In his view, what connects them is that in both cases civilians are killed. Zinn does not, however, distinguish between the terrorist's intention to kill civilians and an army's attempt to avoid killing civilians.

Both of the analogies in the preceding paragraph raise the question of how many points of similarity are necessary to make the analogy valid. In the following example, there appear to be important points of comparison:

Jewish immigrants to the United States have thrived economically due to their strong belief in education and solid family structure. Korean immigrants also value education highly and have tight family networks. Therefore, Korean immigrants will succeed the way the Jews did.

These apparent similarities may not hold up under scrutiny, however. Perhaps the two groups may have different views of the role of education. Other differences may also be significant: Jews came earlier to the United States in large numbers, they have a different religion from the American majority, and they are not racially identifiable. Koreans, on the other hand, have arrived more recently, almost all are Protestants, and they are racially distinct in appearance. Such differences outweigh the similarities given above.

Deduction

Deductive reasoning starts with a generalization (drawn either from induction or stated as an unproven assumption), applies it to a particular case, and draws a conclusion.

Syllogisms

These are the classic format for deductive reasoning. A syllogism has two premises, or propositions, from which a conclusion may be drawn. The following is Aristotle's famous syllogism, illustrating the deductive process:

All men are mortal.   (Major premise)

Socrates is a man.   (Minor premise)

Socrates is mortal.   (Conclusion)

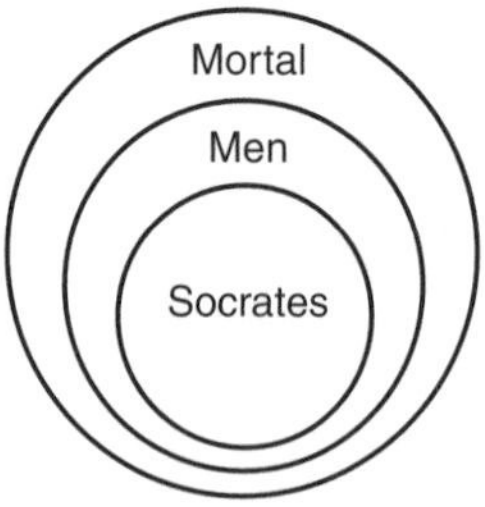

Figure 1-1

Note that here the **major premise** results from an inductive premise (though this is not always the case): all the people who lived in the past eventually died; we know people who have died; we do not know of any exceptions. It thus makes sense to state as a proposition that all men are mortal. The **minor premise** places Socrates in the category of men, that is, he shares the characteristics of men. Given that the entire category of men belongs within the category of mortal being, it makes sense that Socrates, who belongs to the category of men, must also be included within the category of mortal beings. Thus, we can conclude that Socrates is mortal.

To test whether a syllogism is valid, we can both apply rules and diagram the syllogism. Note that validity is not the same as truth. A syllogism may follow all the rules and still not be true because one or both of the premises are not true.

Rule 1. There must be three and only three terms (men, mortal, Socrates), each of which must refer to a discrete entity.
We can draw no secure conclusion from the following premises because the meaning of the middle term shifts. Being a Marxist and teaching Marxism are not the same. Belonging to one group does not mean automatically belonging to the other group:

All Marxists are communists.

Professor Jones teaches Marxism.

Professor Jones is a communist.

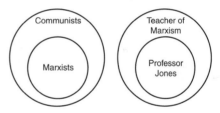

Figure 1-2

Rule 2. The middle term must be distributed at least once.
The **middle term** appears in both premises (in our first example, the middle term is "men") but not in the conclusion. To understand **distribution,** think of the meaning of the statement "all men are mortal." In a positive proposition or statement, the subject term "men" is distributed because "all" refers to every member of the group. Had "men" been modified by "some" or "most" it would not be distributed. The predicate term "mortal" is undistributed. We are essentially saying that men are only some of the mortal beings—others would be dogs, cats, carrots, roses, and so on. Note the illustration of this statement:

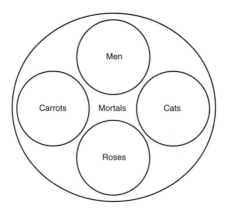

Figure 1-3

In a negative proposition or statement, the subject term is distributed if it is modified by "no." The predicate term is also distributed. In the statement "No cat is a human," we are saying that no member of the class of cats is any part of the class of humans. A diagram illustrates this proposition with two nonintersecting circles:

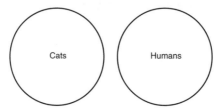

Figure 1-4

Rule 3. If a term is distributed in the conclusion, it must be distributed in the premise.

No local students are dormitory residents.

Some seniors are local students.

Some seniors are not dormitory residents.

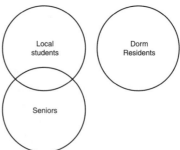

Figure 1-5

The conclusion is valid. Here the term "dormitory residents" is distributed both in the conclusion and in the premise. Look at what happens, though, in the following syllogism:

All local students are dormitory residents.
Some seniors are local students.
All seniors are dormitory residents.

The above conclusion is not valid. We cannot conclude "All seniors are dormitory residents" because the term "seniors" is now distributed in the conclusion where it is undistributed in the premise. We cannot make the extension from "some seniors" to "all." Try to draw your own diagram to illustrate this syllogism.

Rule 4. If a premise is negative, the conclusion must also be negative.

No British are Germans.

Carla is British.

Carla is not German.

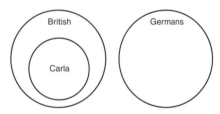

Figure 1-6

In this example, if Carla belongs to one group, she cannot belong to the other. Thus, we cannot logically conclude that "Carla is German."

Rule 5. No conclusion may be drawn from two particular premises.

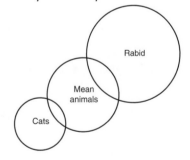

Some cats are mean animals.

Some mean animals are rabid.

Figure 1-7

Here we cannot conclude "some cats are rabid." Since there are, in addition to cats, other members of the class of mean animals, and some of these other mean animals are rabid, we cannot know for certain whether cats are rabid. We could draw a valid conclusion that "some cats are rabid," if we were to say that "all mean animals are rabid" and "some cats are mean animals" because then the middle term would be distributed.

Rule 6. No conclusion may be drawn from two negative premises.

All bimsy are not fimsy.
All fimsy are not mimsy.

We cannot conclude either that "all bimsy **are** mimsy" or "all bimsy **are not** mimsy." They may or may not be:

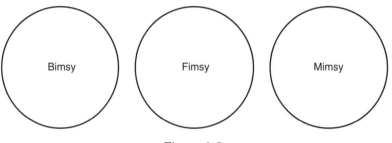

Figure 1-8

Exercises

Test the validity of the following syllogisms both by diagramming them and applying the rules. If no conclusion is supplied, supply the conclusion that will follow logically from the premises.

All humans are rational animals. Mary is a human.	All humans are rational animals. Mary is not a rational animal. Mary is a human.
All good students study for finals. Marge did not study for finals.	Some people are robots. All robots are intelligent. Some people are intelligent.
Some A are B. All B are C. Some A are C.	Some robots are intelligent machines. Some intelligent machines are expensive. Some robots are expensive.
No A are B. No B are C. No A are C.	All A are B. All B are C.

Hypothetical Syllogisms

These syllogisms start with a first premise consisting of an **antecedent** from which a **consequent** follows: If students get 70% or above (antecedent), they will pass the course (consequent). The second premise may either **affirm** or **deny** the antecedent or affirm or deny the consequent. The syllogism is **valid** if the second premise affirms the antecedent or denies the consequent.

If students receive 70% or above,
    they will pass the course.
This student received 70% or above. (Affirms the antecedent, so it is
She will pass the course.   VALID.)

This student did not receive (Denies the antecedent, so it is
    70% or above.   INVALID. There are other
He will not pass the course.   possibilities. Perhaps the teacher
    decided to curve the grade, and
    so the student passed.)

This student will not pass the course. (Denies the consequent, so
She did not receive 70% or above.   it is VALID.)

This student will pass the course. (Affirms the consequent, so
Therefore, she received 70% or   it is INVALID.)
    above.   (That same kind teacher!)

Enthymemes

Enthymemes are shortened syllogisms that we use frequently in speech and sometimes in writing. We might say, John is mortal because he's human. Or John is human, so he's mortal. In such structures, it is usually the major premise we omit, perhaps because it is obvious. Sometimes, though, we may not want to call attention to the major premise because it does not fully meet the test of distribution. For example, in the enthymeme, Professor White is a good writer because she teaches English, we may not be able to preface the major term with *all* but only *nearly all* or *most*. We certainly cannot say that *all* Professors of English are good writers, but we probably can say that *many* or *most* are. The following examples show strategies for expanding the enthymeme. Note that such linguistic clues as "because" and "so" may signal a premise or conclusion:

Because Mary was elected class president, we know she is popular. Since "because" points to a premise—usually the minor premise—the main clause must be the conclusion. So far the syllogism is taking shape like this:

Major premise:	[What belongs here?]
Minor premise:	Mary was elected class president.
Conclusion:	Mary is popular.

"Elected class president" must be the middle term since it appears in a premise, but not in the conclusion, and it also must be distributed at least once. So the major premise must be "All those elected class president are popular." The syllogism is valid, but is it true? Must a student be popular to be class president? Certainly this is often the case, but is it always the case? Might someone be elected because she is competent or a good leader though not popular? Probably the best we can do is say, *most* or *almost all* of those elected class presidents are popular.

When linguistic clues are missing, it can be harder to expand the enthymeme. If we are told, "John must be frugal. He was elected class treasurer," we assume there must be some connection between the two statements, but we cannot assume that the first statement is the premise and the second the conclusion. We can try each statement as the conclusion and work back from there to see if we can derive a major premise that will make a valid syllogism.

If "John is elected class treasurer" is placed as the conclusion, the syllogism would look like one of the following:

Major premise:	Those elected class treasurer are frugal.
Minor premise:	John is frugal.
Conclusion:	John is elected class treasurer.

Or

Major premise:	Frugal people are elected class treasurer.
Minor premise:	John is frugal.
Conclusion:	John is elected class treasurer.

But in the first case the middle term, "frugal," is not distributed at least once. In the second case, there is also a problem because we certainly cannot claim that all frugal people are elected class treasurer. If we make "John is frugal" the conclusion, we can get closer to validity, especially if we qualify the statement: Those elected class treasurers are likely to be frugal; John is elected class treasurer; therefore, John is likely to be frugal.

Exercises

Try your hand at analyzing the following hypothetical syllogisms, rephrasing the statements as necessary to determine their validity. Do not merely apply the rules, but try to think through why the conclusion does not follow from the premises:

1. If you file your taxes late, you will receive a penalty. You received a penalty. Therefore, you must have filed your taxes late.
2. I know you cannot graduate if you don't complete 168 units. Since you will graduate, you must have completed all 168 units.
3. If you don't have your passport, you won't be allowed on the plane for France. You have your passport. So you must have been allowed on the plane.

Expand the following enthymemes to make a valid syllogism. Is the syllogism also true?

4. Martha wears glasses, so she must be studious.
5. George is sick because he ate green apples.
6. Heather is gorgeous. She gets lots of dates.

How Do Deductive Reasoning and Syllogisms Transfer to Longer Arguments?

Essentially, deduction not only logically structures the reasoning process but also provides a framework for the argumentative essay or speech.

In *The Declaration of Independence*, for example, Thomas Jefferson sets up his first or major premise that a "government which becomes destructive of these ends" (ensuring the right to life, liberty, and pursuit of happiness of its citizens) may rightfully be altered or abolished. The body of the argument provides plentiful support for the second or minor premise: The government of Great Britain is destructive of these ends. ("The history of the present King of Great Britain is a history of repeated injuries and usurpations, all having in direct object the establishment of an absolute Tyranny over these States.")

The conclusion of the argument also provides the ineluctable conclusion of the syllogism: The government of Great Britain may rightfully be and is abolished. ("We, therefore, the Representatives of the united States of America . . . are, and of Right ought to be Free and Independent States; that they are Absolved from all Allegiance to the British

Crown, and that all political connection between them and the State of Great Britain, is and ought to be totally dissolved.")

George W. Bush's address to the United Nations (page 223) uses a series of arguments related to the hypothetical syllogism. For example:

> If the Iraqi regime wishes peace, it will "unconditionally foreswear, disclose, and remove or destroy all weapons of mass destruction" [paragraph 27].
> The Iraqi regime has not done so [supported by paragraph 18].
> Therefore, the Iraqi regime does not wish peace.

This syllogism denies the consequent, so it is a valid syllogism. To judge its truth, we must examine the second premise: Are the behaviors listed in paragraph 18 accurate and sufficient on which to base this assertion?

Toulmin Argument: Moving from Certainty to Probability

The contemporary philosopher Stephen Toulmin, has contributed another way of understanding deductive reasoning in his book, *The Uses of Argument* (Cambridge UP), by allowing for a lesser degree of certitude. The Aristotelian syllogism sets up a system that leads ineluctably from a universal statement or major premise to a conclusion. As our discussion of the enthymeme has suggested, though, there are many cases where we cannot argue with complete certainty. How often can we say something that applies to every member of a group? Instead of saying *all*, we may hedge our bets and say *almost all* or *most* or *many*. We often use adverbs to qualify our statements: *usually, frequently, often*. The terms Toulmin uses for the elements of argument reflect this lesser degree of certainty: the **claim** is what is to be proved; **qualifiers** indicate exceptions to or limitations of the claim; the **data** are the evidence or support for the claim; the **warrants** are the assumptions, principles, beliefs—stated or, often, unstated—that both underpin the claims we make and allow us to link the data with the claim. Toulmin includes two other terms, the **backing,** additional support for the warrant, and **rebuttal,** either critiques of an argument or counter-arguments.

The Toulmin method, though quite complex, can be simplified and adapted for the composition classroom; we call this a claim/reasons/specific evidence method, which many students find a useful process for analyzing and constructing arguments. To illustrate how this process works, we have annotated Michael J. Schuck's article, "When the Shooting Stops: Missing Elements in Just War Theory" (see p. 108 in

Casebook). We also provide an illustration of how an enthymeme may be expanded into an argument here:

Claim: What is the proposition to be argued or defended? What, if any, qualifications or exceptions does it have?

Motorcyclists and bikers who do not wear helmets should not be covered by insurance because this risky behavior often contributes to the severity of accidents and to raising their cost.

The **qualifier** here is the word *often*. Is the fact that risky behavior does not always lead to severe accidents or high cost enough to undermine the claim?

Reason I: (or subclaim) for supporting the claim: *Not wearing helmets contributes to the severity of accidents.*

Specific evidence: (data) supporting this reason or subclaim: *frequency and types of severe motorcycle and bike accidents* (**warrants:** *these injuries must clearly relate to having the head unprotected*).

Reason II: *Not wearing helmets helps to raise the cost of accidents.*

Specific evidence: *Head injuries can lead to various types of mental and physical impairment, necessitating costly treatments* (**warrants:** *must show both how the injuries lead to impairments and provide data on the cost of such treatments*).

Reason III: does not apply here, though many arguments have multiple reasons.

Specific evidence

Reason IV and so on: does not apply.

Specific evidence

Warrants: How can one justify connecting each reason with the claim as well as each piece of evidence with the reason it supports? The main warrant for the argument is: *Risky behavior that often contributes to the cost and severity of accidents should not be covered by insurance.* Whether one accepts this reasoning or not probably depends on how much store one places on taking responsibility for one's own acts.

Refutation

Dealing with objections raised about an argument or countering evidence supplied to support an alternative position is an essential strategy to win a hearing from readers who may be leaning to the other side or have already made up their minds. Many readers will raise objections that you fail to raise and may then decide your argument is not worth following because you have not shown yourself to be fair-minded.

Thomas Aquinas' *Summa Theologica* is a kind of rhetorical manual for winning over the audience by gaining their trust. Aquinas is an exemplar of the strategy of refutation: For every question that he debates in the *Summa Theologica* (see p. 69 in Casebook), he first presents the objections, then makes the argument, and then refutes the objections. Though Aquinas saves the refutation or answers for last, he also raises the objections first, not only to get them out of the way but also to reassure the audience that their questions will be answered. Aquinas also takes care to formulate the objections very carefully, giving them due weight and attention.

Unlike Aquinas, who frames his central argument with objections and refutation, Douglas Lackey centers the argument in "Pacifism" (see p. 154 in Casebook) on refutation. At first sight, Lackey's lengthy discussion of the varieties of pacifism seems to be an expository essay of definition. After presenting a fair and refined account of the positions of each type of pacifism—thus gaining his audience's trust in his intellectual honesty—Lackey creates an argument by refuting each position until he comes to his final case, antiwar pacifism. Here he answers objections others might make to this position, but does not add his own refutation, thereby signaling his approval of the position. You will find another example of refutation in the article by Shalom in which he gives a point by point critique of Richard Falk's support for the war in Afghanistan (see p. 194 in Casebook).

Pathos: Weighing Appeals to Emotion

Appeals to emotion can be a very powerful part of argument. Such legitimate appeals often speak to the best parts of our humanity, our sympathy for the sufferings of others, our altruistic desires to improve our world, our outrage against those twisted individuals who inflict harm on the innocent, the unprotected, those who cannot protect themselves.

Through pathos, we also recognize that we are subject to multiple fears that may paralyze us or move us to action. Even when used judiciously, such appeals to emotion may, however, raise the hackles of some readers, so they must be used carefully.

Some useful questions to ask of appeals to emotion are: Does the argument lend itself to emotional support? Most likely a medical discussion of the advisability of taking one drug therapy or another does not lend itself to the use of emotion. Is the audience one that will respond positively or negatively to emotion? An academic audience may be turned off by emotional appeals, for example. Does the emotion strengthen or weaken the argument? Does it replace a weak logical structure?

Appeals to emotion can function legitimately in arguments as an adjunct to the logic they employ. *The Declaration,* for example, appeals for solidarity with the colonists' British brethren: "we have appealed to their native justice and magnanimity, and we have conjured them by the ties of our common kindred to disavow these usurpations." The list of causes, though generally couched in measured terms, does in fact name heinous deeds: "He has plundered our seas, ravaged our Coasts, burnt our towns, and destroyed the lives of our people." The powerful verbs Jefferson uses must heighten the sense of outrage the colonists feel.

Jefferson makes emotional appeals that, while effective, are subordinate to the logical structure. Howard Zinn's article in *The Progressive* (see p. 214 in Casebook), however, relies heavily on emotion in its first half. It seems fair to say that here pathos is not an adjunct to but a primary strategy of the argument. While granting that the war in Afghanistan had a just cause, he argues that the means by which the war was waged are unjust. His inductive list of examples to prove that assertion is very specific and sometimes anecdotal, detailing the attacks on children and the elderly: He notes an AP account of "a child barely two months old, swathed in bloody bandages" and "another child in the hospital because, according to the neighbors, the bombing raid had killed her entire family." Elsewhere he cites a *New York Times* account that "a young boy, his head and one leg wrapped in bloodied bandages, clung to his father's back as the old man trudged back to Afghanistan." For more than a page, Zinn lists the damage to an area, describes the injuries of the people, and tallies the number of dead and injured noncombatants. The cumulative impact of such specificity is powerful.

This discussion of pathos should make us remember our obligations to our readers if we have forgotten them as we become preoccupied with the mechanics of arguments. Readers are flesh and blood people who occupy a moral universe and care what ethos we present. They want to see our character as well as our credentials, reputation, and skill in finding authorities to support us. Readers are intelligent people who dislike being talked down to and recognize when we play fast and loose with logic or evidence. They respect order and clarity and truthfulness. Readers have hearts that make them respond to the predicaments of others, to the poor, the victims, the unfortunate. At the same time, readers resent being manipulated by writers who overdo appeals to emotions by relying on sentimentality or exaggeration. In the next two chapters we will explore both how we can lose the trust of our readers by fallacious reasoning and how we can gain it by careful, respectful reading, research, writing.

2

Avoiding Fallacies

Fallacies, whether deliberate or inadvertent, are failures in logical reasoning and argument. They can be categorized as failures in ethos, in logos, and in pathos. These fallacies may be found at every level of argumentative discourse. The child arguing that she should be allowed to go to bed late because her mother does and the teenager claiming he should be able to have a beer because his father does are both making fallacious claims. Newspaper letters to the editor are gold mines of fallacies with some writers oversimplifying issues, creating false dilemmas, and attacking leaders and candidates based on spurious reasons. Political ads may attack the character of a candidate rather than her positions or misstate the position of a candidate. To sell a product, television commercials, whether selling beer, lingerie, or cars, often appeal to multiple human desires, relying little on the intrinsic worth of the product and more on the product's purported ability to make the buyer happy or desirable.

Recognizing fallacies is important to you as a reader or viewer so that you can evaluate the claims that others make. It is crucial to you as a writer so that you can avoid distorting facts, overstating a claim, or drawing invalid conclusions.

Attacks on Ethos

Usually these are unjustified or irrelevant attacks on the character or credentials of the speaker. Not every attack on credentials or character is unjustified, however. It is necessary to make clear distinctions here.

Making a claim without the credentials to back it up can make the speaker a legitimate target. For example, Linus Pauling, who advocated large doses of vitamin C without the nutritional background or studies to support his claim, was excoriated by the scientific community despite his Nobel Prize. A failure in ethics can also undercut a speaker's credibility. People charged with enforcing laws cannot break them without losing credibility. Both Presidents Nixon and Clinton discovered that the American people take covering up wrongdoing and lying under oath very seriously.

Ad Hominem or Attack on the Person

Here the attack is on the speaker rather than the argument, focusing on something that has nothing to do with the argument:

- He's divorced. How can he have anything to say about funding for childcare?

Tu Quoque or You Too

A favorite of children towards their parents, the claim is that people cannot advise against or prohibit a behavior that they themselves practice.

- You smoke. How can you tell me not to do it?
- You're telling me to save my money? Look how much money you spent last year!

False Authority

We know that legitimate authority is vital to the writer's ethos. In the false authority fallacy, the argument relies on someone without the knowledge, position, or credentials to be an authority on the issue discussed. This fallacy is often seen in ads.

Michael Jordan may be granted authority to promote a brand of athletic shoes. However, this authority most likely does not extend to promoting a particular restaurant or car. There is no reason to think he has those credentials.

Failures in Logos
Errors in Reasoning

Many logical fallacies are related directly to failing to derive valid conclusions or construct valid syllogisms. The following might be called errors in reasoning:

Hasty or Illicit Generalization

Induction requires sufficient relevant examples on which to base a conclusion. A hasty generalization occurs when too small a sample leads to a suspect conclusion:

- I know two redheads who have bad tempers. It's clear that redheads have bad tempers.
- Terrorists who were Muslim were responsible for September 11. Muslims are a threat to the United States.

Stereotyping

Related to hasty generalization, a stereotype begins with a conclusion drawn about a group of people from a too limited sample and then applies that conclusion to a member of the group, implying that every member of the group shares that characteristic:

- Joan must be a gossip. You know what women are like.
- Men are sports freaks. Mark must spend his weekend glued to the TV watching football games.
- The Irish (or the Polish, French, Russians, Jews, Catholics, or Protestants . . .) are all _____ (fill in the blank). What can I say? She's Irish.
- I saw a picture of an Arab terrorist the other day. I'll avoid anyone who looks like him.

Stacked Evidence

Here the evidence supporting an assertion may be valid, but the writer or arguer omits other evidence that may weigh against it. In a criminal trial, for example, if the prosecutor were to omit a relevant fact that might lead to exoneration—perhaps an alibi—that would be stacked evidence.

Invalid Syllogisms

In deductive reasoning, failure to follow the rules of the syllogism, whether categorical or hypothetical, leads to an invalid conclusion, often called a non sequitur. You will recall that hypothetical, categorical, and invalid syllogisms are discussed in Chapter 1.

Faulty Analogy

Analogies can become faulty when similarities are stretched too far, or are outweighed by the differences between the examples being compared:

- A teacher reasons that two students, both named Meghan and both having blond hair, should receive the same grade.

Obviously, the unimportant similarities between the two students are inadequate for reasoning by analogy.

Fuzzy Thinking

These next fallacies may be attempts to sound as if one is arguing logically. Instead, they are fuzzy thinking or replacements for logic.

Begging the Question

Begging the question means restating a claim, in one form or another, without supplying any proof:

- The theory of evolution is just that, a theory. Charles Darwin has not made his case for evolution. Evolution has not been proven.

Circular Reasoning

An attempt at argument that goes nowhere, landing us back at the beginning:

- I have to have a car in order to get to work. And I need to work in order to buy the car.

False Cause

Assigning the wrong cause for an outcome or an incident is a kind of oversimplification, assuming that there is only one cause for an effect:

- Our sales shot up by 25% after we started using an internet pop-up.

This alone *might* have produced the result, but other factors might apply: The product might have been improved or the proximity of Christmas might have stimulated sales.

Post Hoc Ergo Propter Hoc or After This, Because of This

Another type of false cause involves saying that because something happened first in time it caused what followed. Eating spicy food may indeed produce heartburn, but many superstitions ascribe causality to an incident merely because it preceded the effect in time:

- You walked under a ladder today. That's why you had bad luck.
- Your horoscope warned you not to engage in financial transactions today. No wonder you lost money on the stock market.

What's One More or Less?

The question implies that numbers do not really matter, but they do. Too many people in a boat **will** make it capsize. Other examples include:

- I know the registration system says the class is full. Please let me in anyway. One person won't make a difference. (Not true: The teacher will have more work to do and the students will have fewer chances to participate.)
- Why should it matter if we have less than the required number for the tour group? What difference can one person make? (The missing person's fare would have helped cover the expenses of the chaperone.)

Attempts to Deceive

The following fallacies are usually deliberate attempts to deceive, sometimes by oversimplifying, sometimes by misdirection, sometimes by narrowing options:

Straw Man

This fallacy consists of constructing a weak or exaggerated argument in order to tear it down, claiming that it is the argument your opponent is making. However, your opponent has not made this argument:

- Consider this argument against pacifism: Pacifists always oppose violence. They think that the world can be changed by not responding to violence. They clearly do not understand the real world because they are blinded by their idealism. If pacifists were elected, we would be invaded the next day.

Here the arguer, by distorting the pacifist position, makes the argument seem poorly reasoned, even dangerous.

Red Herring

The red herring is named after a strategy used to train hunting dogs to follow the original scent. Dogs learn to ignore a strongly scented object like a herring that has been drawn across a trail. Thus, irrelevant or misleading statements that pull the audience away from the real argument are called red herrings.

- You've argued that our candidate has not been fiscally responsible. She has, however, beautified the city, constructing planters along every major street.

False Dilemma

Sometimes called **black or white reasoning** or the **either/or fallacy,** this fallacy is usually improperly couched as an either/or proposition. As long as there might be another possibility, the statement is fallacious:

- To have peace in the Middle East, either Ariel Sharon or Yasser Arafat must resign. Note that another possibility is that both must resign.
- Either we go to war with Iraq, or Iraq will sell nuclear weapons to terrorists who want to attack us.

Certainly there are other possibilities, including pursuing arms inspection and elimination through the United Nations.

Inappropriate Appeals to Pathos

Though appeals to emotion may be a legitimate adjunct to logic (see Martin Luther King Jr.'s powerful use of the harm that discrimination does to children in *Letter from Birmingham Jail*), they can also be used to *replace* logic.

Ad Populum or Pandering

These are appeals to emotions or desires that many people feel. Commercials and ads might appeal to sexual instincts, selling cars by implying that the gorgeous model will come with them.

At Christmas, children's toys are much more than toys, and Christmas cards more than a seasonal greeting: Ads for these products are targeted to adults as well as children and bring with them happy memories of home and a promise of warmth and good times.

The ad populum fallacy may also involve an appeal to fear. It was used during World War II to justify interning Americans of Japanese descent with the claim that they might aid the Japanese in attacking the United States mainland. In the current war on terror, it might take this form:

- Look at Ground Zero and the grieving survivors. Terrorists are plotting another massive attack on the United States. We must suspend civil liberties in order to prevent this attack.

Bandwagon

This fallacy invites us to join the parade or jump on the bandwagon. Because everyone is doing something, we should too. A favorite ploy of political consultants, the bandwagon appeal often involves showing a large group of people rallying around a candidate. A commercial example is the well-known Coke ad showing a huge group of diverse people while the jingle "I'd like to teach the world to sing" is playing.

Slippery Slope

This is a kind of fear mongering which argues that any step down a path will lead to the worst possible outcome:

- Any restriction of abortion means that *Roe vs. Wade* will be overturned.
- Experiments with gene therapy for diseases will lead to designer or made-to-order babies.

Exercises

1. Work in groups to review the letters to the editor of several newspapers. Read a week's worth of these letters, selecting those letters with weak arguments. In your group decide which fallacies are represented.
2. Also in groups review the ads in several magazines that you read regularly. What needs, instincts, or feelings do these ads appeal to? Which do you think are legitimate appeals; which are not?
3. Identify the fallacious thinking in the following examples:

   - Susan Sarandon, a famous actress, and other entertainment figures used the Academy Awards ceremony to protest the war in Iraq. You should listen to what they have to say.
   - I don't get good grades because my teachers don't like me.
   - 98% of my high school class are attending college, many because "it's what everyone does."
   - Adopting the Equal Rights Amendment will mean that women will be drafted.
   - In his zeal to make his argument a strong one, Joshua presented all the evidence that supported his position, omitting any data that seemed to weaken it.

- After the plane crash, investigators discovered that the airline's ticket agents had allowed several passengers to bring on excess baggage even though they knew the plane was carrying a full cargo load.
- My dad told me that if I do not finish college, I will end up as a waitress or a sales clerk.
- When a ship disappeared after entering the Bermuda Triangle, investigators of paranormal phenomena reasoned that the Bermuda Triangle had triggered the disappearance.

3

Writing the Source-Based Argumentative Paper

Becoming the Arguer: Creating a Conversation Among Writer, Readers, and Authorities

The first two chapters of Part One have focused on understanding how argument works and reading the arguments written by others to determine how they make their argument and whether they avoid fallacious reasoning. The kind of repeated careful analysis that we undertake together in class has undoubtedly honed our analytic skills. As we study how masters of the form make their case, we no longer read passively. We question; we disagree; we put forward our own arguments; we demand additional evidence; we contradict the support that is provided. No longer do we think of reading argument as a private activity, but we enter a conversation with the writer, other readers, and the authorities cited in the text. We say to the writer, Who are you to tell me what I should think? Prove to me that you are competent to make this case. My, you really did make a powerful *Declaration,* Mr. Jefferson. Or, you didn't think I'd let you get away with that, did you, Mr. Bush? With other readers, we dispute their interpretations and evaluations and sometimes reach an agreement: You are just plain wrong that the U.S. bishops are prowar. You convinced me that Howard Zinn does more than make an appeal to pathos. The sources and authorities cited within the text are thus no longer merely providers of dry data but people whose ideas and arguments are so familiar that we feel as if we know Augustine, Aquinas, Colson, or Falk.

No matter how actively we have engaged in the conversation described above, at some point we decide to initiate our own conversation. Sometimes it is our own need to clarify or defend our ideas that urges us to write; often it is an assignment that requires us to do so. Whatever the motive, we need to take charge of the conversation, acquiring and demonstrating expertise, respecting our readers and taking heed of their needs. Most of all we need to lay claim to our position with conviction, passion, and authority, to be as willing to engage with our readers as we were to be critical readers.

The following steps work for any source-based argumentative writing though some may be eliminated for a shorter essay based on a few primary sources. For the longer argumentative research paper, following the process in detail will assure a carefully researched, thoughtful, well-written paper that creates the kind of conversation we have been discussing.

Choosing a Topic

Select a topic that interests you and lends itself to research. For a successful paper, you will need to find multiple relevant and academic sources (that is, from significant journals and magazines, respected national newspapers, books by scholars and experts). Your topic should raise important questions about serious issues.

You will be spending a great deal of time doing research and writing your essay, so you need a project that you will find worthwhile. Even if your topic has been somewhat limited by the topic of this casebook or by your assignment, you can find a way to tailor it to your interests. You might connect your topic with what you have been learning in another class or with a subject in which you are already interested. For example, one student decided to examine the Bush administration speeches that preceded the war in Iraq and used what she had been learning in a communications class to find a framework for analyzing the speeches. Another connected his peace studies class with his topic from the casebook, finding good sources for his support of the pacifist position. Others took historical periods that fascinated them and focused on World War II or the Vietnam War.

A quick survey of the topic will help you decide whether your topic is doable within the time frame and manageable within the parameters of the assignment. Read about the subject in a good encyclopedia like *Britannica.* Look at the bibliography provided after the article, as well as the bibliography provided in the casebook. Does your library have a good selection of these sources or are public and other university libraries easily accessible? Do a quick subject search of your library's catalog and databases and InfoTrac® College Edition to determine whether there is ample and varied material available on your topic.

Narrowing a Topic and Developing a Working Thesis or Claim

Try to narrow your topic as soon as possible. Do not research poverty in general, but research and explore the causes of poverty, the governmental or private remedies for poverty, the impact of poverty on children. Narrow down the topic of capital punishment to the morality of the death penalty, or its deterrent effect, or the question of retribution, or the question of whether capital punishment is fairly administered. Focus on one war, not several; on a few speeches, not ten. Narrowing allows you to focus on more specific sources and to avoid getting lost in reading sources that will not be relevant to your project. Narrowing will also ensure that you can develop adequate support in the time and space you have. Always keep in mind that you need to be able to make a claim, that you will be writing an argument, not merely a report.

As soon as you can, write a working thesis (or claim). It is often helpful to start with a question. Given the information you have already, which questions are most appropriate; for which do you have the most supportive information? For example: Is capital punishment moral? Does it deter murderers? Does it provide retribution? Is it unfair in its application? In a short paper you might want to try to answer only one of these questions; in a longer paper you might want to tackle them all. Go on to provide a tentative answer to your question. This answer is your thesis or claim. Be sure it is arguable, that not everyone is in agreement: Capital punishment is moral because_____. Or capital punishment is unfair in its application because_____.

Your subsequent research will help you determine whether your claim is defensible, whether it will hold up to scrutiny. It is helpful to think of your claim as a hypothesis, one which you will test. Should the evidence not support the claim, you as a responsible and honest arguer will need to reformulate your thesis. Student Frances Ryder, for example, began with a thesis claiming that Just War theory provides an adequate way to deal with nuclear weapons. In the course of doing her research, however, she modified her claim to argue that the theory must change to allow preventive strikes against countries that threaten to use nuclear weapons against another country.

Selecting and Evaluating Sources

Make effective use of library resources to find good sources. Check your library's online catalog of books and articles, as well as locating articles through databases, including InfoTrac® College Edition, for example. Books provide a more comprehensive look at a topic and often include extensive data or thorough development of important ideas; articles are, of course, shorter and more focused on a portion of the topic. Your bibliography should usually include both types of material.

Depending on your topic, your most up-to-date sources will be from journals, magazines, newspapers, and Web sites. Be wary of Web sites as they differ widely in source, reliability, and usable content. Look for those set up by universities, reputable institutions, and authorities. The following are useful questions to ask in order to evaluate sources:

1. Examine the cover of a magazine or journal, the front page of a newspaper, and the opening pages of Web sites. Determine how its images and words affect you. What feelings do you think it is intended to stimulate? What would motivate someone to buy it, if a magazine, or continue reading or subscribe to it, if a newspaper, Web site, or other electronic publication?

2. What is the publication's social and political viewpoint? Who owns or publishes it?

3. Study the table of contents, look at the range of subjects offered, and skim some articles. What can you infer about the political orientation, purpose, and assumptions of this publication?

4. Look at ads and generalize about which sponsors sell their products in this publication. What social class would they appeal to? What kinds of advertisements are missing? How might the advertisers influence the publication's policies and attitudes?

5. Analyze the language in the articles. How does the language indicate the targeted readers and their level of education?

Taking Notes

As you read, you will need to keep track of material helpful to your argument. It is a good idea to print out or copy any sources not in your text since transcribing material directly into your text can lead to many types of errors and, in some cases, to charges of plagiarism. In addition, your instructor may wish you to submit this material with your completed essay in order to check that you have cited material correctly, either by direct and accurate quotation, paraphrase, or summary. Many researchers start by highlighting relevant material in a source. Some researchers are then reluctant to allocate the time to take notes, but omitting this step can make it difficult to locate a quotation or piece of information and arrange material in the best order. When downloading sources, try to find sources which indicate original page numbers, such as PDFs.

We recommend using note cards or fairly small slips of paper for your notes. This way you avoid having too much information on one card and do not lose the flexibility of shuffling cards to determine the correct ordering of the information you have amassed. Usually it is a good idea to have three types of note cards: a card with complete bibliographic information for each source; cards containing the background information, quotations, or evidence you think will be helpful for your argument; and cards on which you jot down ideas, questions, examples, etc., as they occur to you. Bibliography cards can then be alphabetized to serve as the source for your Works Cited or References page. The notes you take on each source should have at least the author and an abbreviated title at the top left and a topic on the right (these topics will help you sort your cards). Be sure to indicate page number (or paragraph number for an Internet source). Use quotations marks to indicate quoted material. For summarized or paraphrased material, be sure to rewrite the material in your own words. Do not merely change a word or two. These three types of cards are invaluable when you write your draft. Many students have told us that after they have arranged their notes in a logical order, the paper almost writes itself. The sample note cards on page 42 will give you an idea of how to proceed. Some students find it convenient to take notes on the computer and then print them out for easy reference.

Yoder, John Howard. <u>When War Is Unjust: Being Honest in Just-War Thinking</u>. Rev. ed. Maryknoll, NY: Orbis Books, 1996.

Excellent list of just war criteria. Appendix on the laws of war. Traces the history of the j.w. tradition. Provides a cautionary note about j.w. Also has a pro-j.w. response by Drew Christiansen.

Yoder   Just War

History

Context: medieval view of legitimacy

"By 'legitimate' we mean 'in conformity with the rules.' Legitimate is less than good, as justified is less than just. War is an evil, a harm, which in a special case may be admitted for the sake of some other value it defends. It is not a good in itself" (11).

My Ideas

It might be interesting to follow how j.w. theory developed over time.

Why does Yoder seem to appreciate j.w. theory and also worry about its potential somehow to make war seem acceptable?

Another possibility—explore how the theory restricts the excesses of war—or does it?

Construct your Works Cited or References page (for example, a minimum of 8–10 sources for an 8–10 page essay) from your bibliography cards. As you add sources, add them to a computer file you have created to list your sources. You can directly copy or download the bibliographic information from your library catalog. Include a wide range of sources: books, articles, and Web sites covering a time frame appropriate for your topic. For each source, do you have complete bibliographic information, including pages or paragraph numbers? Have you used correct MLA or APA bibliographic format?

Annotating a Bibliography

Many instructors require more than an initial list of your sources as a way to help decide if you have the sources you need. The annotated bibliography includes the following steps: Skim each source you have selected. Write your own brief, but specific, summary of the source. Using the abstract in the database is not acceptable as it may often not include the specific information that makes the source valuable to you. Include a paragraph indicating your evaluation of the source: What is its relevance to your project? How pertinent and accurate is the information it contains? Does it make an argument that supports yours or provides important counter-arguments to your position? Keep looking for additional sources as you find holes in your research.

Student Frances Ryder prepared the following entries for her annotated bibliography on the topic of whether Just War theory can adequately deal with the nuclear threat. Note that Frances has succinctly stated the main point of her sources and reflected on their utility for her paper. She has included materials representing diverse viewpoints and drawn from recent and more contemporary sources. She has also been careful to use correct MLA citation form:

Annotated Bibliography

Krauthammer, Charles. "On Nuclear Morality." _Nuclear Arms: Ethics, Strategy, Politics_. Ed. R. James Woolsey. San Francisco: Institute for Contemporary Studies, 1984. 11–21.

This book is an assembly of articles looking to clarify the relationship between moral thinking and military necessity in war. In the section titled "The Argument against Nuclear Deterrence" in Krauthammer's article, he analyzes the bishops' "no-use-ever" stance concerning nuclear weapons. According to the bishops, both counterforce and countervalue deterrence violate the just-war doctrine. Therefore, weapons may be kept but never used. Krauthammer asserts that, according to the bishops, "the only moral nuclear policy is nuclear bluff." This, he believes, is hardly a convincing argument.

Krauthammer's argument will be useful in that it criticizes the bishops' stance, saying that it is too prescriptive and does not provide a feasible solution to the nuclear debate. It seems to me that he is mistaken in his analysis of the bishops' letter. Essentially, the bishops believe there should be no room for negotiation about who can not hold nuclear weapons. There should not be any negotiation about what actions can be taken with nuclear weapons. Nuclear weapons should not exist. The solution to the problem is the destruction of nuclear weapons.

```
Lutz, Charles P. Foreword to the First Edition.
     When War is Unjust: Being Honest in Just
     War Thinking. By John Yoder. 2nd ed. Mary-
     knoll, N.Y.: Orbis Books, 1996. xi-xx.
```

Charles P. Lutz, director of the Office of Church in Society and the American Lutheran Church as well as editor of *Metro Lutheran*, discusses the need for criteria or limits in war. In his section titled "The Need for a Morality of War," he states that, according to popular belief, just-war criteria have not lost their value in modern wartime. He states that just-war criteria are tests that nuclear, biological, and chemical weapons do not pass, making such weapons "morally unacceptable."

Lutz's foreword is useful in that it embodies part of the thesis I would like to propose for my paper. We may say that nuclear weapons may have changed the actions of war, but within the just-war criteria they have not changed the nature of what morality is. Nuclear weapons are immoral in their very nature. There can be no exception for nuclear weapons in a just war. Therefore, there is perhaps no need for alterations in the just-war theory; perhaps it still remains valid.

Focusing the Thesis

Once you have completed your research, you should be able to write a very focused thesis that not only indicates the conclusion you have reached but also provides the reasons or main points of support for your assertions. Such a focused thesis also serves as a kind of road map to the organization of your essay, allowing readers to keep track of where they are in the argument.

1. Capital punishment is moral because it is imposed by the rightful authority of the state, it allows for retribution, it safeguards the community, and it provides avenues of appeal.
2. Capital punishment is unfair in its application because members of minorities and the poor who must use public defenders are more likely to receive the death penalty.
3. Capital punishment is moral except in the case of young offenders, those with low IQs, and those found to be legally insane.

Note how the first two claims include the reasons that support them. The third indicates the exceptions. In both cases, readers will expect you to develop each point in the order given.

Planning an Argument: The Outline or Argument in Brief

Write a plan that will help you discover what you think, that will help you focus on the elements of argument you need to include, and that will help you determine if you need additional material. You should include answers to the following questions:

- In light of your topic, what are your values and what assumptions do you make as **writer?**
- Consider **audience.** Who are your readers? What views may they already have about your issue? What kinds of values does the audience have? How can you make common ground with them? What will your audience need to know?
- What is your **claim** or thesis?
- Consider **reasons** or **subclaims** that will provide the main framework or skeleton of your argument. These can provide the main points of an outline or an argument in brief.
- What kinds of **evidence** or **support** will best substantiate your thesis or claim?
- Think about what kinds of **objections** your readers are likely to raise. Forestall them by raising them first. This tactic helps to keep your readers with you. How will you **refute** these objections?

As you focus your thesis and plan your essay, think about the type of argumentative structure best suited for your topic. For example, if you are setting up general principles of Just War theory against which you will test a particular war, a deductive framework may work for you. In this case, you might find *The Declaration* a useful model: First set up and explain Just War principles as your major premise; use the body of the essay to demonstrate how a conflict fits—or fails to fit—within the Just War criteria; and then draw your conclusion from this evidence: The Korean War does (or does not) conform to Just War criteria.

If you wish to focus your essay on what conclusions may be drawn from specific evidence, an inductive approach, you may decide to use Howard Zinn as a model (see p. 214 in Casebook). Using this approach leads you to collect and present sufficient material about a topic from which you can generalize. After studying a series of presidential speeches concerning war, for example, you might examine the rhetorical devices used to gain acceptance for the war, and then decide how they work and which are most effective. The strategies of Rogerian argument may work well if, for example, you want to make an argument that is particularly difficult for an audience to swallow. Here you would look for the common concerns and values the members of your audience share, and you would take care to illustrate that you understand and accept at least some of the arguments your readers would make.

Another way to proceed is to use the modifications of the syllogism that Toulmin proposes, what we might call the claim/reasons/specific evidence method. Student Emily Fitzgerald has used this method both in the completed essay provided as a sample in the appendix and in her plan for her essay shown below.

Brief for Argument Paper

Claim: The war the United States has launched upon Iraq is unjust and ought not to be waged.

Warrants for the claim: The classic Just War Theory is an appropriate model for judgment of the morality of a war.

- The theory has developed as a respected policy throughout history.
- The tenets of Just War Doctrine are inclusive of many aspects that should be considered before waging war. They consist of the following: just cause, right authority, reasonable hope for success, proportionality, and a last resort. These rules pertain to the many various issues surrounding war and ought to be fully considered. (Sources to support warrants: Alexander, *Just War* casebook, Miller, "When There Is No Peace.")

Reason I: The war with Iraq violates the guidelines for just war.

Specific Evidence: The United States has acted outside of the authority of the United Nations, which is meant to be trusted as an international authority.

- The United States does not have just cause to wage war. A preemptive attack is a violation of the tenets of just war. Iraq has not attacked the United States. The possibility of future attack does not constitute just war. Many nations, including the United States, possess weapons of mass destruction, and have the power to cause tragedies. Security is not guaranteed when so many countries possess such capabilities.
- The hope for success and a good outcome after the war with Iraq is doubtful. There will certainly be extensive loss of life. Innocent civilians and Americans will die. This action is likely to spark more violence against the United States and throughout the world. After military force has ceased, the United States will have a huge mess to clean up, which means further commitment of Americans, soldiers and officials, in the years following the war.
- Iraq is already a country that is hurting. The people of Iraq are facing grave dangers without bombs falling around them. A war will cause more perils to an already suffering people.
- This war is not a last resort. There are other diplomatic means that have not yet been exhausted in the attempt to disarm Iraq. (Sources supporting specific evidence: Arnove, O'Hanlon, Schell, Thistlethwaite, U.S. Bishops.)

Reason II: The arguments that claim Just War Theory supports a war on Iraq extend the meaning of the doctrine to an inappropriate level.

Refutation:

- Many argue that a preemptive war is just. They say that the theory has evolved and must be applied in the context of today. They believe the threat posed by Iraq constitutes just cause for war.
- This extension of the Just War Theory is not compliant with the doctrine itself.

Specific evidence: The Just War Theory does not accept preemptive war. The idea that a threat exists is not enough to justify waging such a war. (Sources: Colson, Gushee, "When There Is No Peace.")

Conferring with Your Instructor

If possible, arrange a conference with your instructor to which you bring your bibliography, sources, notes, argument in brief, etc. Be sure to bring your questions as well. Ask for help if you are having problems finding sufficient information, if your thesis is not as focused as it needs to be, or if any part of your paper is giving you particular trouble.

Drafting the Essay

As you write your **introduction,** think about how you are engaging with your sources and your readers in a kind of conversation. How can you interest your readers in your topic? Can you pose a question that demands an answer, write a scenario that engages them emotionally, jolt them with startling or horrifying statistics, or draw them in with a quotation that provides the pith of your argument? How can you let your readers know both what you are arguing and how you will proceed? A carefully crafted thesis can do both, combining your claim and your reasons and thus providing a road map of your argument.

If you find that you are stalled somewhere in your introduction, move on to the body of your paper. For some readers, laying out the evidence is a very helpful way to get started. Then you can return to the introduction, having discovered what you really want to say. Use your outline or plan to guide the writing of the **body** of your draft. For each point turn to your notes, arranging them in the best order to supply the evidence you need to support each reason or subclaim. Keep checking back with your thesis or claim to see whether what you are writing advances it. As you introduce each section of your essay, be sure to use **topic sentences** that relate that section very specifically to your thesis and that show readers where you are in your argument. For example, if your thesis is *World War II was a just war because the cause was just, the authority was legitimate, and the intention rightful,* you might introduce the section on just cause as follows: *Because entering into war with Japan came as a response to their attack on Pearl Harbor, our cause was just. Defending oneself from attack is the principal criterion for a just war.*

Be careful to introduce your source material accurately, providing parenthetical citation so that you can check later that you have cited material correctly (see Appendix B). Consider whether each quotation, paraphrase, or summary is necessary to make your point. Do not merely drop one into the text but introduce and explain it. Do not allow your text to become a pastiche of quotations. Be true to your sources by presenting them accurately and fairly. Be true to your readers by constantly asking yourself, what do they need to know? How will they respond to what I have written? How can I show that I respect them even if I suspect they will not be sympathetic to my claim?

Even if you are not required to submit a draft with your completed paper, do not give in to the temptation to make your first draft your last! You may encounter difficulties or problems that require time to correct. Write a complete draft, including all the support you have gathered from your sources. This is an invaluable step that allows you to see exactly what you have and where you are missing necessary material. When you see gaps or holes in your research, this is a point at which you must return to your sources for additional information or locate new sources. Sometimes you may discover that the organizational structure you proposed in your plan is not working. To clarify the logical progression of your ideas, you may need to try a different order for your reasons or subclaims or even to employ another argumentative strategy.

Many writers find **conclusions** difficult to write. The temptation is to restate the thesis and leave it at that. Certainly you do need to demonstrate that you have proven your thesis or supported your claim. At this point look back at your introduction to see if you have changed your mind in the course of writing the paper or inadvertently proven a different thesis and adjust your conclusion accordingly. But a mechanical ending does not do justice to the conversation you have been having with your readers and sources. You might inquire whether the conversation about your topic has really been exhausted. What other questions are left to resolve? What problems remain? Where are you least satisfied with what you have discovered? Where do you think additional research needs to be done?

Revising the Draft

Revision means to see again; it implies re-viewing, re-thinking, and re-writing where necessary. Most likely, you have been revising as you write your draft, catching errors as you see them and rearranging the order of material in a kind of ongoing, recursive process. Up until now your writing process has probably been rather solitary. Now it is time to seek out what Donald Murray calls a "test reader" in *The Craft of Revision* (Wadsworth). This reader may be a peer editing partner or group in class or someone you have identified out of class who can provide you with responses to your work. Ask this reader to comment on your work as specifically as possible so you can see how a reader responds to what you have written. Of course, you must be willing to do the same for your reader. The following are questions to guide your reader's response. You might also ask your reader to focus on an area with which you have had particular difficulty.

1. Does the introduction grab your readers and draw them into the discussion? What tactic is used? How can it be improved?
2. Is there a focused claim that predicts the organization of the essay (this should be at the end of the introduction)? What is the claim? Underline it on the draft and write it here. How can it be improved?
3. Does the organization of the essay follow from the thesis? If it deviates from the claim, where does this happen?
4. Does each section of the essay have a topic sentence or subclaim, showing how the section relates to the thesis?
5. Are there transitions that connect sections? Where are transitions needed?
6. Are judiciously chosen quotations included? Are they introduced well and discussed sufficiently or are they merely dropped into the text?
7. Does the essay include ample, pertinent, and specific support from the sources? Where do you need more information? Where is additional support needed?
8. Are in-text citations present and correct? Is the Works Cited or Reference page properly formatted?
9. What are the most successful parts of the essay? Where would you suggest more work is needed?

Proofreading

Proofread carefully. Remember that this is a different process than revision. Check for spelling, punctuation, and typographical errors because an error-ridden paper is distracting or even insulting to the readers.

One helpful technique is to put the paper aside for a few hours or a day so that you can see it with fresh eyes. Then start at the bottom of the page, looking only for errors. Another technique is to keep a list of the errors you make frequently and focus on those. Still another is to read the paper aloud. Often the ear will catch what the eye does not. Many people, including the authors of this text, need to proofread more than once. Check also that you have followed MLA or APA format exactly for both in-text citations and the Works Cited or References page.

Along with your well-edited final essay, submit your annotated bibliography, your argument in brief, copies of your sources, your notes, and your draft. Submit these items in a pocket folder or a manila envelope.

As a guide for your final revision and proofreading, we have also included the kind of checklist many instructors use to evaluate your essay.

Checklist for Argumentative Research Essay

Quality of research
(20 points total)   _____
   Authoritative sources (15)   _____
     Pertinent
     Ample
     Varied
   Notes (5)   _____
     Accuracy
     Documented
     Labeled clearly
     Complete

Success of argument
(50 points total)   _____
   Claim (15)   _____
     Arguable
     Focused
     Provides major points of
       support or subclaims
     Provides map of argument
   Assumptions clearly
     enunciated (5)   _____
   Objections/Refutation (5)   _____
   Subclaims (20)   _____
     Topic sentences
     Complete development
     Necessary definitions
     Specific evidence
   Conclusion (5)   _____
     Valid
     Convincing

Documentation
(10 points total)   _____
     Acknowledgment of all
       borrowed material
     Accurate quotations
     Complete paraphrase
     Smooth inclusion in sentence
     In-text citation
     Works Cited page format

Paragraphs
(10 points total)   _____
     Effective transition sentences
     Logical order of ideas
     Full development
     Appropriate length

Sentences (10 points total)   _____
     Clear
     Grammatical
     Correct spelling, punctuation
     Exact word usage
     Elimination of unnecessary
       words
     Smooth transitions

Total: _____

PART TWO

Just War and Peace Casebook

4

Just War Traditions

The earliest manifestations of Just War thinking are couched in terms of what has been called "holy war." In the Hebrew Bible, both Numbers 33 and Deuteronomy 7 contain God's commands to destroy the inhabitants of Canaan, the Promised Land. Deuteronomy 20 places limits on how subsequent wars should be conducted, listing those who should not go to war, laying out the proper conduct of a siege, and distinguishing between towns far distant from the Israelites and those towns nearby. The New Testament relays Jesus' message of peace, but at the same time it addresses the reality of war. Both Luke and Paul answer ordinary people's concerns about how to follow Christian teaching and yet live in a violent world by recognizing the legitimacy of civil authority. The Muslim tradition also has a notion of holy war, expressed in the term *jihad* or struggle. This struggle may be interior, but it is also external in wars fought to preserve or extend the lands devoted to Allah. The Qur'an in Surahs 2:216 and 22:39–40 expresses the notion of wars fought in the name of Allah.

Both the early Muslim legal scholar al-Shaybani and the medieval Jewish philosopher Maimonides codify and comment upon the rules for war. Al-Shaybani reports the *hadith* or sayings of the prophet Mohammed. Those printed here concern the conduct of war, principally those who should not be killed. Maimonides distinguishes between commanded and optional wars and also sets forth appropriate treatment of conquered peoples.

To read the classics of the Just War tradition in the Christian West is to realize how much the reasoning of one theorist builds upon the reasoning of those who have gone before, creating a conversation over time. The selections here lay out the main lines of the argument, distinguishing the *jus ad bellum*, the just causes or motives for war, from the *jus in bello*, the just way of conducting a war.

The most important early proponents of Just War theory are Augustine, Bishop of Hippo during the invasion of the Vandals, and the great scholastic philosopher Thomas Aquinas. Well acquainted with war, Augustine points out the causes for which good men undertake wars and the authority by which they do so. He turns to Luke's story of John the Baptist to find justification for the soldier's profession. In his *Summa Theologica*, Aquinas raises the central question, "Whether it is always sinful to wage war?" He uses Augustine as his authority to refute arguments based on New Testament passages that seem to prohibit war. His own case for determining when war is just rests on the authority of the sovereign who orders that war be waged, a just cause, and a righteous intention: advancing good or avoiding evil.

During the early sixteenth century, Martin Luther, a key Protestant reformer, and Francisco de Vitoria, a Spanish Catholic theologian, were both concerned with Just War issues. Vitoria, writing at the time of the exploration of the Americas and the concomitant subjection of the indigenous peoples, focuses on what the prince must do *before* going to war; on what limits the prince must place on the way war is to be waged; and how the victory should be handled. Luther, like Augustine, was writing during a time of war. His "Whether Soldiers Too Can Be Saved" strives to resolve a soldier's conflict between the precepts of Christianity and the requirements of his profession. He also considers the reasons for which just wars are fought. Like his contemporary Vitoria, Luther feels free to address—even warn—the princes waging war against each other and against the peasants in the Peasants' Revolt.

The Hebrew Bible: "God's Rules for Commanded Wars"

The Bible is the holy book of Jews and Christians and is important to Muslims as well. The Hebrew Bible is that part holy to Judaism and consists of thirty-nine books divided into three parts—the Five Books of Moses or Pentateuch, called in Hebrew the Torah, The Prophets, and The Writings. Christians refer to these sections of Scripture as the "Old Testament," but Jews do not, since they do not accept the validity of the Christian "new" testament. The Torah, from which the first three excerpts are taken, was completed in the form we know it some time between 950 and 450 B.C.E. Numbers, the fourth book of the Torah, relates the story of the

Israelites in the desert after leaving slavery in Egypt under Moses' leadership. The passage below comes near the end of Numbers and includes God's instructions about invading Canaan (the Promised Land). Deuteronomy, the fifth book of the Torah, contains a series of addresses by Moses as the Israelites began their entrance into Canaan. Chapter 7 in Deuteronomy addresses the key religious problem facing the people of Israel as they encountered idolaters and idolatries for the first time in the forty years after leaving Egypt: how to keep their own religious practices, not yet firmly entrenched, intact. The commanded war against the Canaanites and their culture is severe. Rules for making various wars are given in Chapter 20, including, retrospectively in v. 16–18, the war upon the Canaanite peoples commanded in Chapter 7. Historical evidence indicates that in the actual invasion (about 1200 B.C.E.), no such total extermination took place.

Numbers 33:50–53

[50]And the LORD said to Moses in the plains of Moab by the Jordan at Jericho, [51]"Say to the people of Israel, When you pass over the Jordan into the land of Canaan, [52]then you shall drive out all the inhabitants of the land from before you, and destroy all their figured stones, and destroy all their molten images, and demolish all their high places; [53]and you shall take possession of the land and settle in it, for I have given the land to you to possess it."

Deuteronomy 7:1–5

"When the LORD your God brings you into the land which you are entering to take possession of it, and clears away many nations before you, the Hittites, the Gir'gashites, the Amorites, the Canaanites, the Per'izzites, the Hivites, and the Jeb'usites, seven nations greater and mightier than yourselves, [2]and when the LORD your God gives them over to you, and you defeat them; then you must utterly destroy them; you shall make no covenant with them, and show no mercy to them. [3]You shall not make marriages with them, giving your daughters to their sons or taking their daughters for your sons. [4]For they would turn away your sons from following me, to serve other gods; then the anger of the LORD would be kindled against you, and he would destroy you quickly. [5]But thus shall you deal with them: you shall break down their altars, and dash in pieces their pillars, and hew down their Ashe'rim [sacred posts dedicated to the goddess Asherah], and burn their graven images with fire."

Deuteronomy 20:1–20

"When you go forth to war against your enemies, and see horses and chariots and an army larger than your own, you shall not be afraid of them; for the LORD your God is with you, who brought you up out of the land of Egypt. [2]And when you draw near to the battle, the priest shall come forward and speak to the people, [3]and shall say to them, 'Hear, O Israel, you draw near this day to battle against your enemies: let not your heart faint; do not fear, or tremble, or be in dread of them; [4]for the LORD your God is he that goes with you, to fight for you against your enemies, to give you the victory.' [5]Then the officers shall speak to the people, saying, 'What man is there that has built a new house and has not dedicated it? Let him go to his house, lest he die in the battle and another man dedicate it. [6]And what man is there that has planted vineyard and has not enjoyed its fruit? Let him go back to his house, lest he die in the battle and another man enjoy its fruit. [7]And what man is there that has betrothed a wife and has not taken her? Let him go back to his house lest he die in the battle and another man take her.' [8]And the officers shall speak further to the people, and say, 'What man is there that is fearful and fainthearted? Let him go back to his house, lest the heart of his fellows melt as his heart.' [9]And when the officers have made an end of speaking to people, then commanders shall be appointed at the head of the people. [10]"When you draw near to a city to fight against it, offer terms of peace to it. [11]And if its answer to you is peace and it opens to you, then all the people who are found in it shall do forced labor for you and shall serve you. [12]But if it makes no peace with you but makes war against you, then you shall besiege it; [13]and when the LORD your God gives it into your hand you shall put all its males to the sword, [14]but the women and the little ones, the cattle, and everything else in the city, all its spoil, you shall take as booty for yourselves; and you shall enjoy the spoil of your enemies, which the LORD your God has given you.[15] Thus you shall do to all the cities which are very far from you, which are not cities of the nations here. ¹⁶But in the cities of these peoples that the LORD your God gives you for an inheritance, you shall save alive nothing that breathes, ¹⁷but you shall utterly destroy them, the Hittites and the Amorites, the Canaanites and the Per'izzites, the Hivites and the Jeb'usites, as the LORD your God has commanded; ¹⁸that they may not teach you to do according to all their abominable practices which they have done in the service of their gods, and so to sin against the LORD your God.

¹⁹"When you besiege a city for a long time, making war against it in order to take it, you shall not destroy its trees by wielding an axe against them; for you may eat of them, but you shall not cut them down. Are the trees in the field men that they should be besieged by you? ²⁰Only the trees which you know are not trees for food you may destroy and cut down that you may build siegeworks against the city that makes war with you, until it falls."

Questions about the Passages

1. In the passage from Numbers, "high places" refers to the hilltop locations of pagan cultic worship. Why would the text demand that the idols and even the Canaanites' places of worship be destroyed if the people were driven out?
2. According to Deut. 7:1–2, how will the Israelites be able to conquer the powerful seven nations?
3. Why would Deut. 7:3–4 prohibit the Israelites from intermarrying with the idolaters they were supposed to destroy?
4. According to Deut. 20, why should the Israelites not be afraid when they go into battle?
5. Why should the men listed in Deut. 20:5–8 not go to war? What do they have in common? Would you add anyone else to the list?
6. How should war with far distant towns be conducted? Who should not be killed?
7. How should the nations nearby be treated? Why?
8. Why should the army spare the fruit trees but not the other trees in the field?

Questions about the Arguments

1. Who was the original audience of the Hebrew Bible? Why are the issues raised important to the original audience? Why might they be important to subsequent audiences? How might today's readers respond to the requirement of killing certain populations?
2. How do these passages establish their authority? How effective are they in conveying that authority?

The Christian Bible: "Following the Cross, Yet Carrying the Sword"

The Christian Bible includes the Hebrew Bible and the New Testament. The New Testament consists of twenty-seven books, the most important being the four gospels by Matthew, Mark, Luke, and John telling of the life, teachings, death, and resurrection of Jesus. Also included are the Acts of the Apostles, the history of the spread of Christian faith in its first three decades; letters to congregations and individuals written by followers of Jesus, most notably Paul; and the Book of Revelation. Written within the first century after the death of Jesus, the Christian Bible took its final canonical form in the fourth century. Luke's Gospel includes an account of the John the Baptist's preaching about repentance and his baptism of Jesus. The section below recounts the response of the crowds who came to listen and to be baptized by John. Those who were newly baptized wished to know how they should now live their lives. Paul's Letter to the Romans focuses on God's lordship and also discusses how Christians should act in everyday life. The passage below delineates the role of the state and the duties of the Christian as a citizen.

Luke 3:10–14

[10]And the multitudes asked him, "What then shall we do?" [11]And he answered them, "He who has two coats, let him share with him who has none; and he who has food, let him do likewise." [12]Tax collectors also came to be baptized, and said to him, "Teacher, what shall we do?" [13]And he said to them, "Collect no more than is appointed you." [14]Soldiers also asked him, "And we, what shall we do?" And he said to them, "Rob no one by violence or by false accusation, and be content with your wages."

Romans 13:1–4

Let every person be subject to the governing authorities. For there is no authority except from God, and those that exist have been instituted by God. ²Therefore he who resists the authorities resists what God has appointed, and those who resist will incur judgment. ³For rulers are not a terror to good conduct, but to bad. Would you have no fear of him who is in authority? Then do what is good, and you will receive his approval, ⁴for he is God's servant for your good. But if you do wrong, be afraid, for he does not bear the sword in vain; he is the servant of God to execute his wrath on the wrongdoer.

Questions about the Passages

1. How does Luke connect the tax collectors and soldiers? Why are the soldiers, like the tax collectors, concerned about their professions now that they have been baptized?
2. Why does John tell the soldiers to "be content with your wages"? How does the passage indicate ways soldiers might enrich themselves in addition to their paid wages? How might heeding John's reply change soldiers' behavior?
3. Does Paul, the author of Romans, think that Christians should be afraid of the ruling authorities? Why or why not?
4. Where does the authority of the "governing authorities" ultimately come from, according to Paul?

Questions about the Arguments

1. What audience is John addressing? What audience is Luke addressing? Are they the same audience? Why are John and Luke addressing these audiences?
2. What rhetorical purpose does Luke have in listing the groups who question John?
3. What assumptions underlie Paul's argument in Romans?
4. See if you can rephrase Paul's argument as a syllogism or syllogisms.

Qur'an and Kitab al-Siyar: *"When Allah Commands War"*

Muslims believe that God revealed the Qur'an to the prophet Muhammad between the years 610 and 632. Some of the 114 surahs, or chapters, reflect knowledge of both the Hebrew and Christian Bibles. The Qur'an in Surahs 2:216 and 22:39–40 expresses the notion of holy war fought in the name of Allah. In the second century of the Muslim era, Muhammad ibn al-Hasan al-Shaybani (d. 804 or 805), an eminent jurist of the Hanafite school located in what is today Iraq, wrote the first major Islamic treatise on the law of nations, *Kitab al-Siyar al-Kabir* (book of conduct). Al-Shaybani's text contains detailed laws of war, occupation, treaties, diplomacy and the rights of foreigners; it also reports *hadith* or sayings of the prophet Muhammad. The *hadith* printed here concern how Muslims should treat their enemies in war.

Qur'an

Warfare is ordained for you, though it is hateful unto you; but it may happen that you hate a thing which is good for you, and it may happen that you love a thing which is bad for you. Allah knows, you know not. (2:216)

Sanction is given unto those who fight because they have been wronged; and Allah is indeed able to give them victory; Those who have been driven from their homes unjustly only because they said: Our Lord is Allah—For had it not been for Allah's repelling some men by means of others, cloisters and churches and oratories and mosques, wherein the name of Allah is oft mentioned, would assuredly have been pulled down. Truly Allah helps one who helps Him. Lo! Allah is Strong, Almighty. (22:39–40)

Muhammad ibn al-Hasan al-Shaybani (d. 804 or 805), *Kitab al-Siyar*

Whenever the Apostle of God sent forth an army or a detachment, he charged its commander personally to fear God, the Most High, and he enjoined the Muslims who were with him to do good [i.e., to conduct themselves properly].

And [the Apostle] said:

Fight in the name of God and in the "path of God" [i.e., truth]. Combat [only] those who disbelieve in God. Do not cheat or commit treachery, nor should you mutilate anyone or kill children. Whenever you meet your polytheist enemies, invite them [first] to adopt Islam. If they do so, accept it, and let them alone. You should then invite them to move from their territory to the territory of the *émigrés* [Madina]. If they do so, accept it and let them alone. Otherwise, they should be informed that they would be [treated] like the Muslim nomads (Bedouins) [who take no part in the war] in that they are subject to God's orders as [other] Muslims, but that they will receive no share in either the ghanima (spoil of war) or in the *fay'* [ed. note: booty]. If they refuse [to accept Islam], then call upon them to pay the jizya (poll tax); if they do, accept it and leave them alone. If you besiege the inhabitants of a fortress or a town and they try to get you to let them surrender on the basis of God's judgment, do not do so, since you do not know what God's judgment is, but make them surrender to your judgment and then decide their case according to your own views. But if the besieged inhabitants of a fortress or a town asked you to give them a pledge [of security] in God's name or in the name of His Apostle, you should not do so, but give the pledge in your names or in the names of your fathers; for, if you should ever break it, it would be an easier matter if it were in the names of you or your fathers . . .

He [of the enemy] who has reached puberty should be killed, but he who has not should be spared.

The Apostle of God prohibited the killing of women.

The Apostle of God said: "You may kill the adults of   5
the unbelievers, but spare their minor—the youth."

Whenever the Apostle of God sent forth a detachment he said to it: "Do not cheat or commit treachery, nor should you mutilate or kill children, women, or old men."

Questions about the Passage

1. According to surahs, or verses, of the Qur'an, what are the reasons just wars should be fought?
2. What is Allah's role in warfare?
3. In the *hadith* or sayings of the prophet Mohammed in *Kitab al-Siyar*, which are the groups who should not be killed? Why should they be spared?

Questions about the Argument

1. What are the different categories of groups Muslim soldiers should "leave alone" according to the *hadith*? What principle seems to underlie the way these categories are defined?
2. Compare and contrast the passages from the Hebrew Bible and from the Muslim tradition. On what authority does each base its

laws? What situations in warfare are they concerned about? List any common principles that underlie the laws of warfare.

Moses Maimonides, "Laws of Kings and Their Wars"

Moses ben Maimon (1135–1204), the great medieval Jewish philosopher, known in the West by the Greek version of his name, Maimonides, was born in Cordoba, Spain. His family left Spain because of religious persecution by Muslim rulers, eventually settling in Egypt in 1165. His work reflects a profound knowledge of Jewish, ancient Greek, and Muslim thought, and he influenced not only Jewish thinking but also Muslim philosophy and Christian Scholasticism as well. The *Mishneh Torah* (*Second Law*), written in Hebrew in the 1180s, codifies into a logical system all Jewish law found in the Torah—including laws that applied only in the Land of Israel under an independent Jewish kingdom. The Book of the Commandments, which enumerates the 613 commandments given in the Torah, classifies them as either positive or negative.

Maimonides, "Laws of Kings and Their Wars," from *Mishneh Torah*

Chapter 5

1. At first, the king may wage only a religious war. Which is called a war for religious purposes? The war against the seven nations [of Canaan], the battle against Amalek, in defense of Israel from attacking enemies. Thereafter he may wage an optional war, a war against other peoples, to extend Jewish territory and to augment his military prestige.
2. In the case of a religious war, the king does not have to obtain the sanction of the Supreme [Rabbinical] Court. He may at any time set out independently and compel the people to come out with him. But in case of an optional war, he can bring out the people only by a decision of the [rabbinical] court of seventy-one.

Chapter 6

1. No war is to be waged with anyone in the world before offering him terms of peace, whether it is an optional or a religious war, as it is written: "When you approach a

town to attack it, you shall first offer it terms of peace" (Deut. 20:10). If the inhabitants have responded peaceably and accepted the seven precepts imposed upon the descendants of Noah, none of them should be slain but taxed, as it is written: "They shall do forced labor for you and serve you" (20:11). . . . The tax imposed upon them consists in being prepared to serve the king physically and financially. . . .

3. It is forbidden to prove false to the pact made with them, to deceive them when they have accepted the terms of peace and the seven precepts. . . .

7. When a city is besieged in order to capture it, it must not be surrounded on all four sides but only on three sides, so as to leave room for a refugee, and anyone who wishes to escape. . . .

Maimonides, "Positive Commandment 187"

By this injunction we are commanded to exterminate the Seven Nations that inhabited the land of Canaan, because they constituted the root and very foundation of idolatry. This injunction is contained in His words (exalted be He), (Deut. 20:17): "You must utterly destroy them." It is explained in many texts that the object was to safeguard us from imitating their apostasy. There are many passages in Scripture which strongly urge and exhort us to exterminate them, and war against them is a commanded war.

Questions about the Passage

1. "Religious war" would be literally translated as "commanded war." What is the difference between commanded and optional wars?
2. What sort of system does Maimonides delineate for making optional wars unlikely?
3. Why do the Seven Nations, according to Maimonides, need to be exterminated?

Questions about the Argument

1. By whose authority is a religious or commanded war fought? By whose authority is an optional war fought?

2. Who is Maimonides' audience? There were no kings of Israel in Maimonides' day (or since). What might be his purpose in considering the king's role in different kinds of war?
3. Carefully examine Maimonides' rules in conjunction with the passages from the Hebrew Bible. Does he add or modify any points?

Augustine, "How Should Soldiers Behave?"

Augustine was born in Roman North Africa in 354. As a young man, he became a Manichean, following the dualistic religion founded by Mani in Persia in the third century C.E. Manicheans held that the world was split between two contrary powers: the perfectly good creator and the perfectly evil destroyer. A brilliant thinker and teacher, Augustine was converted to Christianity and baptized by St. Ambrose in 387 in Milan. He returned to Africa and served as bishop of Hippo (in modern Algeria) for thirty-four years, until his death in 430 while the city was under siege by a Vandal army. Augustine's *Reply to Faustus the Manichean* (written about 397–98) was one of a number of his pieces defending Christian teachings against the attacks of the Manicheans on the Bible and Christian beliefs.

> **74.** Now, if this explanation suffices to satisfy human obstinacy and perverse misinterpretation of right actions of the vast difference between the indulgence of passion and presumption on the part of men, and obedience to the command of God, who knows what to permit or to order, and also the time and the persons, and the due action or suffering in each case, the account of the wars of Moses will not excite surprise or abhorrence, for in wars carried on by divine command, he showed not ferocity but obedience; and God, in giving the command, acted not in cruelty, but in righteous retribution, giving to all what they deserved, and warning those who needed warning. What is the evil in war? Is it the death of some who will soon die in any case, that others may live in peaceful subjection? This is mere cowardly dislike, not any religious feeling. The real evils in war are love of violence, revengeful cruelty, fierce and implacable enmity, wild resistance, and the lust of power, and such like; and it is generally to punish these things, when force is required to inflict the punishment, that, in obedience to God or some lawful authority, good men undertake wars,

when they find themselves in such a position as regards the conduct of human affairs, that right conduct requires them to act, or to make others act in this way. Otherwise John, when the soldiers who came to be baptized asked, What shall we do? would have replied, Throw away your arms; give up the service; never strike, or wound, or disable any one. But knowing that such actions in battle were not murderous, but authorized by law, and that the soldiers did not thus avenge themselves, but defend the public safety, he replied, "Do violence to no man, accuse no man falsely, and be content with your wages (Luke 3:14)." But as the Manichaeans are in the habit of speaking evil of John, let them hear the Lord Jesus Christ Himself ordering this money to be given to Caesar, which John tells the soldiers to be content with. "Give," He says, "to Caesar the things that are Caesar's (Matt. 22:21)." For tribute money is given on purpose to pay the soldiers for war. Again, in the case of the centurion who said, "I am a man under authority, and have soldiers under me: and I say to one, Go, and he goeth; and to another, Come, and he cometh; and to my servant, Do this, and he doeth it," Christ gave due praise to his faith; He did not tell him to leave the service (Matt. 8:9, 10). But there is no need here to enter on the long discussion of just and unjust wars.

75. A great deal depends on the causes for which men undertake wars, and on the authority they have for doing so; for the natural order which seeks the peace of mankind, ordains that the monarch should have the power of undertaking war if he thinks it advisable, and that the soldiers should perform their military duties in behalf of the peace and safety of the community. When war is undertaken in obedience to God, who would rebuke, or humble, or crush the pride of man, it must be allowed to be a righteous war; for even the wars which arise from human passion cannot harm the eternal well-being of God, nor even hurt His saints; for in the trial of their patience, and the chastening of their spirit, and in bearing fatherly correction, they are rather benefited than injured. No one can have any power against them but what is given him from above. For there is no power but of God, who either orders or permits. Since, therefore, a righteous man, serving it may be under an ungodly king, may do the duty belonging to his position in the state in fighting by the order of his sovereign—for in some cases it is plainly the will of God that he should fight, and in others, where this is not so plain, it may be an unrighteous command on the part of the king, while the soldier is innocent, because his position makes obedience a duty—how much more must the man be blameless who carries on war on the authority of God, of whom every one who serves Him knows that He can never require what is wrong?

Questions about the Passage

1. According to Augustine, why do good men undertake wars? Would you add any reasons to his list?
2. What are the real evils in war according to Augustine?
3. Augustine collects three scriptural passages to justify a soldier's participation in war. How does he explain each passage to make his case?
4. Who has the power of undertaking war? Why?
5. For what reason should soldiers perform their military duty?

Questions about the Argument

1. Look up Augustine's biblical citations. How does he use them to make his case? Are they good support for his points?
2. Augustine, in referring to Luke 3:14, argues that John could have told the soldiers not to kill. Is offering an alternative answer to the soldiers an effective rhetorical device?
3. Given that soldiers have committed war crimes and atrocities under their superiors' orders, do you think Augustine makes a convincing case that the individual soldier obeying "an unrighteous command on the part of the king" is innocent? Think, for example, of the Nazis tried at Nuremberg or the troops who carried out their orders at My Lai in Vietnam.

Thomas Aquinas, "Whether It Is Always Sinful to Wage War?"

Thomas Aquinas (1225–1274) is a key Scholastic philosopher and one of the most important Roman Catholic theologians. His lasting contribution to theological thought is his reconciliation of Aristotle's philosophy—preserved and commented upon by Muslim scholars and newly available in Latin in the early thirteenth century—with the Church's accepted doctrines. Aquinas synthesized the ideas of Aristotle; of Augustine and other church fathers; of Islamic scholars such as Averroës; of Jewish thinkers such as Maimonides; and of his predecessors in the Scholastic tradition. His greatest work is the *Summa Theologica* (Summary Treatise of Theology, 1265–1273), in three parts (on God, the moral life of man, and Christ), the last of which he did not finish. The following section on war appears in the second part.

Laws of War: First Article: Whether It Is Always Sinful to Wage War?

We proceed thus to the First Article: —

Objection 1. It would seem that it is always sinful to wage war. Because punishment is not inflicted except for sin. Now those who wage war are threatened by Our Lord with punishment, according to Matt. 26:52: *All that take the sword shall perish with the sword.* Therefore all wars are unlawful.

Obj. 2. Further, whatever is contrary to a Divine precept is a sin. But war is contrary to a Divine precept, for it is written (Matt. 5:39): *But I say to you not to resist evil;* and (Rom. 12–19): *Not revenging yourselves, my dearly beloved, but give place unto wrath.* Therefore war is always sinful.

Obj. 3. Further, nothing, except sin, is contrary to an act of virtue. But war is contrary to peace. Therefore war is always a sin.

Obj. 4. Further, the exercise of a lawful thing is itself lawful, as is evident in scientific exercises. But warlike exercises which take place in tournaments are forbidden by the Church, since those who are slain in these trials are deprived of ecclesiastical burial. Therefore it seems that war is a sin in itself.

On the contrary, Augustine says in a sermon on the son of the centurion: *If the Christian Religion forbade war altogether, those who sought salutary advice in the Gospel would rather have been counselled to cast aside their arms, and to give up soldiering altogether. On the contrary, they were told: "Do violence to no man; . . . and be content with your pay." If he commanded them to be content with their pay, he did not forbid soldiering. I answer that,* In order for a war to be just, three things are necessary. First, the authority of the sovereign by whose command the war is to be waged. For it is not the business of a private individual

5

to declare war, because he can seek for redress of his rights from the tribunal of his superior. Moreover it is not the business of a private individual to summon together the people, which has to be done in wartime. And as the care of the common weal is committed to those who are in authority, it is their business to watch over the common weal of the city, kingdom or province subject to them. And just as it is lawful for them to have recourse to the sword in defending that common weal against internal disturbances, when they punish evildoers, according to the words of the Apostle (Rom. 13:4): *He beareth not the sword in vain: for he is God's minister, an avenger to execute wrath upon him that doth evil;* so too, it is their business to have recourse to the sword of war in defending the common weal against external enemies. Hence it is said to those who are in authority (Ps. 81:4): *Rescue the poor: and deliver the needy out of the hand of the sinner;* and for this reason Augustine says *(Contra Faust.* 22. 75): *The natural order conducive to peace among mortals demands that the power to declare and counsel war should be in the hands of those who hold the supreme authority.*

Secondly, a just cause is required, namely that those who are attacked, should be attacked because they serve it on account of some fault. Wherefore Augustine says (QQ. *in Hept., qu. 10, super Jos.): A just war is wont to be described as one that avenges wrongs, when a nation or state has to be punished, for refusing to make amends for the wrongs inflicted by its subjects, or to restore what it has seized unjustly.*

Thirdly, it is necessary that the belligerents should have a rightful intention, so that they intend the advancement of good, or the avoidance of evil. Hence Augustine says *(De Verb. Dom.): True religion looks upon as peaceful those wars that are waged not for motives of aggrandizement, or cruelty, but with the object of securing peace, of punishing evildoers, and of uplifting the good.* For it may happen that the war is declared by the legitimate authority, and for a just cause, and yet be rendered unlawful through a wicked intention. Hence Augustine says *(Contra Faust.* 22. 74): *The passion for inflicting harm, the cruel thirst for vengeance, an unpacific and relentless spirit, the fever of revolt, the lust of power, and such like things, all these are rightly condemned in war.*

Reply Obj. 1. As Augustine says *(Contra Faust.* 22. 70): *To take the sword is to arm oneself in order to take the life of anyone,*

without the command or permission of superior or lawful authority.
On the other hand, to have recourse to the sword (as a private
person) by the authority of the sovereign or judge, or (as a
public person) through zeal for justice, and by the authority,
so to speak, of God, is not to *take the sword*, but to use it as
commissioned by another, wherefore it does not deserve punishment. And yet even those who make sinful use of the
sword are not always slain with the sword, yet they always
perish with their own sword, because, unless they repent,
they are punished eternally for their sinful use of the sword.

Reply Obj. 2. Such like precepts, as Augustine observes (*De
Serm. Dom. in Monte* 1. 19), should always be borne in readi-
ness of mind, so that we be ready to obey them, and, if necessary, to refrain from resistance or self-defense. Nevertheless it
is necessary sometimes for a man to act otherwise for the common good, or for the good of those with whom he is fighting.
Hence Augustine says (*Ep. ad Marcellin.* 138): *Those whom we
have to punish with a kindly severity, it is necessary to handle in
many ways against their will. For when we are stripping a man of
the lawlessness of sin, it is good for him to be vanquished, since
nothing is more hopeless than the happiness of sinners, whence
arises a guilty impunity, and an evil will, like an internal enemy.*

Reply Obj. 3. Those who war justly aim at peace, and so   10
they are not opposed to peace, except to the evil peace,
which Our Lord *came not to send upon earth* (Matt. 10:34).
Hence Augustine says (*Ep. ad Bonif.* 189): *We do not seek peace
in order to be at war, but we go to war that we may have peace. Be
peaceful, therefore, in warring, so that you may vanquish those
whom you war against, and bring them to the prosperity of peace.*

Reply Obj. 4. Manly exercises in warlike feats of arms are not
all forbidden, but those which are inordinate and perilous,
and end in slaying or plundering. In olden times warlike exercises presented no such danger, and hence they were called
exercises of arms or *bloodless wars,* as Jerome states in an epistle.

Questions about the Passage

1. What are the three criteria of Just War according to Aquinas?
2. Must all three criteria be met for a war to be just? Locate a part of
   the text that demonstrates the answer to this question.

3. Choose one objection and its reply. Discuss whether the reply refutes the objection.

Questions about the Argument

1. Aquinas uses a powerful argumentative structure: He raises objections, presents his own case, and then answers the objections one by one. Why do you think he does not answer the objections before proceeding to make his own case?
2. Try to rephrase each objection as a syllogism. Does each syllogism follow the rules of logic?
3. In answering each objection, which kinds of authority does Aquinas use to bolster his refutation? Do you find these refutations convincing? Why or why not?
4. The crux of Aquinas' argument begins with "on the contrary." What are his answers to the question beginning this article? What types of evidence and authority does he bring to support his position?
5. Compare Augustine's and Aquinas' arguments in support of just war. What ideas do they have in common? Do they differ? If so, on what points?

Francisco de Vitoria, "Before, During, and After War"

Francisco de Vitoria (1486?–1546), a Spanish theologian, is credited as the founder of the philosophy of international law. A Dominican like Aquinas, about whom he wrote lengthy commentaries, Vitoria taught at the University of Salamanca, which was famous for its moral analysis of economic subjects. In his *Indiis et de Iure Belli (Of Indians and the Law of War)*, he examined the morality of Spanish treatment of the native peoples of the New World, and he declared that the Indians were not inferior beings who could be enslaved but were human beings equal to Spaniards. Vitoria's views eventually persuaded Charles V and his advisors to put the Indians under the Crown's protection in 1542.

> All this can be summarized in a few canons or rules of warfare. First canon: Assuming that a prince has authority to make war, he should first of all not go seeking occasions and causes of war, but should, if possible, live in peace with all men, as St. Paul enjoins on us (Rom. 12). Moreover, he should reflect that others are his neighbors, whom we are bound to love as ourselves, and that we all have one common Lord,

before whose tribunal we shall have to render our account. For it is the extreme of savagery to seek for and rejoice in grounds for killing and destroying men whom God has created and for whom Christ died. But only under compulsion and reluctantly should he come to the necessity of war.

Second canon: When war for a just cause has broken out, it must not be waged so as to ruin the people against whom it is directed, but only so as to obtain one's rights and the defense of one's country and in order that from that war peace and security may in time result.

Third canon: When victory has been won and the war is over, the victory should be utilized with moderation and Christian humility, and the victor ought to deem that he is sitting as judge between two states, the one which has been wronged and the one which has done the wrong, so that it will be as judge, and not as accuser that he will deliver the judgment whereby the injured state can obtain satisfaction, and this, so far as possible should involve the offending state in the least degree of calamity and misfortune, the offending individuals being chastised within lawful limits; and an especial reason for this is that in general among Christians all the fault is to be laid at the door of their princes, for subjects when fighting for their princes act in good faith and it is thoroughly unjust, in the words of the poet, that—
For every folly their Kings commit the punishment should fall upon the Greeks.

Questions about the Passage

1. What must a prince do *before* he makes war?
2. What limits must be set on a war for a just cause?
3. How should the victor act towards the one who has done the wrong?

Questions about the Argument

1. What is the historical context out of which Vitoria writes?
2. Who is Vitoria's primary audience? How does he direct his teaching to this audience?
3. What rhetorical effect does Vitoria gain by referring to the "canons" or laws of war?

Martin Luther, "Whether Soldiers, Too, Can Be Saved"

Martin Luther (1483–1546), a founder of the Protestant Reformation, was an Augustinian monk when he began to urge reform of the Roman Catholic Church. In 1517 he posted his 95 Theses on the castle church door in Wittenberg, Saxony, an act of protest that ultimately led to his excommunication in 1521 and the founding of the Lutheran Church in 1530. Luther's message advocating the overthrow of the spiritual authority of the church led peasants in southern and western Germany to revolt, demanding more just agrarian economic conditions and freedom from oppression by the nobility. Luther vigorously opposed the Peasants' War (1524–1526), which cost 100,000 peasant lives, denouncing the peasants' revolt against their political and economic authorities. During the war, Assa von Kram, a professional military officer, asked Luther if soldiers could be good Christians, and he wrote "Whether Soldiers, Too, Can Be Saved" (1526) in response.

> To the Worshipful and Honorable Assa von Kram, My Gracious Lord and Friend, [from] Martin Luther. . . .
>
> What men write about war, saying that it is a great plague, is all true. But they should also consider how great the plague is that war prevents. If people were good and wanted to keep peace, war would be the greatest plague on earth. But what are you going to do about the fact that people will not keep the peace, but rob, steal, kill, outrage women and children, and take away property and honor? The small lack of peace called war or the sword must set a limit to this universal, worldwide lack of peace which would destroy everyone. . . .
>
> So too, we must look at the office of the soldier, or the sword, with the eyes of an adult and see why this office slays and acts so cruelly. Then it will prove itself to be an office which, in itself, is godly and as needful and useful to the world as eating and drinking or any other work.
>
> There are some who abuse this office, and strike and kill people needlessly simply because they want to. But that is the fault of the persons, not of the office, for where is there an office or a work or anything else so good that self-willed, wicked people do not abuse it? They are like mad physicians who would needlessly amputate a healthy hand just because they wanted to. Indeed, they themselves are a part of that universal lack of peace which must be prevented by just wars and the sword and be forced into peace. It always happens

and always has happened that those who begin war unnecessarily are beaten. Ultimately, they cannot escape God's judgment and sword. In the end God's justice finds them and strikes, as happened to the peasants in the revolt.

As proof, I quote John the Baptist, who, except for Christ, was the greatest teacher and preacher of all. When soldiers came to him and asked what they should do, he did not condemn their office or advise them to stop doing their work; rather, according to Luke 3:14, he approved it by saying, "Rob no one by violence or by false accusation, and be content with your wages." Thus he praised the military profession, but at the same time he forbade its abuse. Now the abuse does not affect the office. When Christ stood before Pilate he admitted that war was not wrong when he said, "If my kingship were of this world, then my servants would fight that I might not be handed over to the Jews" (John 18:36). Here, too, belong all the stories of war in the Old Testament, the stories of Abraham, Moses, Joshua, the Judges, Samuel, David, and all the kings of Israel. If the waging of war and the military profession were in themselves wrong and displeasing to God, we should have to condemn Abraham, Moses, Joshua, David, and all the rest of the holy fathers, kings, and princes, who served God as soldiers and are highly praised in Scripture because of this service, as all of us who have read even a little in Holy Scripture know well, and there is no need to offer further proof of it here. . . .

Now we will move on to the second point and discuss the question whether equals may wage war against equals. I would have this understood as follows: It is not right to start a war just because some silly lord has gotten the idea into his head. At the very outset I want to say that whoever starts a war is in the wrong. And it is only right and proper that he who first draws his sword is defeated, or even punished, in the end. This is what has usually happened in history. Those who have started wars have lost them, and those who fought in self-defense have only seldom been defeated. Worldly government has not been instituted by God to break the peace and start war, but to maintain peace and to avoid war. Paul says in Romans 13:4 that it is the duty of the sword to protect and punish, to protect the good in peace and to punish the

5

wicked with war. God tolerates no injustice and he has so ordered things that warmongers must be defeated in war. As the proverb says, "No one has ever been so evil that he does not meet someone more evil than he is." And in Psalm 68:30 God has the psalmist sing of him. . . . "He scatters the peoples who delight in war." . . . Let this be, then, the first thing to be said in this matter: No war is just even if it is a war between equals, unless one has such a good reason for fighting and such a good conscience that he can say, "My neighbor compels and forces me to fight, though I would rather avoid it." In that case, it can be called not only war, but lawful self-defense, for we must distinguish between wars that someone begins because that is what he wants to do and does before anyone else attacks him, and those wars that are provoked when an attack is made by someone else. The first kind can be called wars of desire; the second, wars of necessity. The first kind are of the devil; God does not give good fortune to the man who wages that kind of war. The second kind are human disasters; God help in them!

Take my advice, dear lords. Stay out of war unless you have to defend and protect yourselves and your office compels you to fight. Then let war come. Be men, and test your armor. Then you will not have to think about war to fight. The situation itself will be serious enough, and the teeth of the wrathful, boasting, proud men who chew nails will be so blunt that they will scarcely be able to bite into fresh butter.

The reason is that every lord and prince is bound to protect his people and to preserve the peace for them. That is his office; that is why he has the sword, Romans 13:4. This should be a matter of conscience for him. And he should on this basis be certain that this work is right in the eyes of God and is commanded by him. I am not now teaching what Christians are to do, for your government does not concern us Christians; but we are rendering you a service and telling you what you are to do before God, in your office of ruler. A Christian is a person to himself; he believes for himself and for no one else. But a lord and prince is not a person to himself, but on behalf of others. It is his duty to serve them, that is, to protect and defend them. It would indeed be good if he were also a Christian and believed in God, for then he would be saved. However, being a Christian is not princely, and therefore few princes can be Christians; as they say, "A prince is a rare bird in heaven." But even if princes are not Christians, they nevertheless ought to do what is right and good according to God's outward ordinance. God wants them to do this. . . .

A second question: "Suppose my lord were wrong in going to war." I reply: If you know for sure that he is wrong, then you should fear God rather than men, Acts 4 (5:29), and you should neither fight nor serve, for you cannot have a good conscience before God. "Oh, no," you say, "my lord would force me to do it; he would take away my fief and would not give me my money, pay, and wages. Besides, I would be despised and put to shame as a coward, even worse, as a man who did not keep his word and deserted his lord in need." I answer: You must take that risk and, with God's help, let whatever happens, happen. He can restore it to you a hundredfold, as he promises in the gospel, "Whoever leaves house, farm, wife, and property, will receive a hundredfold," etc. (Matt. 19:29).

In every other occupation we are also exposed to the danger   10
that the rulers will compel us to act wrongly; but since God will have us leave even father and mother for his sake, we must certainly leave lords for his sake. But if you do not know, or cannot find out, whether your lord is wrong, you ought not to weaken certain obedience for the sake of an uncertain justice; rather you should think the best of your lord, as is the way of love, for "love believes all things" and "does not think evil," I Corinthians 13 (:4–7). So, then, you are secure and walk well before God. If they put you to shame or call you disloyal, it is better for God to call you loyal and honorable than for the world to call you loyal and honorable. What good would it do you if the world thought of you as a Solomon or a Moses, and in God's judgment you were considered as bad as Saul or Ahab?

Questions about the Passage

1. What terms does Luther use to characterize war? According to Luther, why may a war be necessary?
2. Luther places wars into three categories. What are they? Which type does Luther find most troublesome? Why?

3. Of the antagonists in war, who is always in the wrong?
4. What kind of reason for fighting is required to make a war just?
5. What is the obligation of the individual soldier in the case of an unjust war?
6. Like Augustine and Thomas Aquinas, Luther uses Luke 3:14 to justify the actions of soldiers. Compare and contrast the use each makes of this quotation.
7. What attitudes and rules for war and for rulers would both Vitoria and Luther propose or impose?

Questions about the Argument

1. In the first part of his piece, to whom is Luther addressing his argument? In the second part, who is his audience? In the third part?
2. Who might the "silly lord" in paragraph 6 be? In paragraph 7, who are the "dear lords"? What is the difference between these two groups? How do Luther's adjectives contribute to our understanding of the difference?
3. Luther's use of metaphor and figurative language distinguishes him from the previous writers (see paragraphs 2 and 7, for example). Does he add to his persuasiveness with such language? What sense of Luther's personality do you get?

U.S. Catholic Bishops, "Two Traditions: Nonviolence and Just War"

The U.S. Catholic Bishops' 1993 pastoral letter, *The Harvest of Justice Is Sown in Peace*, revisits and reflects on an earlier pastoral letter, *The Challenge of Peace: God's Promise and Our Response*, concerned with issues of war and peace, especially those facing the U.S. as a superpower in an era of nuclear weapons. The bishops' 1993 letter, a teaching document directed to Roman Catholics in the United States, focuses on a "theology of peace," which is included in Chapter 6. The history of the just war argument that follows makes a forceful claim that "just war teaching has evolved, however, as an effort to prevent war; only if war cannot be rationally avoided does the teaching then seek to reduce its horrors."

B. Two Traditions: Nonviolence and Just War

1. **Nonviolence: New Importance.** As *The Challenge of Peace* observed, "The vision of Christian nonviolence is not passive about injustice and the defense of the rights of others."

It ought not be confused with popular notions of nonresisting pacifism. For it consists of a commitment to resist manifest injustice and public evil with means other than force. These include dialogue, negotiations, protests, strikes, boycotts, civil disobedience and civilian resistance. Although nonviolence has often been regarded as simply a personal option or vocation, recent history suggests that in some circumstances it can be an effective public undertaking as well. Dramatic political transitions in places as diverse as the Philippines and Eastern Europe demonstrate the power of nonviolent action, even against dictatorial and totalitarian regimes. Writing about the events of 1989, Pope John Paul II said,

> It seemed that the European order resulting from the Second World War . . . could only be overturned by another war. Instead, it has been overcome by the nonviolent commitment of people who, while always refusing to yield to the force of power, succeeded time after time in finding effective ways of bearing witness to the truth.

These nonviolent revolutions challenge us to find ways to take into full account the power of organized, active nonviolence. What is the real potential power of serious nonviolent strategies and tactics—and their limits? What are the ethical requirements when organized nonviolence fails to overcome evil and when totalitarian powers inflict massive injustice on an entire people? What are the responsibilities of and limits on the international community?

One must ask, in light of recent history, whether nonviolence should be restricted to personal commitments or whether it also should have a place in the public order with the tradition of justified and limited war. National leaders bear a moral obligation to see that nonviolent alternatives are seriously considered for dealing with conflicts. New styles of preventative diplomacy and conflict resolution ought to be explored, tried, improved and supported. As a nation we should promote research, education and training in nonviolent means of resisting evil. Nonviolent strategies need greater attention in international affairs.

Such obligations do not detract from a state's right and duty to defend against aggression as a last resort. They do, however, raise the threshold for the recourse to force by establishing institutions which promote nonviolent solutions of disputes and nurturing political commitment to such efforts. In some future conflicts, strikes and people power could be more effective than guns and bullets.

2. **Just War: New Questions.** The just-war tradition consists of a body of ethical reflection on the justifiable use of force. In the interest of overcoming injustice, reducing violence and preventing its expansion, the tradition aims at:

a. clarifying when force may be used,
b. limiting the resort to force and
c. restraining damage done by military forces during war.

The just-war tradition begins with a strong presumption against the use of force and then establishes the conditions when this presumption may be overridden for the sake of preserving the kind of peace which protects human dignity and human rights.

In a disordered world, where peaceful resolution of conflicts sometimes fails, the just-war tradition provides an important moral framework for restraining and regulating the limited use of force by governments and international organizations. Since the just-war tradition is often misunderstood or selectively applied, we summarize its major components, which are drawn from traditional Catholic teaching.

First, whether lethal force may be used is governed by the following criteria:

- *Just Cause:* force may be used only to correct a grave, public evil, i.e., aggression or massive violation of the basic rights of whole populations;
- *Comparative Justice:* while there may be rights and wrongs on all sides of a conflict, to override the presumption against the use of force the injustice suffered by one party must significantly outweigh that suffered by the other;
- *Legitimate Authority:* only duly constituted public authorities may use deadly force or wage war;
- *Right Intention:* force may be used only in a truly just cause and solely for that purpose;
- *Probability of Success:* arms may not be used in a futile cause or in a case where disproportionate measures are required to achieve success;

- *Proportionality:* the overall destruction expected from the ·use of force must be outweighed by the good to be achieved;
- *Last Resort:* force may be used only after all peaceful alternatives have been seriously tried and exhausted.

These criteria (*jus ad bellum*), taken as a whole, must be satisfied in order to override the strong presumption against the use of force.

Second, the just-war tradition seeks also to curb the violence of war through restraint on armed combat between the contending parties by imposing the following moral standards (*jus in bello*) for the conduct of armed conflict:

- *Noncombatant Immunity:* civilians may not be the object of direct attack, and military personnel must take due care to avoid and minimize indirect harm to civilians;
- *Proportionality:* in the conduct of hostilities, efforts must be made to attain military objectives with no more force than is militarily necessary and to avoid disproportionate collateral damage to civilian life and property;
- *Right Intention:* even in the midst of conflict, the aim of political and military leaders must be peace with justice, so that acts of vengeance and indiscriminate violence, whether by individuals, military units or governments, are forbidden.

Questions about the Passage

1. How do the bishops distinguish between nonviolence and non-resisting pacifism?
2. What is the connection between nonviolence and Just War according to the bishops?
3. What is the purpose of Just War theory according to the bishops?
4. Can you see any evidence that twentieth-century events have had an impact on the bishops' letter? If so, what?
5. Does the bishops' listing of the tenets of Just War add to or change any points made by earlier theorists?

Questions about the Argument

1. Is the bishops' pastoral letter argumentative writing? Why or why not? Do the bishops present an argumentative thesis (stated or implied)? If so, what is it?

2. What gives the bishops their authority to speak on the issue of war and peace?
3. Who is the primary audience of the letter? Might there be additional audiences? Note that the letter is available on the World Wide Web.
4. Why is it necessary for the bishops to set forth a presumption against the use of force?

Writing Assignments

Conversations

1. Imagine that you are an interviewer on a serious talk show (for example, Charlie Rose or Jim Lehrer). You have invited Augustine, Aquinas, and Luther for a focused discussion about Just War. During the interview, be sure you ask your guests to address the following issues: What do they see as their contribution to the Just War tradition? What do Aquinas and Luther see as their additions to Augustine's original position? Given that all three use the same passage, Luke 3:14, why did they select that passage and how central is it to their argument? Do not structure your show merely as a question-and-answer session but encourage the guests to engage in a discussion with each other. Try to differentiate the voice of each speaker.
2. Suppose you are moderating another discussion, this time in the weeks leading up to a possible war. Your audience has been hearing both pro and antiwar advocates use terms from the Just War traditions such as "just cause," "right intention," "proportionality," and "last resort." To help your audience understand these ideas, you have brought together Vitoria, a U.S. Catholic Bishop, and at least one other discussant of your choice. Be sure they explain the above terms and any others you think are essential in making the difficult decision to go to war.
3. You are the moderator of a round-table discussion during wartime. Your audience is being assaulted by the images of war—firefights, bombing, ruined buildings, corpses, injured children, and POWs. At the table are the writer of Deuteronomy, al-Shaybani, Maimonides, Vitoria, and a representative of the U.S. Catholic Bishops, all of whom have considered how to regulate and limit the conduct of what Luther calls the "great plague"

of war. Ask your guests whether it is possible to conduct war in a just manner. How do their writings provide principles for the just conduct of war?

Sequence One: Exploring Just War Traditions

1. Brainstorm a list of the issues, problems, or questions that these Just War texts raise for you. Identify and explore informally the one or two questions or issues that most interest you. Had you ever heard of Just War theory? Do think that there is a need for such thinking about war? Do these texts help you reflect on and frame current issues connected with war?

2. Write a brief for an argument that takes a position on the Just War issue you explored in the preceding assignment (see Chapter 3). Be sure to identify the audience you are addressing. What will your audience need to know? What assumptions about the issue do you need to make explicit? List the sources (minimum of three) you expect to use to support your position.

3. Write a short argumentative essay (4–5 pages) from your argument in brief. Your position should be stated in a clear thesis. Support for the thesis should come from your reading in this section. Use a minimum of three sources.

Sequence Two: The Rhetoric of Just War Traditions

1. Examine the ethos of either Aquinas or Luther. How trustworthy do you find him? What credentials does he have? How does he create his own authority to speak on the issue of Just War? What are his assumptions?

2. Choose a text that evidently has more than one audience in mind, for example, the U.S. Bishops' Letter or Luke. What can you infer about these audiences? How do the writers keep the assumptions and needs of the audience in mind?

3. Select the text that, in your opinion, gives the most clearly articulated argument (logos). Lay out the argument: its thesis or claim, its main points and support, and its handling of opposing arguments.

4. Of all the Just War theorists included in this section, whom do you find most persuasive or least persuasive? Here consider all the elements of argument—ethos, audience, logos, and pathos. Make your own strong case for the most or least persuasive writer.

5

Changing Over Time: Reworking Just War Traditions

Modern theorists continue to find valuable guidance in the Just War traditions, even as they must confront the realities of modern warfare—such as nuclear bombs, biological weapons, and terrorism—that were unknown to the thinkers of the past. The works included in this chapter all consider the evolution of Just War thinking or contemplate its shortcomings. Majid Khadduri traces the principle of jihad in Muslim thinking from its origins to more modern times. Anyone seriously interested in the conflicts of our world today needs to understand jihad. The political philosopher Michael Walzer carefully examines other sorts of wars that might also be ruled just: preventive wars and interventions for humanitarian causes. In a world filled with left-over landmines and damaged infrastructures, Michael Schuck proposes adding to the duties of the victor, extending traditional Just War thinking with three principles and two accomplishments for a *jus post bellum*, a just conclusion to war. The conditions of modern warfare that so often result in heavy civilian injuries and death lead Laurie Calhoun to question continuing to use Just War thinking at all. For her, too many use the rhetoric of Just War traditions to justify what cannot be justified— the deaths of innocents. Finally, Rabbi Arthur Waskow uses one of the oldest narratives in the Hebrew Bible, the story of Noah's ark, to illuminate his discussion of war in the nuclear age. The chapter ends with Waskow's profound question: do nuclear weapons mean that the category of war itself is no longer possible?

Majid Khadduri, "The Doctrine of Jihad"

Majid Khadduri (1908–) is one of the foremost scholars of Middle Eastern law, politics, and history. Born in Iraq, he attended the American University of Beirut and the University of Chicago. Professor Khadduri was a member of the Iraqi delegation to the founding sessions of the United Nations in 1945, where he worked on the drafting of the U.N. Charter. He spent the bulk of his career at Johns Hopkins University's School of Advanced International Studies, where he founded and directed its Middle East Studies Center, and is the author, editor, or translator of sixteen books and many major articles about Islamic law and Middle Eastern history, politics, and society.

> "Every nation has its monasticism, and the monasticism of this
> [Muslim] nation is the jihād," a hadīth.

The Meaning of Jihād

The term jihād is derived from the verb jāhada (abstract noun, juhd) which means "exerted";[1] its juridical-theological meaning is exertion of one's power in Allah's path, that is, the spread of the belief in Allah and in making His word supreme over this world. The individual's recompense would be the achievement of salvation, since the jihād is Allah's direct way to paradise. This definition is based on a Qur'ānic injunction which runs as follows:

> O ye who believe! Shall I guide you to a gainful trade which will save you from painful punishment? Believe in Allah and His Apostle and carry on warfare (jihād) in the path of Allah with your possessions and your persons. That is better for you. If ye have knowledge, He will forgive your sins, and will place you in the Gardens beneath which the streams flow, and in fine houses in the Gardens of Eden: that is the great gain.[2]

The jihād, in the broad sense of exertion, does not necessarily mean war or fighting, since exertion in Allah's path may be achieved by peaceful as well as violent means. The jihād may be regarded as a form of religious propaganda that can be carried on by persuasion or by the sword. In the early Makkan revelations, the emphasis was in the main on persuasion. Muhammad, in the discharge of his prophetic functions, seemed to have been satisfied by warning his people against idolatry and inviting them to worship Allah. This is evidenced by such a verse as the following: "He who exerts himself (jāhada), exerts only for his own soul,"[3] which expresses the jihād in terms of the salvation of the soul rather than a struggle for proselytization.[4] In the Madīnan revelations, the jihād is often expressed in terms of strife, and there is no doubt that in certain verses the conception of jihād is synonymous with the words war and fighting.[5]

The jurists, however, have distinguished four different ways in which the believer may fulfill his jihād obligation: by his heart; his tongue; his hands; and by the sword.[6] The first is concerned with combatting the devil and in the attempt to escape his persuasion to evil. This type of jihād, so significant in the eyes of the Prophet Muhammad, was regarded as the greater jihād.[7] The second and third are mainly fulfilled in supporting the right and correcting the wrong. The fourth is precisely equivalent to the meaning of war, and is concerned with fighting the unbelievers and the enemies of the faith.[8] The believers are under the obligation of sacrificing their "wealth and lives" (Q [ur'an]. LXI, 11) in the prosecution of war.[9]

The Jihād as *Bellum Justum*

War is considered as just whether commenced and prosecuted   5
in accordance with the necessary formalities required under a certain system of law, or waged for justifiable reasons in accordance with the tenets of the religion or the mores of a certain society. In Islam, as in ancient Rome, both of these concepts were included in their doctrine of the *bellum justum,* since a justifiable reason as well as the formalities for prosecuting the war were necessary. In both Islam and ancient Rome, not only was war to be *justum,* but also to be *pium,* that is, in accordance with the sanction of religion and the implied commands of gods.[10]

The idea that wars, when institutionalized as part of the mores of society, are just may be traced back to antiquity. It was implied in the concept of vendetta as an act of retaliation by one group against another. In the *Politics,* Aristotle refers to certain wars as just by nature.[11] The Romans instituted the *jus fetiale,* administered by a *collegium fetialium* (consisting of twenty members, presided over by *magister fetialium*), embodying the proper rules of waging war in order to be just.[12] In medieval Christendom, both St. Augustine and Isodore de Seville were influenced in their theory of just war by Cicero. St. Thomas Aquinas, who was acquainted with Muslim writings, formulated his theory of just war along lines similar to the Islamic doctrine of the jihād.[13] St. Thomas and other Medieval writers influenced in their turn the natural law theories of the sixteenth, seventeenth, and eighteenth centuries. Grotius, the father of the modern law of nations, developed his system under the impact of the natural law theory of just war, and his ideas remained predominant until the end of the eighteenth century.[14] Although the doctrine of war during the nineteenth century was by far less influenced by natural law than in previous centuries, the concept of just war reappeared after the First World War in the form of a doctrine of outlawing war, save that against an aggressor.

Recurring as a pattern in the development of the concept of war from antiquity, it assumed in Islam a special position in its jural order because law and religion formed a unity; the law prescribed the way to achieve religious (or divine) purposes, and religion provided a sanction for the law.

In Muslim legal theory, Islam and shirk (associating other gods with Allah) cannot exist together in this world; it is the duty of the imām as well as every believer not only to see that God's word shall be supreme, but also that no infidel shall deny God or be ungrateful for His favors (ni'am).[15] This world would ultimately be reserved for believers;[16] as to unbelievers, "their abode is hell, and evil is the destination."[17] The jihād in other words, is a sanction against polytheism and must be suffered by all non-Muslims who reject Islam, or, in the case of the dhimmīs (Scripturaries), refuse to pay the poll tax. The jihād, therefore, may be defined as the litigation between Islam and polytheism; it is also a form of punishment to be inflicted upon Islam's enemies and the renegades from the faith.[18] Thus in Islam, as in Western Christendom, the jihād is the *bellum justum*.

In Islam, however, the jihād is no less employed for punishing polytheists than for *raison d'état* [reason of state]. For inherent in the state's action in waging a jihād is the establishment of Muslim sovereignty, since the supremacy of God's word carries necessarily with it God's political authority. This seems to be the reason why the jihād, important as it is, is not included—except in the Khārijī legal theory—among the five pillars of Islam. The reason is that the five pillars are not necessarily to be enforced by the state; they must be observed by the individuals regardless of the sanction of authority. The jihād, in order to achieve *raison d'état,* must, however, be enforced by the state. In the technical language the five pillars—the basic articles of the faith—are regarded as individual duties (fard 'ayn), like prayer or fasting, which each believer must individually perform and each is held liable to punishment if he failed to perform the duty. The jihād, on the other hand—unless the Muslim community is subjected to a sudden attack and therefore all believers, including women and children, are under the obligation to fight—is regarded by all jurists, with almost no exception, as a collective obligation of the whole Muslim community.[19] It is regarded as fard al-kifāya, binding on the Muslims as a collective group, not individually. If the duty is fulfilled by a part of the community it ceases to be obligatory on others; the whole community, however, falls into error if the duty is not performed at all.[20]

The imposition of the jihād duty on the community rather than on the individual is very significant and involved at least two important implications. In the first place, it meant that the duty need not necessarily be fulfilled by all the believers. For the recruitment of all the believers as warriors was neither possible nor advisable.[21] Some of the believers were needed to prepare food and weapons, while the crippled, blind, and sick would not qualify as fighters.[22] Women and children were as a rule excused from actual fighting, although many a woman contributed indirectly to the war effort.

In the second place, the imposition of the obligation on the community rather than on the individual made possible the employment of the jihād as a community and, consequently, a state instrument; its control accordingly, is a state, not an individual, responsibility. Thus the head of the state can in a more effective way serve the common interest of the community than if the matter is left entirely to the discretion of the individual believer. Compensation for the fulfillment of such an important public duty has been amply emphasized in both the authoritative sources of the creed[23] and in formal utterances of public men.[24] All of them give lavish promises of martyrdom and eternal life in paradise immediately and without trial on resurrection and judgment day for those who die

10

in Allah's path. Such martyrs are not washed but are buried where they fall on the battlefield, not in the usual type of grave, after washing in a mosque. It is true that a promise of paradise is given to every believer who performs the five basic duties, but none of them would enable him to gain paradise as surely as participation in the jihād.[25]

The Jihād as Permanent War

War, however, was not introduced into Arabia by Islam. It was already in existence among the Arabs; but it was essentially a tribal war. Its nature was peculiar to the existing social order and its rules and procedure were thoroughly integrated as part of the sunna [Muslim law supplementary to the Qur'an]. Since the tribe (in certain instances the clan) was the basic political unit, wars took the form of raids; mainly for robbery or vendetta (tha'r). This state of affairs had, as observed by Ibn Khaldūn, developed among the Arabs a spirit of self-reliance, courage, and co-operation among the members of the single tribe.[26] But these very traits intensified the character of warfare and rivalry among the tribes and created a state of instability and unrest.

The importance of the jihād in Islam lay in shifting the focus of attention of the tribes from their intertribal warfare to the outside world; Islam outlawed all forms of war except the jihād, that is, the war in Allah's path. It would, indeed, have been very difficult for the Islamic state to survive had it not been for the doctrine of the jihād, replacing tribal raids, and directing that enormous energy of the tribes from an inevitable internal conflict to unite and fight against the outside world in the name of the new faith.

The jihād as such was not a casual phenomenon of violence; it was rather a product of complex factors while Islam worked out its jural-doctrinal character. Some writers have emphasized the economic changes within Arabia which produced dissatisfaction and unrest and inevitably led the Arabs to seek more fertile lands outside Arabia.[27] Yet this theory—plausible as it is in explaining the outburst of the Arabs from within their peninsula—is not enough to interpret the character of a war permanently declared against the unbelievers even after the Muslims had established themselves outside Arabia. There were other factors which created in the minds of the

Muslims a politico-religious mission and conditioned their attitude as a conquering nation.

To begin with, there is the universal element in Islam which made it the duty of every able-bodied Muslim to contribute to its spread. In this Islam combined elements from Judaism and Christianity to create something which was not in either: a divine nomocratic state [a state governed by codified laws] on an imperialistic basis. Judaism was not a missionary religion, for the Jews were God's chosen people; a holy war was, accordingly, for the defense of their religion, not for its spread. Christianity on the other hand was a redemptive and, at the outset, a non-state religion. Even when it was associated with politics, the Church and state remained apart. Islam was radically different from both. It combined the dualism of a universal religion and a universal state. It resorted to peaceful as well as violent means for achieving that ultimate objective. The universality of Islam provided a unifying element for all believers, within the world of Islam, and its defensive-offensive character produced a state of warfare permanently declared against the outside world, the world of war.

Thus the jihād may be regarded as Islam's instrument for carrying out its ultimate objective by turning all people into believers, if not in the prophethood of Muhammad (as in the case of the dhimmis), at least in the belief in God. The Prophet Muhammad is reported to have declared "some of my people will continue to fight victoriously for the sake of the *truth* until the last one of them will combat the anti-Christ."[28] Until that moment is reached the jihād, in one form or another, will remain as a permanent obligation upon the entire Muslim community. It follows that the existence of a dār al-harb is ultimately outlawed under the Islamic jural order; that the dār al-Islām [abode of peace] is permanently under jihād obligation until the dār al-harb [abode of war] is reduced to nonexistence; and that any community which prefers to remain non-Islamic—in the status of a tolerated religious community accepting certain disabilities—must submit to Islamic rule and reside in the dār al-Islam or be bound as clients to the Muslim community. The universalism of Islam, in its all-embracing creed, is imposed on the believers as a continuous process of warfare, psychological and political if not strictly military.

Although the jihād was regarded as the permanent basis of Islam's relations with its neighbors, it did not at all mean continuous fighting. Not only could the obligation be performed by nonviolent means, but relations with the enemy did not necessarily mean an endless or constant violent conflict with him. The jihād, accordingly, may be stated as a doctrine of a permanent state of war, not a continuous fighting. Thus some of the jurists argued that the mere preparation for the jihād is a fulfillment of its obligation.[29] The state, however, must be prepared militarily not only to repel a sudden attack on Islam, but also to use its forces for offensive purposes when the caliph deems it necessary to do so.

In practice, however, the jihād underwent certain changes in its meaning to suit the changing circumstances of life. Islam often made peace with the enemy, not always on its own terms. Thus the jurists began to reinterpret the law with a view to justifying suspension of the jihād, even though temporarily. They seem to have agreed about the necessity of peace and the length of its duration. When Muslim power began to decline, Muslim publicists seem to have tacitly admitted that in principle the jihād as a permanent war had become obsolete; it was no longer compatible with Muslim interests. The concept of the jihād as a state of war underwent certain changes. This change, as a matter of fact, did not imply abandonment of the jihād duty; it only meant the entry of the obligation into a period of suspension—it assumed a dormant status, from which the imām may revive it at any time he deems necessary. In practice, however, the Muslims came to think of this as more of a normal condition of life than an active jihād.

The shift in the conception of the jihād from active to dormant war reflects a reaction on the part of the Muslims from further expansion. This coincided with the intellectual and philosophical revival of Islam at the turn of the fourth century of the Muslim era (tenth century A.D.), when the Muslims were probably more stirred by the controversy between orthodoxy and rationalism than by fighting Byzantine encroachments on the frontiers. To certain Muslim thinkers, like Ibn Khaldūn (d. 1406),[30] the relaxation of the jihād marked the change in the character of the nation from the warlike to the civilized stage. Thus the change in the concept of the jihād was not merely an apologia for weakness and failure to live up to a doctrine, but a process of evolution dictated by Islam's interests and social conditions.

* * *

The Jihād and Secular War

Islam, it will be recalled, abolished all kinds of warfare except   20
the jihād. Only a war which has an ultimate religious purpose, that is, to enforce God's law or to check transgression against it, is a just war. No other form of fighting is permitted within or without the Muslim brotherhood.

Throughout the history of Islam, however, fighting between Muslim rulers and contending parties was as continuous as between Islam and its external enemies. The *casus foederis* of a jihād was frequently invoked on the grounds of suppressing innovations and punishing the leaders of secession from the faith. Not infrequently the naked ambition of opposition leaders who resorted to war for the sake of a throne or high political offices was too apparent to be ignored. When the caliph's prestige and power declined, lack of respect for and opposition to the central authority became fashionable among local rulers. This state of affairs accentuated the struggle for power and created instability and anarchy in the world of Islam. Ignoring existing realities, the jurists continued to argue— following the example of al-Māwardī—that ultimate authority belonged to the caliph and that no one else had the right to renounce it even if the caliph proved to be unjust and oppressive, since tyranny, it was then contended, was preferrable to anarchy[31]—a sad comment on existing conditions.

A few publicists, in their reflections on the state of affairs as they then existed, have said that wars, in forms other than the jihād, had often recurred in the Islamic society. Paying lip service to the jihād as a religious duty, they looked upon wars as dangers which Muslim rulers should avoid. Al-Tartūshī (died A.H. 520) described "war crises" as social anomalies[32] and al-Hasan ibn 'Abd-Allah compared them to diseases of society.[33] Both of these writers, who expatiated on the ways and means of conducting fighting, advised their rulers that the best way to win wars, if they found it impossible to avert them, was to be adequately prepared militarily. Thus Muslim publicists,

like their Roman predecessors, seemed to have been convinced that *si vis pacem, para bellum.*

It was, perhaps, Ibn Khaldūn (A.D. 1332–1406) who for the
first time recognized that wars were not, as his Muslim predecessors thought, casual social calamities. He maintained that
war has existed in society ever since "Creation." Its real cause,
which accounts for its persistence in society, is man's will-to-
revenge. Man, in other words, is by nature warlike. He is for-
ever moved to fight either for his own selfish interests or by
such emotional motives as jealousy, anger, or a feeling of
divine guilt. Thus the members of one group or nation, in
order to attain their objectives, combined against others and
the inevitable result was war.

Wars, according to Ibn Khaldūn, are of four kinds. First is the
tribal warfare, such as that which existed among the Arabian
tribes; second, feuds and raids which are characteristic of primitive people; third, the wars prescribed by the sharī'a i.e., the
jihād; fourth, wars against rebels and dissenters. Ibn Khaldūn
contends that the first two are unjustified, because they are
wars of disobedience; the other two are just wars ('adl).

* * *

It is to be noted that Muslim thinkers, from the rise of Islam   25
to the time of Ibn Khaldūn, regarded secular wars as an evil to
be avoided since they were inconsistent with God's law which
prohibited all forms of war except those waged for religious
purposes. A close examination of society taught Muslim
thinkers that secular wars were not easily avoided by fallible
human beings; peace within the Muslim brotherhood needed
the inspiring influence of a Prophet or the prestige and power
of an 'Umar I. When the caliphs departed from the sunna of
the Prophet, holy wars were no longer the only kind of warfare waged; nor were they always devoid of secular purposes.
A war, called harb, in distinction from a holy war (jihād), was
looked upon as an unnatural phenomenon which befell society
only because of man's carelessness and sins. Ibn 'Abd-Allah, it
will be remembered, described wars as diseases; but Ibn
Khaldūn thought that their frequency in society, arising from
the very nature of man, makes their recurrence as permanent
as social life itself. Ibn Khaldūn based his conclusions not only

on his own personal observations on the state of constant warfare that existed among the petty Muslim states in North Africa, but also on the experiences of various nations with whose history he was acquainted. Ibn Khaldūn's observation, which shows keen insight in understanding human society, is corroborated by modern research, which has demonstrated that early societies tended to be more warlike and that peace was by no means the normal state of affairs.[34] As Sir Henry Maine stated, "it is not peace which was natural and primitive and old, but rather war. War appears to be as old as mankind, but peace is a modern invention."[35] Islam, unlike Christianity, sought to establish the Kingdom of Heaven on earth; but, like Christianity, could not produce that world brotherhood and God-fearing society which would live permanently in peace. War was as problematic to our forefathers as to ourselves; they sought earnestly to abolish it by the faiths they honored no less than we do by our own faith in the scientific approach.

Notes

1. For the literal meaning of jihād, see Fayrūzabādī, *Qāmūs al-Muhīt* (Cairo, 1933), Vol. I, p. 286. For the Quar'ānic use of jihād in the sense of exertion see Q. VI, 108; XXII, 77.
2. Q. LXI, 10–13. See also jurjānī, *kitāb al-Ta'rīfāt*, ed. Gustavus Flügel (Leipzig, 1845), p. 84.
3. Q. XXIX, 5.
4. See Shāfi'ī, *Kitāb al-Umm* (Cairo, A. H. 1321), Vol. IV, pp. 84–85; 'Abd al-Qāhir al-Baghdādī, *Kitāb Usūl al-Dīn* (Istanbul, 1928) Vol. I, p. 193; Shaybāni, *al-Siyar al-Kabīr,* with Sarakhsī's Commentary (Hyderabad, A.H. 1335), Vol. I, p.126.
5. See Q. II, 215; IX, 41; XLIX, 15; LXI, 11; LXVI, 9.
6. See Ibn Hazm, *Kitāb al-Fasl fī al-Milal wa'l-Ahwā wa'l-Nihal* (Cairo, A.H. 1321). Vol. IV, p. 135; Ibn Rushd, *Kitāb al-Mugaddimāt al-Mumahhidāt* (Cairo, A.H. 1325), Vol. I, p. 259; Buhūtī, *Kashshāf al-Qinā' 'An Matn al-Iqnā'* (Cairo, A.H. 1366), Vol. III, p. 28.
7. Ibn al-Humām, *Sharh Fath al-Qadīr* (Cairo, A.H. 1316), Vol. IV, p. 277.
8. Ibn Hazm distinguishes between the jihād by the tongue and the jihād by ra'y and tadbīr (i.e., reason) and he maintains that the Prophet Muhammad showed preference for reason over the sword. Ibn Hazm, Vol. IV, p. 135.

9. Bukhārī, *Kitāb al-Jāmi' al-Sahīh*, ed. Krehl (Leiden, 1864), Vol. II, p. 199; Abū Dā'ūd *Sunan* (Cairo, 1935), Vol. III, p. 5; Dārimī, *Sunan* (Damascus, A.H. 1349), Vol. II, p. 213.

10. See J. Von Elbe, "The Evolution of the Concept of the Just War in International Law," *American Journal of International Law*, Vol. XXXIII (1939), pp. 665–88; and Coleman Phillipson, *The International Law and Custom of Ancient Greece and Rome* (London, 1911), Vol. II, p. 180.

11. *Politics*, Bk. I, chap. VIII.

12. In the *Offices*, Cicero, who may be regarded as the representative legal philosopher of ancient Rome, has discussed the rules and formalities which constitute the *bellum justum*. See Cicero, *Offices, Essays, and Letters* (Everyman's edition), Bk. I, § 11–12.

13. See A. P. D'Entreves, *Aquinas: Selected Political Writings* (Oxford, 1948) pp. 59–61; John Epstein, *The Catholic Tradition of the Law of Nations* (London, 1935); William Ballis, *The Legal Position of War: Changes in its Practice and Theory* (The Hague, 1937), pp. 32–60.

14. Hugo Grotius, *De Jure Belli ac Pacis*, first published in 1625 (Oxford, 1925).

15. The Prophet Muhammad is reported to have said: "I am ordered to fight polytheists until they say: 'there is no god but Allah.'" The validity of the rule of fighting polytheists is also based on a Qur'ānic injunction, in which Allah said to His Apostle, as follows: "slay the polytheists wherever you may find them" (Q. IX, 5). See also Tāj al-Dīn al-Subkī, *Kitāb Mu'īd al-Ni'am wa Mubīd al-Niqam*, ed. David W. Myhrman (London, 1908), p. 27.

16. The idea that Islam would ultimately replace other religions (except perhaps the tolerated religions) is not stated in the Qur'ān, but it is implied in the objective of the jihād and expressed in the hadīth. See note 15, above.

17. Q. IX, 74.

18. For the forms or types of jihād.

19. Sa'īd ibn al-Musayyib said that the jihād duty is fard 'ayn. Awzā'ī and Thawrī; however, advocated a defensive jihād (Shaybānī, *op.cit.*, Vol. I, p. 125) and an extremely pacifist sect, known as the Māziyāriyya, dropped both the jihād against polytheists and fasting from the articles of faith. See 'Abd al-Qāhir al-Baghdādī, *Mukhtasar Kitāb al-Farq Bayn al-Firaq*, summarized by al-Ras'anī and edited by Hitti (Cairo, 1924), p. 163.

20. For a definition of this term, see Suyūtī, *al-Ashbāh wa'l-Nazā'ir* (Cairo, 1938), pp. 496–503; Ibn Qudāma, *al-Mughnī*, ed. Rashīd Rida (Cairo, A.H. 1367), Vol. VIII, pp. 345–6; Ibn al-Humām, *op. cit.*, p. 278.

21. Q. IX, 123: "The believers must not march forth all to war."

22. Q. XXIV, 60: "There is no blame on the blind man, nor on the lame, nor on the sick. . . ."

23. Q. III, 163: "Count not those who are killed in the path of Allah as dead; they are alive with their Lord." A woman complained to Muhammad about the death of her son in the battle of Badr, and then she asked whether her son went to hell or paradise, Muhammad replied: "Your son is in the higher Paradise!" (Bukhrārī, Vol. II, p. 202.) Another hadīth runs as follows: "There are one hundred stages in Paradise that are provided by Allah for those who fight in His path" (Bukhārī, II, p. 200). See also Ibn Hudhayl, *Tuhfat al-Anfus wa Shi'ār Sukkān al-Andalus*, ed. Louis Mercier (Paris, 1936), chaps. 10 and 20.

24. See a speech given by Caliph Abū Bakr to Syrian expedition in Tabarī; *Ta'rīkh*, ed. de Goeje (Leiden, 1890), Series I, Vol. IV, p. 1850.

25. Shaybānī, *op. cit.*, Vol. I, p. 20; and Herman Theodorus Obbink, *De Heilige Oorlog Volgen den Koran* (Leiden, 1901), pp. 110–1.

26. Ibn Khaldūn, *al-Muqaddima*, ed. Quatremère (Paris, 1858), Vol. II, pp. 220–1.

27. The economic factors are discussed by Carl H. Becker in *The Cambridge Medieval History* (Cambridge, 1913), Vol. II, pp. 329 ff; Henri Lammens, *Le Berceau de l'Islam* (Rome, 1914), Vol. I, pp. 114 ff; the Semitic migratory theory is discussed in Prince Caetani, *Annali dell'Islam* (Milan, 1907) Vol. II, 831–61.

28. Abū Dā'ūd, *Sunan* (Cairo, 1935), Vol. III, p. 4.

29. Ibn Hudhayl, *op. cit.*, p. 15.

30. Ibn Khaldūn, *op. cit.*, Vol. I, pp. 309 ff.

31. Badr al-Dīn Ibn Jamā'a, *Tahrīr al-Ahkām fī Tadbīr Ahl al-Islām*, ed. H. Koefler in *Islamica*, Vol. VI (1934), p. 365.

32. Tartūshī, *Sirāj al-Mulūk*, pp. 150–153.

33. Ibn 'Abd-Allah, who wrote his book in A. H. 708, gives seven reasons for the recurrence of war in society: First, for the establishment of a new state (dawla) or dynasty; second, for the consolidation of an already established state or dynasty; third, the wars of a just state (dawla 'ādila) against rebels and dissenters; fourth, wars between two nations or tribes in the form of raids; fifth, the annex-

ation of one state by another, regardless of whether the latter was just or unjust; sixth, wars for the purpose of mere robbery, not for any political purpose; seventh, intertribal warfare as those existed in pre-Islamic Arabia. Al-Hasan ibn 'Abd-Allah, Āthār al-Uwal fi Tartīb al-Duwal (Cairo, A. H. 1295), pp. 167–8.

34. Ibn Khaldūn is not the first thinker who said that warfare is the normal state in society, but he was the first Muslim thinker to say so. Plato (*The Laws*, Bk. I. 2) before him as well as others after in Medieval and modern times have expressed similar ideas. Hobbes, in an often quoted statement, said: "Hereby it is manifest, that during the time men live without a common power to keep them all in awe, they are in that condition which is called war; and such a war, as is of every man, against every man. For war, consisteth not in battle only, or the act of fighting; but in a tract of time, wherein the will to contend by battle is sufficiently known: and therefore the notion of time, is to be considered in the nature of war; as it is in the nature of weather. For as the nature of foul weather, lieth not in a shower or two of rain; but in an inclination thereto of many days together: so the nature of war consisteth not in actual fighting; but in the known disposition thereto, during all the time there is no assurance to the contrary. All other time is peace." (Hobbes, *Leviathan*, Chap. 13). See also Leo Strauss, *The Political Philosophy of Hobbes* (Oxford, 1936), pp. 160–3.

35. Sir Henry Maine, *International Law* (London, 1888), p. 8. See also Quincy Wright, *A Study of War* (Chicago, 1942), Vol. I, Chapters 6, 7, appendices, 6, 8, 9, and 10.

Questions about the Passage

1. What is the definition of jihad? What are the four ways a believer may fulfill his jihad obligation?
2. How is the jihad a just war (*bellum justum*)?
3. Who are the sanctioned enemies of the jihad?
4. Why is the jihad not one of the five pillars of Islam?
5. What is the significance of jihad being a community duty rather than an individual one?
6. Why is jihad a permanent state of war? Does that mean Muslims must always be fighting?
7. How did the idea of jihad change over time?
8. What was Ibn Khaldun's view of war?

Questions about the Argument

1. Who is Khadduri's audience? What does he assume about their knowledge about Islam and their general education? Their religious background?
2. Comment on Khadduri's authority and credibility.
3. Do you consider this text to be an argument? Why or why not?
4. Khadduri is a historian and scholar of Islamic law. Is it possible for historians to be objective? How do historians put forward their point of view? Do you see any signs of Khadduri's views?
5. Why does Khadduri compare Islam to Christianity and Judaism in his discussion? Why might these comparisons and contrasts be effective teaching tools?

Michael Walzer, "Preventive War" and "Humanitarian Intervention"

Michael Walzer (1935–) is a distinguished political philosopher, social scientist, and historian. Educated at Brandeis, Cambridge (as a Fulbright Fellow), and Harvard Universities, he taught at Princeton University and at Harvard before becoming Professor of Social Science at the Institute for Advanced Study, Princeton, New Jersey, in 1980.

Walzer is the author of twenty-three books and many scholarly articles, and he is the editor of *Dissent*, a member of the editorial board of *Philosophy and Public Affairs, Political Theory*, and a contributing editor of *The New Republic*. In *Just and Unjust Wars*, now in its third edition, he asserts the value of Just War theory and examines how it has been used to critique the conduct of war and misused to justify unjust wars. In the passages reprinted below, he examines two concepts not included in the Just War traditions we have read so far—preventive war and humanitarian intervention.

In order to understand his argument, we need to be familiar with his definition of the legalist paradigm. The legalist paradigm, or model of behavior, "consistently reflects the conventions of law and order" and is the "fundamental structure for the moral comprehension of war." International society, like all societies, has laws which establish the rights of its members, in this case rights to respond violently to acts of aggression by another state.

Preventive War and the Balance of Power

Preventive war presupposes some standard against which danger is to be measured. That standard does not exist, as it were, on the ground; it has nothing to do with the immediate security of boundaries. It exists in the mind's eye, in the idea of a balance of power, probably the dominant idea in international politics from the seventeenth century to the present day. A preventive war is a war fought to maintain the balance, to stop what is thought to be an even distribution of power from shifting into a relation of dominance and inferiority. The balance is often talked about as if it were the key to peace among states. But it cannot be that, else it would not need to be defended so often by force of arms. "The balance of power, the pride of modern policy . . . invented to preserve the general peace as well as the freedom of Europe," wrote Edmund Burke in 1760, "has only preserved its liberty. It has been the original of innumerable and fruitless wars."[1] In fact, of course, the wars to which Burke is referring are easily numbered. Whether or not they were fruitless depends upon how one views the connection between preventive war and the preservation of liberty. Eighteenth century British statesmen and their intellectual supporters obviously thought the connection very close. A radically unbalanced system, they recognized, would more likely make for peace, but they were "alarmed by the danger of universal monarchy."[2] When they went to war on behalf of the balance, they thought they were defending, not national interest alone, but an international order that made liberty possible throughout Europe.

That is the classic argument for prevention. It requires of the rulers of states, as Francis Bacon had argued a century earlier, that they "keep due sentinel, that none of their neighbors do overgrow so (by increase of territory, by embracing of trade, by approaches, or the like) as they become more able to annoy them, than they were."[3] And if their neighbors do "overgrow," then they must be fought, sooner rather than later, and without waiting for the first blow. "Neither is the opinion of some of the Schoolmen to be received: that a war cannot justly be made, but upon a precedent injury or provocation. For there is no question, but a just fear of an imminent danger, though no blow be given, is a lawful cause of war." Imminence here is not a matter of hours or days. The sentinels stare into temporal as well as geographic distance as they watch the growth of their neighbor's power. They will fear that growth as soon as it tips or seems likely to tip the balance. War is justified (as in Hobbes' philosophy) by fear alone and not by anything other states actually do or any signs they give of their malign intentions. Prudent rulers assume malign intentions.

The argument is utilitarian in form; it can be summed up in two propositions: (1) that the balance of power actually does preserve the liberties of Europe (perhaps also the happiness of Europeans) and is therefore worth defending even at some cost, and (2) that to fight early, before the balance tips in any decisive way, greatly reduces the cost of the defense, while waiting doesn't mean avoiding war (unless one also gives up liberty) but only fighting on a larger scale and at worse odds. The argument is plausible enough, but it is possible to imagine a second-level utilitarian response: (3) that the acceptance of propositions (1) and (2) is dangerous (not useful) and certain to lead to "innumerable and fruitless wars" whenever shifts in power relations occur; but increments and losses of power are a constant feature of international politics, and perfect equilibrium, like perfect security, is a utopian dream; therefore it is best to fall back upon the legalist paradigm or some similar rule and wait until the overgrowth of power is put to some overbearing use. This is also plausible enough, but it is important to stress that the position to which we are asked to fall back is not a prepared position, that is, it does not itself rest on any utilitarian calculation. Given the radical uncertainties of power politics, there probably is no practical way of making out that positions—deciding when to fight and when not—on utilitarian principles. Think of what one would have to know to perform the calculations, of the experiments one would to conduct, the wars one would have to fight—and leave unfought! In any case, we mark off moral lines on the anticipation spectrum in an entirely different way.

It isn't really prudent to assume the malign intent of one's neighbors; it is merely cynical, an example of the worldly wisdom which no one lives by or could live by. We need to make judgments about our neighbor's intentions, and if such judgments are to be possible we must stipulate certain acts or sets of acts that will count as evidence of malignity. These stipulations are not arbitrary; they are generated, I think, when we reflect upon what it means *to be threatened*. Not merely *to be afraid,* though rational men and women may well respond fearfully to a genuine threat, and their subjective experience is not an unimportant part of the argument for anticipation. But we also need an objective standard, as Bacon's phrase "just fear" suggests. That standard must refer to the threatening acts of some neighboring state, for (leaving aside the dangers of natural disaster) I can only be threatened by someone who is threatening me, where "threaten" means what the dictionary says it means: "to hold out or offer (some injury) by way of a threat to declare one's intention of inflicting injury."[4]

* * *

Humanitarian Intervention

A legitimate government is one that can fight its own internal   5
wars. And external assistance in those wars is rightly called counter-intervention only when it balances, and does no more than balance, the prior intervention of another power, making it possible once again for the local forces to win or lose on their own. The outcome of civil wars should reflect not the relative strength of the intervening states, but the local alignment of forces. There is another sort of case, however, where we don't look for outcomes of that sort, where we don't want the local balance to prevail. If the dominant forces within a state are engaged in massive violations of human rights, the appeal to self-determination in the Millian sense of self-help is not very attractive. That appeal has to do with the freedom of the community taken as a whole; it has no force when what is at stake is the bare survival or the minimal liberty of (some substantial number of) its members. Against the enslavement or massacre of political opponents, national minorities, and religious sects, there may well be no help unless help comes from outside. And when a government turns savagely upon its own people, we must doubt the very existence of a political community to which the idea of self-determination might apply.

Examples are not hard to find; it is their plenitude that is embarrassing. The list of oppressive governments, the list of massacred peoples, is frighteningly long. Though an event like the Nazi holocaust is without precedent in human history, murder on a smaller scale is so common as to be almost ordinary. On the other hand—or perhaps for this very reason—clear examples of what is called "humanitarian intervention" are very rare.[5] Indeed, I have not any, but only mixed cases where the humanitarian motive is one among several. States don't send their soldiers into other states, it seems, only in order to save lives. The lives of foreigners don't weigh that heavily in the scales of domestic decision-making. So we shall have to consider the moral significance of mixed motives.[6] It is not necessarily an argument against humanitarian intervention that it is, at best, partially humanitarian, but it is a reason to be skeptical and to look closely at the other parts

* * *

The Indian invasion of East Pakistan (Bangladesh) in 1971 is a[n] . . . example of humanitarian intervention—not because of the singularity or purity of the government's motives, but because its various motives converged on a single course of action that was also the course of action called for by the Bengalis. This convergence explains why the Indians were in and out of the country so quickly, defeating the Pakistani army but not replacing it, and imposing no political controls on the emergent state of Bangladesh. No doubt, strategic as well as moral interests underlay this policy: Pakistan, India's old enemy, was significantly weakened, while India itself avoided becoming responsible for a desperately poor nation whose internal politics was likely to be unstable and volatile for a long time to come. But the intervention qualifies as humanitarian because it was a *rescue*, strictly and narrowly defined. So circumstances sometimes make saints of us all

I shall not say very much about Pakistani oppression in Bengal. The tale is a terrible one and by now fairly well documented.[7] Faced with a movement for autonomy in what was then its eastern province, the government of Pakistan, in March, 1971, literally turned an army loose on its own people—or rather, a Punjabi army loose on the Bengali people, for the unity of east and west was already a broken thing. The resulting massacre only completed the break and made it irreparable. The army was not entirely without direction; its officers carried "death lists" on which appeared the names of the political, cultural, and intellectual leaders of Bengal. There was also a systematic effort to slaughter the followers of these people: university students, political activists, and so on. Beyond these groups, the soldiers ranged freely, burning, raping, killing. Millions of Bengalis fled into India, and their arrival, destitute, hungry, and with incredible stories to tell, established the moral foundation of the later Indian attack. "It is idle to argue in such cases that the duty of the neighboring people is to look on quietly."[8] Months of diplomatic maneuvering followed, but during that time, the Indians were already assisting Bengali guerrillas and offering sanctuary not only to refugees but also to fighting women. The two-week war of December 1971 apparently began with a Pakistani air strike, but the Indian invasion required no such prior attack; it was justified on other grounds.

The strength of the Bengali guerrillas and their achievements between March and December are matters of some dispute; so is their role in the two-week war. Clearly, however, it was not the purpose of the Indian invasion to open the way for the Bengali struggle; nor does the strength or weakness of the guerrillas affect our view of the invasion. When a people are being massacred, we don't require that they pass the test of self-help before coming to their aid. It is their very incapacity that brings us in. The purpose of the Indian army, then, was to defeat the Pakistani forces and drive them out of Bangladesh, that is, to win the war. The purpose was different from that of a counter-intervention, and for an important moral reason. People who initiate massacres lose their right to participate in the normal (even in the normally violent) processes of domestic self-determination. Their military defeat is morally necessary.

Governments and armies engaged in massacres are readily   10
identified as criminal governments and armies (they are guilty, under the Nuremberg code of "crimes against humanity"). Hence humanitarian intervention comes much closer than any other kind of intervention to what we commonly regard, in domestic society, as law enforcement and police work. At the same time, however, it requires the crossing of an international frontier, and such crossings are ruled out by the legalist paradigm—unless they are authorized, I suppose, by the society of nations. In the cases I have considered, the law is unilaterally enforced; the police are self-appointed. Now,

unilateralism has always prevailed in the international arena, but we worry about it more when what is involved is a response to domestic violence rather than to foreign aggression. We worry that, under the cover of humanitarianism, states will come to coerce and dominate their neighbors; once again, it is not hard to find examples. Hence many lawyers prefer to stick to the paradigm. That doesn't require them, on their view, to deny the (occasional) need for intervention. They merely deny legal recognition to that need. Humanitarian intervention "belongs in the realm not of law but of moral choice, which nations, like individuals must sometimes make . . ."[9] But that is only a plausible formulation if one doesn't stop with it, as lawyers are likely to do. For moral choices are not simply *made;* they are also judged, and so there must be criteria for judgment. If these are not provided by the law, or if legal provision runs out at some point, they are nevertheless contained in our common morality, which doesn't run out, and which still needs to be explicated after the lawyers have finished.

Morality, at least, is not a bar to unilateral action, so long as there is no immediate alternative available. There was none in the Bengali case. No doubt, the massacres were a matter of universal interest, but only India interested itself in them. The case was formally carried to the United Nations, but no action followed. Nor is it clear to me that action undertaken by the UN, or by a coalition of powers, would necessarily have had a moral quality superior to that of the Indian attack. What one looks for in numbers is detachment from particularist views and consensus on moral rules. And for that, there is at present no institutional appeal; one appeals to humanity as a whole. States don't lose their particularist character merely by acting together. If governments have mixed motives, so do coalitions of governments. Some goals, perhaps, are cancelled out by the political bargaining that constitutes the coalition, but others are super-added; and the resulting mix is as accidental with reference to the moral issue as are the political interests and ideologies of a single state.

Humanitarian intervention is justified when it is a response (with reasonable expectations of success) to acts "that shock the moral conscience of mankind." The old-fashioned language seems to me exactly right. It is not the conscience of political leaders that one refers to in such cases. They have other things to worry about and may well be required to repress their normal feelings of indignation and outrage. The reference is to the moral convictions of ordinary men and women, acquired in the course of their everyday activities. And given that one can make a persuasive argument in terms of those convictions, I don't think that there is any moral reason to adopt that posture of passivity that might be called waiting for the UN (waiting for the universal state, waiting for the messiah . . .).

> Suppose . . . that a great power decided that the only way it could continue to control a satellite state was to wipe out the satellite's entire population and recolonize the area with "reliable" people. Suppose the satellite government agreed to this measure and established the necessary mass extermination apparatus . . . Would the rest of the members of the U.N. be compelled to stand by and watch this operation merely because [the] requisite decision of U.N. organs was blocked and the operation did not involve an "armed attack" on any [member state] . . . ?[10]

The question is rhetorical. Any state capable of stopping the slaughter has a right, at least, to try to do so. The legalist paradigm indeed rules out such efforts, but that only suggests that the paradigm, unrevised, cannot account for the moral realities of military intervention.

The second, third, and fourth revisions of the paradigm have this form: states can be invaded and wars justly begun to assist secessionist movements (once they have demonstrated their representative character), to balance the prior interventions of other powers, and to rescue peoples threatened with massacre. In each of these cases we permit or, after the fact, we praise or don't condemn these violations of the formal rules of sovereignty, because they uphold the values of individual life and communal liberty of which sovereignty itself is merely an expression. The formula is, once again, permissive, but I have tried in my discussion of particular cases to indicate that the actual requirements of just interventions are constraining indeed. And the revisions must be understood to include the constraints. Since the constraints are often ignored, it is sometimes argued that it would be best to insist on an absolute rule of nonintervention (as it would be best to insist on an absolute rule of a nonanticipation). But the absolute rule will also be ignored, and we will then have no standards by which to judge what happens next. In fact, we do have standards, which I have tried to map out. They reflect deep and valuable, though in their applications difficult and problematic, commitments to human rights.

Notes

1. Quoted from the *Annual Register,* in H. Butterfield, "The Balance of Power," *Diplomatic Investigations,* pp. 144–45.
2. The line is from David Hume's essay "Of the Balance of Power," where Hume describes three British wars on behalf of the balance as having been "begun with justice, and even, perhaps, from necessity." I would have considered his argument at length had I found it possible to place it within his philosophy. But in his *Enquiry Concerning the Principles of Morals* (Section III, Part I), Hume writes: "The rage and violence of public war: what is it but a suspension of justice among the warring parties, who perceive that this virtue is now no longer of any *use* or advantage to them?" Nor is it possible, according to Hume, that this suspension itself be just or unjust; it is entirely a matter of necessity, as in the (Hobbist) state of nature where individuals "consult the dictates of self-preservation alone." That standards of justice exist alongside the pressures of necessity is a discovery of the *Essays.* This is another example, perhaps, of the impossibility of carrying over certain philosophical positions into ordinary moral discourse. In any case, the three wars Hume discusses were none of them necessary to the preservation of Britain. He may have thought them just because he thought the balance generally useful.
3. Francis Bacon, *Essays* ("Of Empire"); see also his treatise *Considerations Touching a War With Spain* (1624), in *The Works of Francis Bacon,* ed. James Spedding *et al.* (London, 1874), XIV, pp. 469–505.
4. *Oxford English Dictionary,* "threaten."
5. Ellery C. Stowell suggests some possible examples in *Intervention in International Law* (Washington, D.C., 1921), ch. II. For contemporary legal views (and newer examples), see Richard Lillich, ed., *Humanitarian Intervention and the United Nations* (Charlottesville, Virginia, 1973).
6. The case is different, obviously, when the lives at stake are those of fellow nationals. Interventions designed to rescue citizens

threatened with death in a foreign country have conventionally been called humanitarian, and there is no reason to deny them that name when life and death are really at issue. The Israeli raid on Entebbe airport in Uganda (July 4, 1976) seems likely to become a classic case. Here there is, or ought to be, no question of mixed motives: the only purpose is to rescue *these* people towards whom the intervening power has a special commitment.

7. For a contemporary account by a British journalist, see David Loshak, *Pakistan Crisis* (London, 1971).

8. John Westlake, *International Law*, vol. I, *Peace* (2nd ed., Cambridge 1910), pp. 319–20.

9. Thomas M. Franck and Nigel S. Rodley, "After Bangladesh: The Law of Humanitarian Intervention by Military Force," 67 *American Journal of International Law* 304 (1973).

10. Julius Stone, *Aggression and World Order*, p. 99.

Questions about the Passage

1. In the first section, what was the argument of British philosophers in favor of preventive war? What is Walzer's judgment of their arguments?

2. What is Bacon's critique of the classic Just War position of the "Schoolmen" (medieval Christian philosophers and teachers, including Aquinas)?

3. What are the utilitarian arguments for and against preventive war?

4. How does Walzer define a legitimate threat that might justify a preventive war?

5. In the second section, what distinction does Walzer make between counter-intervention and intervention for humanitarian causes?

6. Why do mixed motives need to be considered when examining humanitarian intervention?

7. What does Walzer say about unilateralism in humanitarian interventions? What is the role of the "society of nations" or the United Nations?

Questions about the Argument

1. Who are Walzer's readers? What sort of assumptions does he make about their knowledge, education, and interests?

2. How does Walzer establish his authority and credibility as a writer in these passages?

3. Like Khadduri, Walzer traces the development of ideas and beliefs over time. Is Walzer presenting arguments? If so, what claims does he make, and how well does he support them?
4. Is India's 1971 intervention in Bangladesh a good example of humanitarian intervention? Why or why not? Is Walzer's use of the example persuasive? Can you think of any other examples?
5. Walzer's example of preventive war, not included in the passage here, is the War of the Spanish Succession (1701–1714). Drawing upon your knowledge of history and current events, how would you apply his criteria for preventive war to past or current interventions? You may wish to do some research. For example, you might examine Israel's bombing of the Iraqi Osirak nuclear facilities in 1981 or the U.S. government's March 2003 invasion of Iraq.

Michael J. Schuck, "When the Shooting Stops: Missing Elements in Just War Theory"

Michael Schuck (1953–) has degrees from the University of Chicago and teaches Christian Ethics at Loyola University Chicago, where he specializes in Roman Catholic social thought. He is the author of *That They Be One: The Social Teaching of Papal Encyclicals 1740–1989* (1991) and of a number of articles. Of himself, he says, "I am not a Christian pacifist, but I do support any and all efforts at solving international conflict through nonviolent means. I think this is the fundamental rationale behind the Just War Theory." In the article below, Schuck extends Just War theory to include what occurs after "the shooting stops."

> A recent article in the *Toronto Star* listed 35 wars currently under way on the planet. Often as we hear and read about these wars, what stays with us most are the sad and gruesome pictures—from Bosnia, Somalia, South Africa, Rwanda, Israel and elsewhere. The most shocking picture for me was one I saw in a weekly newsmagazine after the 1991 Gulf War. It showed General Norman Schwarzkopf, commander of the allied forces, leading a victory parade down Disneyworld's main street, with Mickey Mouse and Donald Duck at his side. This was a scandalous trivialization of war.
>
> One could explore the curious reversal by which the "Magic Kingdom" has alchemized in American culture—how, for instance, a fantasy main street has become real and, on it, a

real war has become fantasy. But my shock at Schwarzkopf's march at Disneyworld had a more personal dimension. I felt compelled to hide the magazine from my seven-year-old daughter. Beginning with the evening bombing of Baghdad on January 16, 1991, my daughter's bedtime prayers had asked God to stop the war, her request generally voiced with a quiver of fear and a quick sniff to hold back tears. This was my first war with my first child; while we were not near the action, we were nonetheless newly struggling—for different reasons—with the spiritual and moral horror of war. When the Schwarzkopf picture appeared I was not prepared to explain to my daughter how the horrible reality she had prayed about for five weeks had become a Magic Kingdom.

If one assumes for the moment—as most Christians do—that the rubrics of the just war theory are morally tenable and that the bulk of those rubrics were satisfied in the Gulf War by the American side, then such postwar behavior must come under moral scrutiny. If Christians are called upon to probe the moral propriety of entering and conducting war by using the seven *jus ad bellum* principles (which concern justification for using force) and two *jus in bello* principles (which apply to conduct in war), should they not also be called upon to monitor the moral propriety of concluding a war through some set of *jus post bellum* principles?

I would suggest as a start that right conduct after a war entails three principles and two accomplishments. First, the principles.

The centerpiece of the *jus post bellum* conditions of a just war would be the principle of repentance. Victors would be expected to conduct themselves humbly after a war. Where public display is called for, victors should show remorse for the price of war paid not only by their comrades but also by the vanquished. Did Augustine not say that even a just war constitutes a mournful occasion? Proscribed by the principle of repentance would be nationalistic, ethnocentric celebrations of victory—celebrations disregarding the profound pain experienced by those on both sides of a conflict. There is a real, though subtle, moral difference between appropriately celebrating the return of sons and daughters from war and celebrating the defeat of one's enemies. Such a distinction may seem marginal, but as the famous Roman Catholic just

5

war theorist John Courtney Murray once said, in morality, margins often make all the difference.

My second moral principle would be operative before the public return of the victors. Just wars generally end with formal surrender. A seemingly necessary *jus post bellum* principle, then, would be a principle of honorable surrender. Victors would be expected to construct the terms and method of surrender in a manner that protects the fundamental human rights of the vanquished. Proscribed by such a principle would be punitive terms (such as those of the 1919 Versailles Treaty) as well as methods that degrade the defeated.

The Civil War offers an illustration of honorable surrender. Joshua L. Chamberlain was commander of the 20th Maine Infantry Regiment, the regiment best known for its defense of Little Round Top at the Battle of Gettysburg. Chamberlain remains most famous, however, for his actions during the Confederate surrender at Appomattox in 1865. General Grant had selected Chamberlain for the daunting task of formally receiving the surrendering army. Only days before, the two armies had been at each other's throats. The potential humiliation was almost intolerable for the Confederates, and the opportunity for venting pent-up rage and ridicule was almost irresistible for the Union. At nine o'clock in the morning on April 12, on a hilltop overlooking the Appomattox courthouse, the Confederate soldiers began falling in for their march to surrender. The troops moved forward without band or drum; they were exhausted, dirty, wounded. At their head was Major General John B. Gordon, astride his horse with head bowed.

The significance of the occasion impressed Chamberlain. He had already decided to mark the moment by saluting his former enemies. In her book *In the Hands of Providence: Joshua L. Chamberlain and the American Civil War* (1992), Alice Trulock describes what took place.

As Gordon reached the right of the Federal column where Chamberlain and his officers waited, a bugle sounded. Immediately, the whole Union line snapped to attention, and the slapping noise of hands on shifting rifles echoed in the stillness as regiment after regiment in succession down the Union line came to the old manual of arms position of "salute" and then back to "order arms" and "parade rest."

. . . When Gordon heard the sounds of the drill, he instantly 10
recognized their significance and wheeled to face Chamberlain.
As he did, his spurs touched the sides of his horse, causing it to
rear, and as his horse's head then came down in a bow, the gal-
lant young general dropped his sword point to his boot toe in a
graceful salute to the man whom he would call "one of the
knightliest soldiers of the Federal army."

Turning to his men, the Confederate leader gave an order,
which was repeated through the ranks, and the large Confederate banner dipped. The men of the vanquished army then
answered with the same salute given them as they marched
by, "honor answering honor," as Chamberlain described it.

Chamberlain's salute order was "one for which I sought no
authority nor asked forgiveness," he later explained. "Before
us in proud humiliation," he wrote, "stood the embodiment of
manhood. . . . Men whom neither toils and sufferings, nor
the fact of death, nor disaster, nor hopelessness could bend
from their resolve; standing before us now thin, worn, fam-
ished, but erect, and with eyes looking level into ours, waking
memories that bound us together as no other bond." Such is
the spirit of honorable surrender.

The horrible effects of war on the former fields of battle continue long after the surrender. The losing society's infrastructure may be utterly devastated. At the same time, violence may
still be meted out by abandoned weaponry. The United Nations
estimates that at least 105 million land mines remain uncleared
in 62 countries. The American Red Cross calculates that
uncleared mines kill 800 people a month and injure another 450
worldwide. The continued presence of such weaponry makes
land too dangerous for farming and refugee resettlement.

Given this situation, I would add a third *jus post bellum*
principle to just war theory: the principle of restoration. As a
minimal requirement, victors must return to the fields of battle and help remove the instruments of war. As a maximal
requirement, victors must assist in the repair of the social
infrastructure. Proscribed by such a principle would be neglect of the vanquished and disregard of the fact that, for many
innocent victims, the war continues after surrender.

What might the principles of repentance, honorable surrender 15
and restoration accomplish? First, they could expand—like

the already existing *jus ad bellum* and *jus in bello* principles—
the moral sensibilities of people who believe that war, while
evil, is sometimes necessary for the protection of human life.
Second, the principles could serve as a litmus test for the
sincerity of the just war claims made before and during the
conflict. Would nationalistic celebrations, punitive terms of
surrender and neglect for the field of battle not discredit the
victor's earlier claims to moral propriety? According to existing
just war theory, disproportionate and indiscriminate violence
in the conduct of war discredits moral claims for entering the
war. Abuse of the *jus post bellum* principles would do the
same. Would this not establish for subsequent discussions of
war a higher moral standard, one that would probe deeper
into the victor's actual motives?

The issue of motivation recalls Augustine—the Christian
thinker generally identified as the originator of the just war theory. Of course, Augustine did not present the full-blown theory
as we know it today. Indeed, it could be argued that he only
clearly offered two moral principles in direct reference to war:
just cause and legitimate authority. The remainder of the theory
has been drawn out of Augustine's thought over the centuries,
especially from his writings on murder and capital punishment.
Similarly, a case could be made for the propriety of the *jus post
bellum* principles in the context of Augustine's thought.

For Augustine, the critical factor in determining the possibility of a person's involvement in war as a Christian is
attitude. Improper attitudes, not actions alone, account for the
civil of war. Augustine wrote:

> What is the evil in war? Is it the death of someone who will
> soon die in any case, that others may live in peaceful subjec-
> tion? This is merely cowardly dislike, not any religious feel-
> ing. The real evils in war are love of violence, revengeful cru-
> elty, fierce and implacable enmity, wild resistance, and the
> lust of power, and such like; and it is generally to punish
> these things, when force is required to inflict the punishment,
> that, in obedience to God or some lawful authority, good
> men undertake wars.

Augustine thought that anyone, Christian or not, could participate in a just war and escape legal culpability. But to

escape divine culpability a soldier must conduct himself in a
manner free of cruelty, enmity and lust. Christians as Christians can kill only if they are devoid of such attitudes. As a
result, Augustinian thought may well accommodate the *jus
post bellum* principles as a test for discerning the warrior's true
attitudes before and during war.

In his excellent study *On War and Morality* Robert L. Holmes   20
doubts whether it is humanly possible for a soldier, amid
chaos and slaughter, to remain free of the attitudes Augustine
identifies as evil. For Christians, this doubt opens the question
of the moral adequacy of the Just War theory as a whole.
Related sentiments may well have inspired the surprising editorial in the Vatican-connected Jesuit publication *La Civilta Cat-
tolica* which, soon after the Gulf War, called for the abandonment of the theory.

Is just war theory inadequate as a form of moral discourse
about war? This question challenges many Christians today.
For now, however, the theory is with us and will no doubt
remain so for some time to come. I ask anyone who thinks the
theory credible to consider it nonetheless incomplete without
a set of *jus post bellum* principles such as repentance, honorable surrender and restoration.

Questions about the Passage

1. After reporting that he has seen numerous gruesome pictures
   from recent wars, Schuck says that he found the sight of General
   Schwarzkopf leading a victory parade in Disneyland "the most
   shocking picture" he saw. How does Schuck justify using that
   adjective in the superlative form?
2. Explain what Shuck means by each of his principles of postwar
   behavior: repentance, honorable surrender, and restoration. Can
   you think of any others he might have included?
3. How do these principles lead to what Schuck calls "accomplishments"? Are these important outcomes? Why or why not? What
   other outcomes might there be from following the principles?

Questions about the Argument

1. Schuck uses two scenes in his introduction to set up the argument. Who is his audience? How do you think they are likely to

respond to this strategy? How do you respond? Is the use of his daughter a legitimate appeal to pathos?

2. To illustrate his first principle, Schuck provides an extended example of a Civil War surrender. Is the example pertinent, of appropriate length, effective?

3. How does Schuck draw upon Augustine's view of war to support his overall argument?

4. Review the elements of argument—ethos, concern for the audience, logos, and pathos—found in this article. Is this a well-constructed argument? Do you find it convincing?

5. Review postwar actions in Afghanistan and Iraq in the light of Schuck's article. Do they meet his principles?

Laurie Calhoun, "Violence and Hypocrisy"

Laurie Calhoun (1961–) holds degrees in chemistry and in philosophy and has taught both at the college level. She is the author of *Philosophy Unmasked: A Skeptic's Critique* (1997) as well as articles on ethics and epistemology, and has been writing specifically on the philosophy of war since the 1999 NATO bombing of Kosovo. A member of an international and interdisciplinary project group aiming to develop new strategies for human security and conflict resolution, Calhoun has given presentations on ethics and international affairs at the International Studies Association annual meetings, in addition to being a part of the Ethics Lecture Series on war and terrorism for 2003–2004 at Villanova University. Calhoun lives in Cambridge, Massachusetts and currently works as an administrator at Harvard University.

> Imagine: You awaken in the middle of the night to the sound of piercing sirens. Suddenly the ceiling comes crashing down. You are trapped under rubble, bones broken, joints popped from sockets. Blood pours down your face from the gash on your head. Children are shrieking in the next room. The bombs continue to fall; your head begins to throb. You don't know how much longer you have to live or if you'll ever see your family again.

Have You Been Wronged?

I presume that you need no further information to answer this question. You have been wronged. Regardless of your political affiliations, regardless of where you happen to live, regardless of who you are, you have been wronged. Even if you were a convicted felon, guilty of a heinous crime, the above treatment would constitute "cruel and unusual punishment," prohibited by law. Yet, according to just war theorists, whether or not you have been wronged is supposed to be a function of the past actions of another person altogether, your leader. If your leader is a criminal, then you are "collateral damage," regrettable but unavoidable. If your leader has committed no crimes against humanity, then you have been unjustly attacked, unjustly terrorized, and unjustly harmed.

Let us make the case a bit more detailed. You voted for the opposition. Your candidate did not win the most recent election. The winner went on to abuse power and commit crimes. Are you responsible, in any sense, for the crimes committed by your leader, whom you never supported in any way whatsoever? Are you any less the victim of an unjust attack than are the people unlucky enough to have been on board an airplane hijacked by fanatics?

We could make the case more controversial and complex. You voted for your leader, whom you believed at the time to be a person of integrity and moral vision. You were wrong. Your leader victimized innocent people and abused his power to achieve personal ends. Despite these facts, have you not still been wronged?

Of course some inhabitants of nations led by criminals support their government. So let us consider this possibility too: You voted for and continue to support the government in power. Your leader carefully explained to you and your compatriots that national self-interest and honor mandated the invasion of territories that had been unjustly appropriated by "The Evil Enemy." You never heard any other version of the story. Does being brutally attacked by your leader's enemies have any more tangible effect than to strengthen your belief in the lies of your leader?

The options are simple: Either you support or once supported the regime in power or you do not and never did. (Children always fall into the latter category.) But your personal attitude toward your own government does not seem to be particularly relevant in determining culpability for the unfortunate circumstances in which you currently find yourself. You are trapped under fallen beams and rubble, injured, frightened, traumatized, and uncertain whether you will escape alive. Yet,

5

as far as you can tell, you have personally committed no crime. If you are a soldier, you were legally obliged to follow the orders of your superior officer. That you happen to have believed your leader's lies seems to be irrelevant to the question of whether you have been wronged. How could the answer to that question be a function of your personal beliefs? What do your leader's actions have to do with what is being done to you? Certainly you have an interpretation, true or false, plausible or implausible, of your leader's actions, at least of the ones that you know about. But what does your interpretation have to do with the actual wrongness of your leader's policies?

Even if you are among the soldiers who committed crimes against other people, what is being done to you right now, as you lie in your pajamas, months after having followed the orders of your leader, does not seem to be right. If you are guilty of a crime, then you should be tried. But what does your guilt have to do with the children shrieking next door, even if they are your children, and even if you committed (unwittingly, since no soldier follows orders "to murder") crimes?

The Just War Tradition

War has long been supported by human societies, through the funding of military institutions and the production of deadly weapons. Many people therefore assume that war is sometimes just and permissible, or even obligatory. Wars do occur, and the pressing question, according to many thinkers, is how to distinguish the just from the unjust. Basic tenets of "Just War theory" were articulated by a cluster of medieval thinkers, who maintained that war would be morally justified if and only if certain conditions were met. Although there have been some disagreements over the precise articulation of the theory, the just war tradition has since the seventeenth century distinguished two broad sets of conditions, *jus ad bellum,* for the just initiation of a war, and *jus in bello,* for the just conduct of a war.

Tradition has it that a just war must be waged with right/ moral intention and must have an objective, not merely subjective or selfish, aim. The gravity of the situation must warrant the extreme measure of war, and there must be a reasonable chance for success. War must be publicly declared by a legitimate authority, and recourse to force must be a "last resort."

Once war has been waged, the following additional precepts apply: The means deployed may not exceed what is warranted by the cause. Combatants are through capture rendered noncombatants, and noncombatants are immune from belligerent attack.

Noncombatant Immunity

Given the inevitability of civilian casualties in modern war, one might think that, according to the requirements of just war theory, all wars are unjust. But the "immunity" of non-combatants has been understood historically to permit war. Most notably, Catholic theologians have interpreted noncombatant immunity using "the doctrine of double effect." This principle specifies that bad consequences such as civilian deaths (euphemistically referred to by modern military personnel as "collateral damage") are permissible during wartime, even if foreseen, so long as they are unintended (neither as ends in themselves nor indirectly as means). Whether "collateral damage" victims have been wronged is supposed to be a function of the intentions of the people who dropped the bombs and the relative weight of devastation vis-à-vis the military objective achieved. Somewhat suspiciously, the answer given by military authorities always seems to be "no." Though now dead, "collateral damage" victims have not been wronged by their killers, for the war is a just one, the victims were not targeted, and an important objective was achieved through bombing in the vicinity.

By emphasizing the importance of objectives achieved, just war theorists underscore the requirement of proportionality, as Robert Phillips explains in *War and Justice:* "the permission of collateral evil must be justified by considerations of proportionate moral weight." But the "proportionality" requirement is problematic, as Michael Walzer openly admits in *Just and Unjust Wars:* "Certainly we want political and military leaders to worry about costs and benefits. But they have to worry; they can't calculate, for the values at stake are not commensurate—at least they can't be expressed or compared mathematically, as the idea of proportion suggests. How do we measure the value of a country's independence against the value of the lives that might be lost in defending it?"

10

The most important question that Walzer raises (apparently unintentionally) is this: costs to whom? Centuries ago, when just war theory originated, political leaders were simultaneously military leaders whose willingness to fight courageously alongside their soldiers evinced their own sincerity regarding their causes. In contrast, modern leaders do not seriously risk damage to their own persons when they wage conventional wars against other nations. Today civilians and low-ranking soldiers bear the brunt of leaders' decisions to engage their nations in war.

Military authorities apply the "doctrine of double effect" to cases such as the scenario described above, explaining that you have not been wronged by your killers, since the requirements of *jus ad bellum* and *jus in bello* have been satisfied. Certainly you have been harmed, but your leader, who acted in ways that provoked military action on the part of his enemies, is ultimately responsible. However, from your own perspective, you are in effect being punished for another person's crimes.

Although its military utility cannot be denied, "the doctrine of double effect" ultimately exonerates everyone who kills for what he takes to be good reasons. The actual deaths effected can always be construed as foreseen but unintended. Tragically, the history of warfare is a long concatenation of deadly conflicts between groups led by commanders who have claimed to be fighting for justice and peace. But what rational person would act for what he or she takes to be bad reasons?

A Closer Look at History and Grounds

The most influential just war theorists throughout history have been Christians such as Augustine, Thomas Aquinas, and Francisco Suárez. To some this comes as a surprise, given the apparent pacifism of Jesus Christ, who famously exhorted his followers to "turn the other cheek" in the face of violent assault. Countless Christians have found ways to reconcile the apparent teachings of Christ with their own acts of violence in religious war after war. Upon closer analysis, this apparent conundrum is easily resolved.

Augustine, arguably the father of just war theory, distinguishes the "City of Man" from the "City of God," maintaining that, practically speaking, we should adhere to the conventions

15

of our societies while inwardly attempting to align our souls with God. Leaders were believed by Augustine to be in some sense doing God's will, since everything on earth is in its place through the grace of God. This picture was of course capitalized upon by leaders throughout the Middle Ages. But with the separation of church and state in the modern world, leaders cannot, with any shred of plausibility, claim to derive their policy decisions directly from God. One of the legacies of the Protestant Reformation was a thorough unmasking of pretentious religious and political leaders who claimed to have special connections to the Almighty. In democratic societies, political authorities no longer can seriously claim to have more direct access to God than has the person on the street. In the modern world, political leaders are given the legal power to wage wars despite the fact that political leaders are people on the street, appointed as leaders by themselves or their citizenry. So just as it seems safe to say that some of the people walking the street are bad, evil, immoral, and/or ignorant, we can be sure that some leaders are no less. When two leaders adept at the use of moral rhetoric come into conflict, we can be sure that at least one of them is mistaken, since the claims that they make are mutually inconsistent.

Just war theory evolved out of controversial metaphysical assumptions of Christianity, most notably that there is an afterlife. Augustine maintained that what really matters, in the grand scheme of things, is purity of conscience, and this God alone can assess. Although we may think that the actions of some of our fellow human beings are wrong or evil, we cannot know the motives behind their actions, nor whether they had any but the best of intentions. Given his skepticism about human moral judgment, Augustine concluded that it is best to abide by the laws of the society in which we live, to follow the orders of our leaders, and to know that, ultimately, justice will be done regardless of the injustices suffered during our ephemeral time as terrestrial beings.

A profoundly important point emerges: given Augustine's metaphysical beliefs, anything that transpires on this planet is of relatively little consequence. Obviously, to one who believes that justice will be done in the afterlife, the harsh reality of "collateral damage" killings of the innocent is not a particularly grave problem. For justice always prevails in a worldview such as Augustine's. Human beings may mistakenly harm, punish, even execute other people, but in the grand scheme of things, justice will be done. Although Augustine (along with some other Christians) is skeptical about the power of human beings to render judgment upon others (given the inaccessibility of others' intentions), he is not at all skeptical about the existence of God, the ultimate arbiter in matters of justice. There is no question that the falsely executed will be recompensed, and undetected sinners, including murderers, will be punished.

What is peculiar about the influence of just war theory in later centuries is the extent to which its tenets have been retained while the metaphysics have been abandoned. Today a secularized version of just war theory is built into military protocol. Leaders of all nations appeal to some version of just war theory in motivating their populace to conduct war when "duty calls." In fact, what survives as "just war theory" is a powerful rhetorical weapon, involving fallacious appeals to authority and tradition and playing upon human frailty, especially the need to believe that we are good and our adversaries evil. Through appeals to "justice," leaders miraculously galvanize their troops to kill people who have nothing whatsoever to do with the criminal actions supposedly justifying recourse to war. In the modern Western world, the ongoing development of weapons of mass destruction progressively exacerbates the danger to civilians of decisions to wage war. Were the early expositors of just war theory alive today, some might very well declare that its requirements cannot be satisfied, given the nature of modern warfare. Wars are no longer fought at sites far removed from civilian life. Wars are no longer fought by chivalric men on horseback armed with spears and protected by shields.

Democracy

"Collateral damage" apologies suggest a lamentable lesson: 20
the civilian noncombatants of enemy nations, including children, have less of a right to be spared violence and destruction than do the civilians of the attacking nations. While accidental killings are still considered criminal acts within the borders of one's own nation, "collateral damage" killings of the civilians

of other nations are briefly mentioned in a tone of regret and then forgotten. Democratic leaders may preach that "all men are created equal," but their practice, the use of military force against enemy nations, which always results in the deaths of innocent people (including children), betrays the fact that they do not believe what they say. For leaders presume that it would be preferable to kill rather than convince soldiers and civilian inhabitants of the enemy nation that their leader is mistaken in the claims he has made. The use of destructive and deadly force against other nations reveals an implicit belief that "The Evil and Irrational Enemy" and all inhabitants of his land are beyond the reach of reason. Although leaders often say that they are waging war in the name of democratic values, in fact, their resort to deadly force belies such claims.

John Stuart Mill, in *On Liberty*, defends the free marketplace of ideas as necessary to the discovery of policies just and fair to all. The marketplace of ideas presumably allows people eventually to arrive at the truth, since criticism of currently prevalent views is always possible. In this way, formerly popular views, for example, regarding the moral permissibility of slavery and the legal possession of wives by their husbands, have been rejected after due consideration of much trenchant criticism. The marketplace of ideas requires an input of ideas, and this source derives from individual thinkers, who must be provided with the opportunity to voice opinions so that their merits and deficiencies can be assessed by all. We may find some views offensive, but in order to ascertain what is wrong with those opinions, we must permit them to be aired. Mill and those of his ilk insist that people are themselves capable of sifting the wheat from the chaff in the thresher of ideas. In order to adjudicate the claims made by the disputants, they must be permitted not only to speak their views, but also to hear what others claim to be true.

In a democratic nation, people elect their leaders and legislators. The laws are proposed by delegates and approved by the people. Many different interests compete and, ultimately, out of the disagreement emerges a winner, the majority opinion. The fundamental presupposition of democracy is that people are capable and desirous of ascertaining the truth. The fundamental value of democracy is freedom, freedom of thought, action and speech. Speech is the *sine qua non* of belief revision. The use of deadly force against any human being is decidedly undemocratic, for it annihilates the possibility of speech.

Human beings are fallible, and the mechanism by which democracy deals with this fundamental fact is the court of law, where both sides are given the right to be heard. Those accused of harming a fellow citizen or breaking the law in some other way are brought before a jury of peers and judged. Once the evidence has been weighed, a judgment is then made. But the burden of proof lies with the prosecution. The only thing worse than to deprive an innocent person of freedom would be to deprive him or her of life. "Vigilante justice" is undemocratic because it involves a refusal to articulate the grievances at issue and to permit one's peers to assess the available evidence. In all conflicts, both sides claim to be right and that their adversaries are wrong. One of the two parties must be mistaken. "Vigilante justice" is illegal because in punishing another person without trial, even if he be guilty of a crime, one undermines the democratic basis of the legal system. Vigilante killings of allegedly just retribution prevent the accused from defending him- or herself and invert the burden of proof. The victim is presumed guilty until proven innocent.

In international conflicts, no less than in courts of law, both sides claim to be right. Thus, military intervention can quite plausibly be analogized to vigilante violence. In fact, military attacks upon nations are far worse than vigilante violence, because the victims are, in many cases, not even candidates for guilt. Most contemporary just war theorists maintain that agents who are doing what they would have been doing anyway, were there no war, are immune from attack. In *The Ethics of War and Peace*, Paul Christopher observes that, in the Gulf War, "in addition to identifying command and control centers as targets, American planners also planned to destroy much of the support infrastructure of Baghdad: namely, sewage treatment plants, water purification facilities, and electrical power generators. The destruction of these facilities affected the civilian population and its health, safety, and living standards as much, and perhaps even more, than it affected the military. In this case it seems at least questionable whether the destruction of targets of these types is permitted under the condition of double effect." Even in heavily militarized nations, only a small percentage of the population participates in the armed forces.

Terrorism

In addition to rejecting "vigilante justice," representatives of stable nations also regularly condemn terrorist actions by extremist factions. The rationale for refusing to negotiate with terrorists is that even if they have been wronged, it is no less wrong to deploy violent means against innocent victims. Unfortunately, some of the most outspoken critics of factional terrorism seem utterly incognizant that their own destructive military policies are not so different from the crimes they decry. What, after all, is terrorism, if not the threat of the use of force against another party with the intention of achieving one's aims? From the perspective of the victims of terrorism, whether their killers be members of extremist groups or the professional soldiers of well-established nations matters not. The most nocent terrorists are those who act under the aegis of an institution such as the Third Reich.

A victim of terrorism is arbitrarily targeted, not for having committed any crime, but because he or she is unlucky enough to be in the wrong place at the wrong time. When nations undertake bombing campaigns, noncombatant civilians are subjected to the sound of bombs raining overhead and unnerving alarms in the vicinity. Even when these civilians believe that they are not being singled out, they know that bombs do not always land on their intended targets. In nations under attack, civilians wait huddled in fear, knowing full well that they may be the next to die. Consider, for example, the 1999 bombing of the Chinese Embassy in Belgrade during the NATO campaign against the regime of Slobodan Milosevic. Political leaders and war supporters excuse men in uniform for mistakes that result in the deaths of civilians, claiming that the soldiers did not intend to kill noncombatants. But the victims of a military bombing campaign are no less the victims of a terrorist act than are the persons unfortunate enough to have been on board an airplane hijacked by political fanatics. If it is always wrong to punish the innocent

25

for the crimes of the guilty, then those killed through "collateral damage" are no less victims of immoral actions than are those arbitrarily killed by smaller, less stable terrorist factions.

For just war theorists, declaration by "legitimate authority" is the criterion distinguishing individual acts of murder or renegade acts of terrorism from justifiable instances of military violence. Here the conservatism of just war theory manifests itself. It is allegedly permissible for established nations to use deadly force in achieving their aims, but not smaller groups, though they can sometimes with great plausibility be construed as inchoate nations. Certainly political organizations represent the interests of a group of people no less than do the spokesmen for established nations. In reality, the nations for which people kill and die are temporal and transitory. People find themselves in nations, which they assume to be stable, persistent things, but it is clear from even a cursory consideration of history that they are not. The nations of today are not the same as those in existence only fifty years ago, much less five hundred years ago.

If moral persons are defined as beings in possession of sentience, intelligence, and consciousness, then nations, lacking all of these properties, are not moral persons and, therefore, do not possess rights. A "right" is a moral concept and as such applies only to moral persons. Nations are formed by the association of consenting persons into groups. Accordingly, there is no principled distinction between nations and smaller subgroups, which can be viewed as "proto-nations" comprising people bound by certain interests and concerns. The distinction between violent intervention undertaken by smaller groups and those undertaken by military institutions cannot be made out in any morally significant way.

By deploying deadly force against the people of other countries, national leaders display their belief that recourse to force is morally permissible. Political leaders invariably invoke "just war" rhetoric in defending such decisions to wage war. They insist that war is not merely permissible but obligatory, whenever the cause is just and proportional and all pacific proposals have proven infeasible. But terrorist factions are often morally driven and claim to have been denied any legal avenue through which to express their grievances. Some terrorist groups foment against oppressive and inegalitarian regimes denying rights to the minority inhabitants of the land. In the end, all parties who offer reasons for their acts of violence offer moral reasons. The leaders of first world nations hypocritically decry terrorist acts by minority factions, while simultaneously providing them with a role model counterproductive to the abolition of terrorism in the modern world. Each bombing campaign is a graphic display of how force can be used to achieve one's own aims.

Moral Responsibility

Military campaigns against nations led by criminals convey   30
an odd lesson regarding moral responsibility and criminal justice, a lesson that contradicts the burden of proof requirement
governing our legal proceedings within society. In civil society, we place the burden of proof upon the prosecution
because we recognize that the false conviction and punishment of an innocent person would constitute a travesty of
justice. The law is commonly thought to reflect, albeit imper-
fectly, morality, but in cases where an innocent person is
falsely convicted and executed, the putative institution of
justice itself perpetrates gross injustice. So we are willing to
err to the side of caution, insisting that all people are innocent
until proven guilty, even though some offenders may be
acquitted and roam at large. But we accept what we consider
to be the lesser of two evils. In stark contrast, leaders who initiate bombing campaigns against enemy nations consider it
permissible to punish (through terrorism) or even terminate
innocent lives for the crimes of their leader.

In other words, moral responsibility is construed in a
strange way when it comes to nations. For example, in his
speech on January 16, 1991, then-president George Bush in
effect proclaimed that, in order to avoid attack, the Iraqi people would have to persuade Saddam Hussein to withdraw his
troops from Kuwait: "It is my hope that somehow the Iraqi
people can, even now, convince their dictator that he must lay
down his arms, leave Kuwait, and let Iraq itself rejoin the family of peace-loving nations." In general, we hold persons
accountable only for actions that they voluntarily intend and
execute. Yet the possibility of a "just war" in the modern

world presumes that it is perfectly acceptable to hold civilians accountable for their leader's crimes.

The erroneous ascription of moral responsibility to civilians is seldom mentioned in discourse about war. It is perhaps often thought that when a people freely selects its leaders, the citizens themselves bear at least some responsibility for their government's mistakes. Unfortunately, some leaders are dictators. Moreover, although many people assume that democratically determined leaders are obviously "legitimate," leaders are never elected unanimously in democratic nations. When a leader wins by majority vote, the minority selected someone else altogether. And so the question arises again: how can it be morally acceptable to punish, terrorize, or even kill people for their leader's crimes if they never selected the leader, or even tried to prevent him from becoming their leader?

One might retort that since citizens share the benefits of their society, they should share its burdens, some of the worst of which are incurred during wartime. But an analogous argument would seem to apply no less to the parent–child relation. It seems ludicrous to suppose that because a child benefits from being a part of a family (for example, by provision of food and shelter), the child should be held responsible for the crimes of its parents. Of course, if one can in good conscience hold a child responsible for its parents' crimes, then one will also be able to hold innocent citizens responsible for their leaders' abominations.

Force and Judgments

Throughout history, soldiers have been honored and praised for carrying out missions that terminate the lives of their fellow human beings. But no stable international tribunal exists for assessment of the alleged crimes against humanity ordered by national leaders. Accordingly, many people continue to condone the use of military means, pointing to the lack of any international analog to the court systems found within democratic societies. However, the Nuremberg Trials of Nazi war criminals were analogous to the legal system within civil society. It is obviously possible for international tribunals to render judgments upon the activities of egregious political criminals. In fact, it is plausibly none other than the nearly continuous use of military force by powerful nations that prevents any strides from being made toward the establishment of an effective international legal system. Were such a system implemented by representatives of mutually self-interested nations, then measures that decrease rather than increase the domestic political power of criminal leaders could be taken. No nation is a political island, for all depend upon imports and exports. A leader truly spurned by the international community (some members of which have armed criminals with their deadly weapons) could not remain in power for long.

Scenarios such as that sketched at the opening of this essay are neither ineluctable nor acceptable. On the contrary, to terrorize, assault, and even execute without trial the inhabitants of a land governed by a criminal is to indulge in an inexcusable act of myopic tyranny. Despotism is no less despicable in the name of a nation than for a leader. Least of all can despotic military destruction be coherently defended in the name of democracy. The true spirit of democracy will prevail only when the inhabitants of other nations are treated as fellow citizens of the world community, as rational beings capable and desirous of learning the truth.

35

Questions about the Passage

1. Trace your responses to the first seven paragraphs of Calhoun's article. What is your emotional response after each paragraph? How do you answer the question she asks at the end of paragraphs 3–7? By the end of the section have your responses changed appreciably from your responses to the first paragraph or two? Try to account for this change or lack of change.
2. Be sure you can define the following terms as Calhoun uses them in the "Noncombatant Immunity" section of her argument: "immunity of noncombatants"; "collateral damage"; "the doctrine of double effect"; "proportionality." How is understanding these terms crucial to following the argument?
3. Break into groups to scour each section for word choices that indicate Calhoun's views of Just War theory, especially its position on noncombatants. Adverbs, adjectives, verbs, and the connotations of nouns can all be used to indicate such viewpoints.

Place each word you select on a scale ranging from negative to neutral to positive. Where do most of these words cluster?

4. Calhoun writes, "In fact, what survives as 'Just War theory' is a powerful rhetorical weapon, involving fallacious appeals to authority and tradition and playing upon human frailty, especially the need to believe that we are good and our adversaries evil." What does she mean, and what do you think of her statement?

Questions about the Argument

1. Is Calhoun qualified to write about the topic? Check her credentials and reputation by rereading the introduction and glancing at reviews of her book. What evidence is there in the text of her personal authority, that is, how does she demonstrate her competence in handling this material, as well as her use of authorities?

2. In the chapter on argument, we discussed Calhoun's introduction as a Rogerian strategy to find common ground with her audience. Does the introduction also make an emotional appeal? If so, what emotions are engaged? What specific language does Calhoun use to create this effect? Does the remainder of the article focus on emotional response as well?

3. Calhoun devotes the middle section of her article to explaining the principle of noncombatant immunity as it has been traditionally understood. Is her explication accurate and unbiased?

4. Summarize the section entitled "Democracy," paying particular attention to how Calhoun's view differs from the traditional view of noncombatant immunity. How do her assumptions based on the principles of democracy differ from the traditional assumptions based on a God-oriented world view?

5. In "Democracy," Calhoun makes analogies between military intervention and vigilante justice. Explain both terms in order to discover whether the analogy is valid.

6. In "Terrorism," Calhoun uses two hypothetical syllogisms. Locate these syllogisms. Are they valid, that is, do they follow the rules? Are they true? Examine the premises carefully.

7. In "Terrorism," Calhoun implies that from the perspective of the victims an identical definition should apply both to war and terrorism. Do you accept that these concepts are equivalent? See also Howard Zinn's definition of war and terrorism (p. 214). What argumentative purpose does it serve to make the two concepts identical in definition?

8. Based on evidence in this article, is Calhoun a pacifist? If so, what kind of pacifist would she be (see Lackey p. 154 for categories of pacifism)?

The Hebrew Bible: "Noah's Flood" and Arthur Waskow, "Nuclear War or Nuclear Holocaust: How the Biblical Account of the Flood Might Instruct Our Efforts"

The career of Rabbi Arthur Waskow (1933–) demonstrates his continuing commitment to justice and peace. He attended Johns Hopkins University, received a Ph.D. in U.S. history from the University of Wisconsin, and was a policy analyst for the Institute for Policy Studies from 1963–1977 and a Fellow of the Public Resource Center from 1977–1982. He has published more than twenty books on peace, nuclear strategy, race, and Jewish spirituality. In the 1960s, Waskow was an antiwar activist and a secular Jew. In 1968, he experienced a spiritual awakening at a Passover Seder. Since that time, he has become one of the leaders of the Jewish Renewal Movement, working for justice, peace, the healing of the earth, and inter-religious dialogue. He is the director of that movement's Shalom Center, which he founded in 1983 as a source for Jewish perspectives in preventing nuclear war. The essay below appeared in a collection of responses from various religious thinkers to the U.S. Catholic Bishops' pastoral letter *The Challenge of Peace* (1983). We have included for your reference the passage from Genesis 6:5–9:17 that tells the story of Noah.

Genesis 6:5–9:17
Chapter 6

⁵The LORD saw that the wickedness of man was great in the earth, and that every imagination of the thoughts of his heart was only evil continually. ⁶And the LORD was sorry that he had made man on the earth, and it grieved him to his heart. ⁷So the LORD said, "I will blot out man whom I have created from the face of the ground, man and beast and creeping things and birds of the air, for I am sorry that I have made them." ⁸But Noah found favor in the eyes of the LORD. ⁹These are the generations of Noah. Noah was a righteous man, blameless in his generation; Noah walked with God. ¹⁰And Noah had three sons, Shem, Ham, and Japheth. ¹¹Now the earth was corrupt in God's sight, and the earth was filled with violence. ¹²And God saw the earth, and behold, it was corrupt; for all flesh had corrupted their way upon the earth. ¹³And God said to Noah, "I have determined to make an end of all flesh; for the earth is

filled with violence through them; behold, I will destroy them with the earth. [14]Make yourself an ark of gopher wood; make rooms in the ark, and cover it inside and out with pitch. [15]This is how you are to make it: the length of the ark three hundred cubits, its breadth fifty cubits, and its height thirty cubits. [16]Make a roof for the ark, and finish it to a cubit above; and set the door of the ark in its side; make it with lower, second, and third decks. [17]For behold, I will bring a flood of waters upon the earth, to destroy all flesh in which is the breath of life from under heaven; everything that is on the earth shall die. [18]But I will establish my covenant with you; and you shall come into the ark, you, your sons, your wife, and your sons' wives with you. [19]And of every living thing of all flesh, you shall bring two of every sort into the ark, to keep them alive with you; they shall be male and female. [20]Of the birds according to their kinds, and of the animals according to their kinds, of every creeping thing of the ground according to its kind, two of every sort shall come in to you, to keep them alive. [21]Also take with you every sort of food that is eaten, and store it up; and it shall serve as food for you and for them." [22]Noah did this; he did all that God commanded him.

Chapter 7

[1]Then the LORD said to Noah, "Go into the ark, you and all your household, for I have seen that you are righteous before me in this generation. [2]Take with you seven pairs of all clean animals, the male and his mate; and a pair of the animals that are not clean, the male and his mate; [3]and seven pairs of the birds of the air also, male and female, to keep their kind alive upon the face of all the earth. [4]For in seven days I will send rain upon the earth forty days and forty nights; and every living thing that I have made I will blot out from the face of the ground." [5]And Noah did all that the LORD had commanded him. [6]Noah was six hundred years old when the flood of waters came upon the earth. [7]And Noah and his sons and his wife and his sons' wives with him went into the ark, to escape the waters of the flood. [8]Of clean animals, and of animals that are not clean, and of birds, and of everything that creeps on the ground, [9]two and two, male and female, went into the ark with Noah, as God had commanded Noah. [10]And after seven

days the waters of the flood came upon the earth. [11]In the six hundredth year of Noah's life, in the second month, on the seventeenth day of the month, on that day all the fountains of the great deep burst forth, and the windows of the heavens were opened. [12]And rain fell upon the earth forty days and forty nights. [13]On the very same day Noah and his sons, Shem and Ham and Japheth, and Noah's wife and the three wives of his sons with them entered the ark, [14]they and every beast according to its kind, and all the cattle according to their kinds, and every creeping thing that creeps on the earth according to its kind, and every bird according to its kind, every bird of every sort. [15]They went into the ark with Noah, two and two of all flesh in which there was the breath of life. [16]And they that entered, male and female of all flesh, went in as God had commanded him; and the LORD shut him in. [17]The flood continued forty days upon the earth; and the waters increased, and bore up the ark, and it rose high above the earth. [18]The waters prevailed and increased greatly upon the earth; and the ark floated on the face of the waters. [19]And the waters prevailed so mightily upon the earth that all the high mountains under the whole heaven were covered; [20]the waters prevailed above the mountains, covering them fifteen cubits deep. [21]And all flesh died that moved upon the earth, birds, cattle, beasts, all swarming creatures that swarm upon the earth, and every man; [22]everything on the dry land in whose nostrils was the breath of life died. [23]He blotted out every living thing that was upon the face of the ground, man and animals and creeping things and birds of the air; they were blotted out from the earth. Only Noah was left, and those that were with him in the ark. [24]And the waters prevailed upon the earth a hundred and fifty days.

Chapter 8

[1]But God remembered Noah and all the beasts and all the cattle that were with him in the ark. And God made a wind blow over the earth, and the waters subsided; [2]the fountains of the deep and the windows of the heavens were closed, the rain from the heavens was restrained, [3]and the waters receded from the earth continually. At the end of a hundred and fifty days the waters had abated; [4]and in the seventh month, on the

seventeenth day of the month, the ark came to rest upon the mountains of Ar'arat. [5]And the waters continued to abate until the tenth month; in the tenth month, on the first day of the month, the tops of the mountains were seen. [6]At the end of forty days Noah opened the window of the ark which he had made, [7]and sent forth a raven; and it went to and fro until the waters were dried up from the earth. [8]Then he sent forth a dove from him, to see if the waters had subsided from the face of the ground; [9]but the dove found no place to set her foot, and she returned to him to the ark, for the waters were still on the face of the whole earth. So he put forth his hand and took her and brought her into the ark with him. [10]He waited another seven days, and again he sent forth the dove out of the ark; [11]and the dove came back to him in the evening, and lo, in her mouth a freshly plucked olive leaf; so Noah knew that the waters had subsided from the earth. [12]Then he waited another seven days, and sent forth the dove; and she did not return to him any more. [13]In the six hundred and first year, in the first month, the first day of the month, the waters were dried from off the earth; and Noah removed the covering of the ark, and looked, and behold, the face of the ground was dry. [14]In the second month, on the twenty-seventh day of the month, the earth was dry. [15]Then God said to Noah, [16]"Go forth from the ark, you and your wife, and your sons and your sons' wives with you. [17]Bring forth with you every living thing that is with you of all flesh—birds and animals and every creeping thing that creeps on the earth—that they may breed abundantly on the earth, and be fruitful and multiply upon the earth." [18]So Noah went forth, and his sons and his wife and his sons' wives with him. [19]And every beast, every creeping thing, and every bird, everything that moves upon the earth, went forth by families out of the ark. [20]Then Noah built an altar to the LORD, and took of every clean animal and of every clean bird, and offered burnt offerings on the altar. [21]And when the LORD smelled the pleasing odor, the LORD said in his heart, "I will never again curse the ground because of man, for the imagination of man's heart is evil from his youth; neither will I ever again destroy every living creature as I have done. [22]While the earth remains, seedtime and harvest, cold and heat, summer and winter, day and night, shall not cease."

Chapter 9

[1]And God blessed Noah and his sons, and said to them, "Be fruitful and multiply, and fill the earth. [2]The fear of you and the dread of you shall be upon every beast of the earth, and upon every bird of the air, upon everything that creeps on the ground and all the fish of the sea; into your hand they are delivered. [3]Every moving thing that lives shall be food for you; and as I gave you the green plants, I give you everything. [4]Only you shall not eat flesh with its life, that is, its blood. [5]For your lifeblood I will surely require a reckoning; of every beast I will require it and of man; of every man's brother I will require the life of man. [6]Whoever sheds the blood of man, by man shall his blood be shed; for God made man in his own image. [7]And you, be fruitful and multiply, bring forth abundantly on the earth and multiply in it." [8]Then God said to Noah and to his sons with him, [9]"Behold, I establish my covenant with you and your descendants after you, [10]and with every living creature that is with you, the birds, the cattle, and every beast of the earth with you, as many as came out of the ark. [11]I establish my covenant with you, that never again shall all flesh be cut off by the waters of a flood, and never again shall there be a flood to destroy the earth." [12]And God said, "This is the sign of the covenant which I make between me and you and every living creature that is with you, for all future generations: [13]I set my bow in the cloud, and it shall be a sign of the covenant between me and the earth. [14]When I bring clouds over the earth and the bow is seen in the clouds, [15]I will remember my covenant which is between me and you and every living creature of all flesh; and the waters shall never again become a flood to destroy all flesh. [16]When the bow is in the clouds, I will look upon it and remember the everlasting covenant between God and every living creature of all flesh that is upon the earth." [17]God said to Noah, "This is the sign of the covenant which I have established between me and all flesh that is upon the earth."

Nuclear War or Nuclear Holocaust: How the Biblical Account of the Flood Might Instruct Our Efforts

In this paper I would like to shed light on the issue of nuclear arms and war by using the classical Jewish process called *midrash*. Midrash, drawn from the verb meaning "to search," is the process of looking into the Torah to arrive at an accurate understanding of the spirit of the text. It is the effort to understand the meaning contained within the text, although not at an explicit level. As the rabbis of the Talmud said, the text of the Torah is not written in black ink on white parchment; it is written in black fire on white fire. There is as much truth in the white fire, that is, the spaces, as there is in the black fire, the letters themselves. This ancient rabbinic process has reawakened in considerable richness within American Jewish life, for various complicated reasons. But midrash has always been present. Through the ages, it has been the process by which generation after generation of the Jewish people coped with the transformations of Jewish life and of the larger society within which they lived.

The Torah is central to this process. The study of the Torah is itself a form of prayer, a direct contact with God. The blessing with which we traditionally begin the process—and which I shall repeat here—is: "Blessed is the Holy One of Being, Who is the Breath of Life, Who makes us holy by means of the study of the Torah."

Three years ago when the people of the Jewish community first began in a serious way to ask the question, "What would Jewish tradition have to teach about the possibility of nuclear war?" the passage that surfaced and we found ourselves responding to was not the passage concerning just or unjust wars. What arose in this context was the passage that describes the Flood, Noah's Ark, and the Rainbow. Given that this passage came to us almost like a dream arising from the unconscious, we asked, "What does it mean for us that this is what arises? What would it mean for our generation to study this text carefully?"

It should be added that in classic rabbinic writing the Noah text, which sets forth the three-concerned covenant between God, Noah, and all human life, is the origin of most Jewish thought regarding the obligation that *all* human beings have to God, to each other, and to the created universe. The Noah text is, in classical Jewish thought, the text from which questions of the universal character of the human race arise.

Upon examination of the Noah text, it was obvious to us   5
why it had arisen. This is the one passage of the Torah that

talks about the danger of the destruction of all life on the planet. Within the text are some extraordinarily powerful symbols, such as the Flood itself, the Ark, the Rainbow, and the dove. However, we were not satisfied with simply the possibility of the power of these symbols, even though that power could awaken our own and others' spiritual energy toward dealing with the danger of the destruction of all human life. We wanted more than that as a teaching from the text.

The initial two levels of learning are fairly obvious. The first is the obligation of all persons to deal with the potential of the destruction of all life on the planet. The command to Noah is to protect every species of life on the planet, not just the human race or one section of the human race. Although only one portion of the human race was preserved in the Noah account, one realizes in reading the story that it was God's intent to make possible the re-creation of the entire human race and all the rest of life. For us it is clear that when the destruction of all life is threatened, we are commanded to preserve life. We must also take seriously our knowledge that there is no Ark capable of preserving all life—except this planet. No area smaller than the planet can do this; no cavern under the Smokies with corporate records, no concrete-lined bunker under the Rockies designed to protect some faint part of the Strategic Air Command, no fallout shelter will suffice. Only the planet will do.

The second level of learning from the text teaches us that God's command comes to a very "special" unspecial type of human being. The "specialness" of Noah is that he is unspecial. Noah is not an expert. He is not an expert on rain or on animals. The rabbinic midrash contains wonderful accounts of the difficulties Noah had dealing with all the animals on the Ark. Nor is Noah an expert at shipbuilding. He has to be told how to build his very peculiar ship. Noah is simply a reasonably righteous individual. In fact, the rabbis question how fully righteous an individual he was. They compare Noah to Abraham and Moses, who, when there were threats of destruction, as at Sodom and Gomorrah, and at Mt. Sinai, argued with God and prevailed. Noah never argued. So, the rabbis conclude, Noah was righteous for his generation, but when measured against others, he was not "super"-righteous.

This "unspecial" quality to Noah should serve as a powerful reminder to us not to defer to experts on the question of nuclear arms. Many of us have the habit of saying, on the question of nuclear weapons, that this issue is so complicated and advanced in its technicalities that it should be left to generals, or scientists, or international diplomats, or priests, rabbis, and theologians. Our typical reaction often is: "Don't come to me! What do I know?" But our understanding of Noah should refute this reaction.

We should also remember that Noah was not the leader of any government. Noah was, in a sense, a private citizen of the earth. This also raises some profound questions. To whom is the Noah text directed? Only to private citizens? To government leaders? Or to both? If to private citizens, what should be the impact on public policy?

As we studied the text further, an unexpected teaching came   10
from it. The question we had put to the text was, What does it have to teach us about nuclear war? In the process of studying and reflecting on the text, we realized that the text rejects, through a very powerful silence, talking about war at all. The text does not want to deal with the danger of the destruction of all life on the planet as if it were a war. So, we asked ourselves, of what use is this teaching? One use of the teaching is to raise a profound question as to whether war is the appropriate category to apply to exchanges of nuclear weapons.

This question strikes at the logical root of the bishops' pastoral letter. The dominant logic of the pastoral letter is centered on the issue of just and unjust wars. Nonetheless, the pastoral letter also alludes to other ways of thinking about this issue. One strain of the bishops' thought approaches the understanding that has evolved for us. This strain of thought is found in the references in the letter to the fact that what is at risk is the whole of God's creation.[1] The insight is, however, weakened in that the letter fails to use it as the basis for any call to action or for the development of any new systematic ethics, any new approach to knowing what action to take. It remains as powerful rhetoric. There may be an implicit connection between this insight and ideas of proportionality or the pursuit of justice, but such connections are not made explicit.

To return to the Noah text: We concluded that there was a serious danger in using the category of war, even when framed in terms of just or unjust war, when dealing with the issue of nuclear arms. The primary danger is that the category of war is one that the human race is accustomed to controlling. We have traditionally thought of war in terms of justice and injustice, in terms of gain and loss, and in terms of proportionate damage for the gain. It appeared to us that by pushing the category of war to its limits we had perhaps pushed beyond its limits. Some of us have become accustomed to saying that in nuclear war there would be no winners. Far fewer of us are accustomed to saying and absorbing the statement, "In a nuclear war there might be no losers." Although some political leaders have said such words in public, these concepts have not *in fact* been absorbed into the strategic theories and operational plans of either the United States or the Soviet Union; both nations' strategic plans still seek to "prevail" in nuclear war. What strategists and most of the rest of us have failed to internalize is the essentially different character of nuclear war. Once one realizes that in a nuclear "war" there might be no winners or losers, one questions the very usefulness of the category of war.

It is not only "winners" and "losers" that might be missing in a nuclear "war," but also "justice" and "injustice." For if no human community remains after a nuclear exchange, can there be justice or injustice? Or, are the standards dissolved and the category of war inappropriate? This question cuts close to the heart of the logic of the pastoral letter, which has at its root a call for justice.

A third aspect of this problem of the inadequacy of the category of war deals with our attitudes toward the weapons of war. Keeping in mind that the human race is accustomed to war and knows the painful consequences that ensue from both winning and losing a war, the human race in its various parts, when it notes an advantage, still prepares to win the war. The way to win a war ordinarily is to have a greater number of weapons, and more powerful weapons, than the anticipated opponent. This is the source of arms races. Such actions make sense if one thinks in the category "war." The notion that there might emerge a weapon that, given a certain number, would obliterate life on the planet has been a difficult notion to absorb.

We now know that the number beyond which nuclear bombs cease to be weapons is considerably lower than we had surmised 20 years ago. Scientists have reported that there is clear evidence that perhaps as few as 100 one-megaton nuclear bombs detonated on major cities might create a dust cloud so thick that sunlight could not reach the earth for an extended period of time. This period of time would be long enough to cause the cessation of photosynthesis and the death of all life on the planet. One hundred is a small number, taking into account that at present there are 50,000 nuclear "bombs" in the arsenals of the two superpowers.[2]

In the light of the foregoing, we must ask ourselves whether   15
the Noah text is teaching us to leave the category "war" altogether. The text might powerfully be teaching us to stretch ourselves, to think in different categories. If one thinks in the category of war, one is much more likely to participate in that category. Employing the category "war," nations are prone to go forward with the nuclear arms race, as such a race makes sense within the category "war." One is also prone to attempt fine-tuned analyses of just and unjust war. The high probability that such a "war" would result in universal destruction does not enter the equation

The Noah text and traditional midrash on it intimates at the destruction that would follow a nuclear exchange. In the text, humanity is destroyed by a flood of water. Paralleling this text, however, is an ancient rabbinic midrash that notes that while God promised not to send a flood of water at the end of the world, God did not promise that the world would not end in fire. This midrash has even entered southern Black culture in a song that says, "God gave Noah the rainbow sign—no more water—the fire next time."

We shall now attend to the text. The text first conveys the fact that *khamas*, i.e., violence, corruption, and ruination, were appearing everywhere on earth. God is still present in this process, however, maintaining that what the human race sows, so it shall reap. If humankind floods the earth with violence and corruption, then this violence and corruption will overflow and the world will be flooded.

The text, however, refuses to do what the category of war would require, i.e., define a "them" and an "us," a good side and a bad side. The Noah text refuses to have a good side and a bad side. There is only a tiny family. This family is not defined politically or ethnically. Noah and his family are not Jewish. Neither is it suggested that they are set against the rest of the human race. One might conclude that where the destruction of all life is threatened, the text cautions us not to expend energy searching for a bad side or a good side.

There is a strong tendency in every culture to find a good side and a bad side. This is seen even in peace movements. Among some of those active in the peace movement in this country, there is sometimes a tendency to say that since the United States is building nuclear bombs, the United States must be at fault. Among Americans who favor building more bombs, there is a tendency to say that the United States is morally superior to the Russians. (Among Soviet dissidents and apparatchiks there are obverse reactions. Soviet dissidents tend to identify the U.S.S.R. as the uniquely evil power; Soviet apparatchiks see the U.S.S.R. as uniquely good.) The Torah warns against all these outlooks. Rather than attempting to fix blame, the text teaches us to be on guard for the springs of violence that can overflow in every human society.

When we began dealing with the concept, "flood of fire," it   20
echoed, especially for Jewish ears, with the modern English word "holocaust," which literally means the burning of everything. Flood of fire—Holocaust—in the life experience of the Jewish people brings to mind the fact that a "high civilization," the society of Goethe and Beethoven, acted not only brutally but irrationally in its decision to try to obliterate the Jewish people even at great cost to itself. In trying to come to terms with the historical record, one realizes that the Nazis' decision to implement the Holocaust was made despite the fact this diversion of resources, labor, and energy made their victory in World War II less likely. By normal definitions this is not rational behavior. The notion that a government of a highly "advanced" and "civilized" Western society might commit an act of extraordinary evil ultimately harmful to itself is difficult to believe. But the Jewish people is a witness to this action, not in a vague sense, but in the tangible sense of having had the crime perpetrated on its own body. As a result, the Jewish people is available to state to the world: "We know that *the* most

dangerous statement can be made in the face of danger is that nobody would ever do such a crazy thing, that acts of supreme irrationality can never be committed." This is the most dangerous statement that can be made because it weakens efforts to prevent the "unthinkable" from being *done.*

We discovered not only an unexpected silence, but an unexpected speaking in the text, as well. The Noah text is full of dates. In the entire book of Genesis, no dates are provided for some very important events. There are no dates provided for the creation of the world, or for Abraham's departure for and arrival in Canaan, or for Joseph's journey to Egypt and his appointment as prime minister of Egypt. In contrast, there is a plethora of dates in the Noah story. There is a date for the beginning of the Flood. We learn not only that the rain falls for 40 days and nights, but also how much time elapsed before the water reached its crest. There are dates for the receding of the water, for the appearance of the mountain tops, and then the appearance of dry ground on the rest of the planet, and finally the exit from the Ark and the experience of the Rainbow. We were startled to realize the presence of all these dates and the extraordinariness of this in the context of Genesis.

In Jewish tradition, as in all religious traditions, it is clear what is to be done with important dates. They are made into moments in the cycle of the year, in which the event is re-addressed and re-experienced. Thus, the date of the Exodus is made into Passover and the date of the rededication of the Temple is made into Hannukah. In the Christian tradition, the use of dates is seen with the Crucifixion, the Resurrection, Advent, and so forth. The Passover Haggadah, the service read on the first night of Passover, teaches that the Passover event is not to be taken only as history. The participants themselves in their own lives each year re-experience the liberation from slavery.

There was, however, no observance of the dates of the Flood, either its beginning or its end. It became clear to us why this lack of observance was so. There was never any generation of the human race that had faced the practical possibility of the destruction of life on the planet—until our own. So it seemed to us that these dates had been "stored away" by the Torah to address our present generation, which faces this danger. Taking into account the way religious traditions deal with dates, we are now to understand a command to experience this danger, this deliverance, and to participate in the Rainbow Covenant, in order to make the deliverance a reality.

Jewish communities began to respond to this command in 1982. That first year, possibly 20 communities observed the call. I would estimate that in 1984, 1,000 communities have held or will hold observances. Increasingly, Jewish communities holding such observances, recognizing that the Flood was a universal event and nuclear holocaust a universal danger, are inviting other religious communities to join them.

These observances must not simply be "faddish" events. 25
They must be built into the liturgy, life cycle, of the people. I have visited synagogues where the reaction has been, "We covered the nuclear issue last year." Compare this response to Passover. We "did" liberation from Pharaoh last year and we will "do" it again this year, and 1,000 years from now, until the Messiah comes. It is now clear that the danger posed by nuclear bombs will be with us just as long a time. Even if all the bombs were physically eliminated, we would still have to deal with the fact that the knowledge to produce these bombs will always be with us

Such an incorporation into the liturgical calendar means that the nuclear issue can never be avoided. It is a means of defeating the American tendency to deal with issues only periodically, while it is fashionable to do so. In the period 1959–64, nuclear arms was an important question on the agendas of the two superpowers. It was in this period that the heads of the Soviet Union and the United States agreed that general and complete disarmament was essential. The deputies of these two leaders initialed an agreement on the general principles of how to proceed toward disarmament. (See the McCloy-Zorin Pact.) But beginning in 1964, disarmament fell out of fashion and little else was done. Placing this concern in the liturgy of the people will help prevent any future loss of interest and will teach our bodies, our emotions, and our spirits—as well as our minds—to go deeper into the Wellspring of Life in order to prevent the flood of fire. For these reasons, I hope the Church as well as the Synagogue will create such liturgies.

The liturgy that we feel is called for is a flexible one and is based around the Rainbow Sign. The Rainbow is a powerful element in the midrash on the Noah text. The Rainbow represents a covenant between God and humankind promising the preservation of all life. The giving of the Rainbow Sign to Noah was accompanied by the following passage: "While the earth remains, seedtime and harvest, cold and heat, summer and winter, day and night, shall not cease." This passage evokes a concern with cycles. It suggests that one of the things that had gone wrong in the period leading up to the Flood was that the cycles had been disrupted.

The concern for cycles is strengthened by other elements in the account. If one adds up the periods of time mentioned in the text, one finds that it equals a Jewish lunar year, plus 11 days. This is precisely a solar year. Hidden within the text are other indications of a concern for cycles. When the Flood waters abated, Noah sent forth a raven and a dove to search for land. The word raven in Hebrew is *arvah*, very close to the Hebrew word *erev*, "evening." And the Hebrew word for dove, *yonah*, is very close to Hebrew *yom*, "day." So first Noah sends out the dark of night and then the light of day. Heightening this symbolism, it should also be noted that the raven is a bird of carrion that would bring to a full end the last cycle of time before the Flood, by eating the carcasses bestrewing the flooded earth; and the dove returns with the olive branch, the first growth of the new cycle. The use of the raven and the dove at this point suggests that Noah knew that the cycles had been disrupted, both the micro-cycle of day and night, and the macro-cycle of life and death.

We realized that this insight has application to today. One of the great failings of the modern period is its destruction of the cycles of life. Modern society no longer considers the cycles important. Modern society has become so skilled at creating things, manufacturing things, that the notion of sacred time, a time where you stop producing and rest—contemplate—meditate—has been obliterated. We no longer know how to make sabbath. Both Jewish life through the great festivals and Christian life through feast days and saints' days respected the fact that there are times and days that are sacred and holy. This sacred time was recognized through ceasing the normal daily routine and meditating. But the modern Western world of the last several hundred years has forgotten how to do this.

What is the connection between this loss of sacred time and the bomb? The connection is that when you produce, and make, and manufacture, and never rest, the result is destruction. Artists recognize this fact of life. Artists begin a painting with great creativity, but if the artist works too long, if the artist makes one brushstroke too many, the painting is not finished, it is finished off. One act of creativity too many leads to ruination.

One can compare the flood to the story of creation. The creation account illustrates that it is necessary not to create in order to create. The crucial final act of creation was the Sabbath, the day on which God rested. God's rest sealed creation.

Cycles are crucial in both a large sense and a small sense. These last 500 years, we have done some extraordinary things. We have invented technologies that have transformed the planet. The oceans are chemically different from what they were 500 years ago. The face of the moon has been touched. The human life span is appreciably longer. New elements, such as californium, which have not existed since the first few minutes of creation, have been created. We must now stop, catch our breath, and make sabbath. Failure to do so will finish off the painting that is the earth.

Modernity and religious traditions must become reconciled. Our religious traditions have been very skeptical toward the technological and scientific developments of the last 500 years. It is now time to integrate what the human race has learned these last 500 years into the religious traditions. If one sees the last 500 years as a moment in the cycle of a great harvest of human knowledge, then the thing to do after the harvest is to recognize that last year's growing season is dead and that all that is left are seeds. It is a time for taking stock, the close of one harvest and the beginning of another season.

The Rainbow itself also provides important symbolism. It is an extraordinary symbol of unity in diversity. The Rainbow is not white light; if it were, it would be invisible. The Rainbow is a pattern made from all the colors of the spectrum, red, orange, yellow, green, blue, indigo, violet. It is infinite variety.

But the Rainbow is not merely infinite variety. There is also   35
an aspect of unity: a pattern. A nuclear-age midrash illustrates this point. People who have seen the hydrogen bomb tested say that the mushroom cloud is a thing of terrifying beauty. The bomb so disrupts the electromagnetic patterns that it creates sparks and flashes of all the colors. All the colors of the Rainbow are found in the mushroom cloud, but shattered into a billion pieces. This suggests that only seeing the diversity is not enough, just as seeing only a unity is not sufficient. There must be a way to recognize that the Rainbow unites dissimilarities.

Related to this is the role Mt. Ararat plays in the account. Ararat was for the writers of the Torah what satellites are to us—the satellites from which the entire Earth could be seen as a ball of blue and white. From Ararat, the entire Middle East—the "world" of the Torah—can be seen as a unity. In fact, the Middle East forms a sort of great arc, the great fertile crescent. The Rainbow might be seen as a reflection in the sky of this crescent of many cultures. From Ararat, one would see the whole of the great crescent in the sky.

I wish to close by reflecting on Noah. Noah, as mentioned earlier, is not a political leader. This raises the question, how are we called to act against the flood of *khamas,* violence, on the planet? What does it mean that *each* human being is obligated to act to prevent the destruction of all life on the planet and is obligated not to cooperate with the structures and rules that proceed inexorably toward this destruction? What does it mean that every human being is obligated to build the Ark that is this planet?

The bishops' pastoral letter takes only tentative steps toward addressing this question of personal responsibility, although a number of bishops have begun to set honorable personal examples. I hasten to add that most other communities—including the organized Jewish community—have not yet done any better. I should also add that the publishing of the pastoral letter may prove to be one of the key moments of world history—even of "Earth history," defined more broadly than the history of the human race alone. It will not be the only key moment, however; standing alone, it is not enough. It is now our duty, acting in fraternal/sororal unity—in the tradition of the Rainbow—to push beyond this noble beginning.

Notes

1. The pastoral letter, in its discussion of the Pontifical Academy of Sciences' "Statement on the Consequences of the Use of Nuclear Weapons," recognizes that what is at risk in the nuclear age is the survival of the entire planet. The pastoral moves from this recognition to the conclusion that the appropriate moral corollary is the prevention of nuclear war. (See *The Challenge of Peace*, nn. 126–131.) The pastoral, however, somewhat anomalously given this recognition, also maintains a just-war analysis.

   Moreover, the anomaly is not just theoretical—but goes to the heart of certain policy issues. In addressing *how* to prevent nuclear "war," the pastoral letter does not examine the possibility that if in the real world any use of nuclear weapons is very likely to result in world nuclear holocaust, then the proclamation of this fact by nuclear powers as truth and even its translation into weapons targeting may be a less immoral version of "deterrence" than false and phony claims that nuclear weapons are not being targeted on civilians.

   To make that point more precise: The pastoral letter, out of a just-war analysis, says that any version of deterrence based on an explicit intention and warning of the deliberate destruction of cities is immoral. I would suggest that if *any* version of nuclear deterrence is less immoral than any other—itself a doubtful proposition—the version most likely to be least immoral is one that says: "Since any nuclear war is very liable to turn into a world holocaust, and since attempting to prepare for a 'limited nuclear war' is liable to bring one on and therefore liable to bring on a world nuclear holocaust, we will eschew all rhetoric or practical steps looking toward a 'limited nuclear war' altogether. We are therefore abandoning all but a small number of weapons, and these are targeted on cities, purely to deter anyone from using nuclear weapons against us. We invite all other nuclear powers to do the same, but this is not a precondition. We will pursue with great vigor the elimination of these remaining weapons by all nuclear powers." The explicit statement that a "minimum deterrent" is targeted on cities seems to be excluded by the pastoral letter—which I think is the (unwise) result of its inappropriate use of just-war theory.

2. There is now very persuasive evidence on the devastating effects of the detonation of even the "small" number of 100 megatons of nuclear bombs. See, R. P. Turco, O. B. Toon, T. P. Ackerman, J. B. Pollock, and C. Sagan, "Nuclear Winter: Global Consequences of Multiple Nuclear Explosions," *Science* 222, 4630 (December 23, 1983), pp. 1283–1292; P. R. Ehrlich, J. Harte, M. A. Harwell, P. H. Raven, C. Sagan, G. M. Woodwell, J. Berry, E. S. Ayensu, A. H. Ehrlich, T. Eisner, S. J. Gould, H. D. Grover, R. Herrera, R. M, May, E. Mayr, C. P. McKay, H. A. Mooney, N. Myers, D. Pimentel, and J. M. Teal, "Long Term Biological Consequences of Nuclear War," *Science* 222, 4630 (December 23, 1983), pp. 1293–1300. See also Scientists' Report to Pope John Paul II, "The Nuclear Winter," *Origins*, Vol. 13, 38 (March 1, 1984), pp. 625–627.

Questions about the Passage

1. What is *midrash?* What is the connection between studying the Torah and *midrash?*
2. What are the three levels of learning, or teachings, that Waskow finds in the Noah text?
3. Why does Waskow put "war" in quotation marks when referring to nuclear war?
4. How does the Noah text encourage abandoning the category of war?
5. Why does Waskow believe it is important to incorporate the Rainbow Covenant into regular liturgical observance?
6. Why are cycles and "sacred time" important as part of the lesson of the Noah text?
7. At the end of the essay, what does Waskow want his readers to do?

Questions about the Argument

1. Reread the introduction to this piece. What in Waskow's background helps to create his authority as a writer?
2. Who is the "we" of Waskow's essay? Is this "we" the same as his audience?

3. Define Waskow's audience. What does he assume the members of his audience know and do not know? How does he address his readers—what does he do to help make them comfortable with novel ideas and practices?
4. Spell out the implied analogy in paragraph 20 comparing attitudes towards Nazi actions and towards the potential for governments to launch nuclear war. Evaluate the effectiveness of the analogy.
5. Consider Waskow's use of metaphors and how they contribute to his argument (see, for example, paragraphs 1–2, 33–35).
6. Examine how Waskow uses the Noah text to support his argument. Which elements of the biblical narrative does he employ? How do they function?
7. How does Waskow's view of nuclear war challenge just war thinking?

Writing Assignments

Conversation

You have had one of the authors of this chapter as a speaker on campus who then joins you for a late-night dorm conversation. What questions would you want to ask him or her? Do you want to challenge the speaker? Do you want clarification on specific points? Do you want to know how the speaker views current events? Can you infer from the text how the speaker might respond? You may present this as an informal discussion.

Writing Sequence: Is "Just War" an Outmoded Concept?

1. Consider the following claim: Just war is an outmoded concept in an age of terrorism and weapons of mass destruction. Explore your ideas about both sides of this issue, pro and con. Would you attach any qualifications (in a Toulmin sense) to this claim?
2. What do Walzer, Shuck, Calhoun, and Waskow have to say about the above claim? Summarize their positions on this point in one or two paragraphs each. Then respond briefly to each position.
3. Construct a debate, written or in class, about the proposition—Resolved: That just war is an outmoded concept in an age of terrorism and weapons of mass destruction. Use the writers of this

chapter to support one side or the other of the debate. Join the debate on the side you support. Would you include any of the writers from Chapter 4? Given that they had no knowledge of modern terrorism or weapons, what constructive ideas could they add to the debate? Or—Write a persuasive essay supporting one side or the other in this debate, drawing your evidence from the writers of this chapter and of Chapter 4, if you believe they have ideas to buttress your position.

6

The Peace and Non-Violent Positions

Some might say, with Martin Luther, that the Just War position responds to a world where "people will not keep the peace, but rob, steal, kill, outrage women and children, and take away property and honor." The just war thus becomes a kind of pragmatic compromise in which "the small lack of peace called war or the sword must set a limit to this universal, worldwide lack of peace which would destroy everyone."

There is another more idealistic tradition that privileges peace. The U.S. Catholic Bishops stand at an intersection between war and peace. They recognize that some wars are just. But they value the peace treasured in the psalms and by the prophets of the Hebrew Bible and esteem the peacemakers whom Jesus blessed and to whom he promised the peace of the kingdom of heaven. Their 1993 pastoral letter *The Harvest of Justice Is Sown in Peace* enunciates a "theology of peace [that] should ground the task of peacemaking solidly in the biblical vision of the kingdom of God." The letter has a strong section entitled "The Value of Non-violence" which traces the history of the pacifist position and affirms the validity of this position. The bishops favor a "presumption in favor of peace and against war."

Douglas Lackey separates the various strands of pacifist traditions in his book *Ethics of War and Peace* (1989). First are those who believe killing is always wrong. Second are those who say any kind of violence is wrong. The third group argues that personal violence is always wrong, but political violence is sometimes right. The fourth group justifies some personal violence but rejects war as always wrong.

Peace Churches, which include groups like the Quakers and Mennonites, take a resolutely pacifist stand. The *Confession of Faith in a Mennonite Perspective,* Article 22, is uncompromising: "As disciples of Christ, we do not prepare for war, or participate in war or military service." Though not based on Christianity, Gandhi's position is, if anything, more uncompromising than the Peace Church position. He not only rejects violence of any sort, but he says that *Ahimsa* (non-killing) "really means that you may not offend anybody; you may not harbor an uncharitable thought, even in connection with one who may consider himself to be your enemy."

Another strand of the peace position is secular. This stand denounces war and violence but bases the denunciation on humanistic rather than religious values and scriptural support. Howard Zinn's argument against the war in Afghanistan (in Chapter 7) probably belongs in this category, as might Laurie Calhoun's (in Chapter 5).

U.S. Catholic Bishops, "A Vision for Peacemaking"

This section included below opens the U.S. Catholic Bishops' letter and discusses both the virtues necessary for peacemaking as well as providing a "clear vision for a peaceful world." Only after an exploration of peacemaking do the bishops reexamine the Just War tradition (included in Chapter 4).

I. Theology, Spirituality and Ethics for Peacemaking

An often neglected aspect of *The Challenge of Peace* is the spirituality and ethics of peacemaking. At the heart of our faith lies "the God of peace" (Rom. 15:33), who desires peace for all people far and near (Ps. 85; Is. 57:19). That desire has been fulfilled in Christ in whom humanity has been redeemed and reconciled. In our day, the Holy Spirit continues to call us to seek peace with one another, so that in our peacemaking we may prepare for the coming of the reign of God, a kingdom of true justice, love and peace. God created the human family as one and calls it to unity. The renewed unity we experience in Christ is to be lived out in every possible way. We are to do all we can to live at peace with everyone (Rom. 12:18). Given the effects of sin, our efforts to live in peace with one another depend on our openness to God's healing grace and the unifying power of Christ's redemption.

Change of mind and heart, of word and action are essential to those who would work for peace (Rom. 12:2). This conversion to the God of peace has two dimensions. On the one hand, in imitation of Christ we must be humble, gentle and patient. On the other, we are called to be strong and active in our peacemaking, loving our enemies and doing good generously as God does (Lk. 6:35–36, 38), filled with eagerness to spread the gospel of peace (Eph. 6:15).

Likewise, discovering God's peace, which exceeds all understanding, in prayer is essential to peacemaking (Phil. 4:7). The peace given in prayer draws us into God, quieting our anxieties, challenging our old values and deepening wells of new energy. It arouses in us a compassionate love for all humanity and gives us heart to persevere beyond frustration, suffering and defeat. We should never forget that peace is not merely something that we ourselves as creatures do and can accomplish, but it is, in the ultimate analysis, a gift and a grace from God.

By its nature, the gift of peace is not restricted to moments of prayer. It seeks to penetrate the corners of everyday life and to transform the world. But, to do so, it needs to be complemented in other ways. It requires other peaceable virtues, a practical vision of a peaceful world and an ethics to guide peacemakers in times of conflict.

A. Virtues and a Vision for Peacemakers

Peaceable Virtues. True peacemaking can be a matter of policy   5
only if it is first a matter of the heart. In the absence of repentance and forgiveness, no peace can endure; without a spirit of courageous charity, justice cannot be won. We can take inspiration from the early Christian communities. Paul called on the Corinthians, even in the most trying circumstances, to pursue peace and bless their persecutors, never repaying evil for evil, but overcoming evil with good (Rom. 12:14, 17, 21).

Amid the violence of contemporary culture and in response to the growing contempt for human life, the Church must seek to foster communities where peaceable virtues can take root and be nourished. We need to nurture among ourselves *faith and hope* to strengthen our spirits by placing our trust in God, rather than in ourselves; *courage and compassion* that move us to action; *humility and kindness* so that we can put the needs and interests of others ahead of our own; *patience and perseverance* to endure the long struggle for justice; and *civility and charity* so that we can treat others with respect and love.

"The goal of peace, so desired by everyone," as Pope John Paul has written, "will certainly be achieved through the putting into effect of social and international justice, but also through the practice of the virtues which favor togetherness and which teach us to live in unity."

1. **A Vision of Peace.** A practical complement to the virtues of peacemaking is a clear vision of a peaceful world. Thirty years ago Pope John XXIII laid out before us a visionary framework for peace in his encyclical letter *Pacem in Terris (Peace on Earth)*, which retains its freshness today. *Pacem in Terris* proposed a political order in service of the common good, defined in terms of the defense and promotion of human rights. In a prophetic insight, anticipating the globalization of our problems, Pope John called for new forms of political authority adequate to satisfy the needs of the universal common good.

   Peace does not consist merely in the absence of war, but rather in sharing the goodness of life together. In keeping with Pope John's teaching, the Church's positive vision of a peaceful world includes:

   a. the primacy of the global common good for political life,
   b. the role of social and economic development in securing the conditions for a just and lasting peace, and
   c. the moral imperative of solidarity between affluent, industrial nations and poor, developing ones.

   a. *The Universal Common Good.* A key element in Pope John's   10
   conception of a peaceful world is a global order oriented to the full development of all peoples, with governments committed to the rights of citizens, and a framework of authority which enables the world community to address fundamental problems that individual governments fail to resolve. In this framework, sovereignty is in the service of people. All political authority has as its end the promotion of the common good, particularly the defense of human rights. When a government clearly fails in this task or itself becomes a central impediment to the realization of those rights, the world community has a right and a duty to act where the lives and the fundamental rights of large numbers of people are at serious risk.

   b. *The Responsibility for Development.* A second element consists of the right to and the duty of development for all peoples. In the words of Pope John Paul II, "[J]ust as there is a collective responsibility for avoiding war, so too there is a collective responsibility for promoting development." Development, the Holy Father reasoned, will contribute to a more just world in which the occasions for resorting to arms will be greatly reduced:

> [It] must not be forgotten that at the root of war there are usually real and serious grievances: injustices suffered, legitimate aspirations frustrated, poverty and the exploitation of multitudes of desperate people who see no real possibility of improving their lot by peaceful means.

Development not only serves the interest of justice, but also contributes greatly to a lasting peace.

c. *Human Solidarity.* A third imperative is to further the unity of the human family. Solidarity requires that we think and act in terms of our obligations as members of a global community, despite differences of race, religion or nationality. We are responsible for actively promoting the dignity of the world's poor through global economic reform, development assistance and institutions designed to meet the needs of the hungry, refugees and the victims of war. Solidarity, Pope John Paul II reminds us, contributes to peace by providing "a firm and persevering determination" to seek the good of all. "Peace," he declares, will be "the fruit of solidarity."

Questions about the Passage

1. How must people change in order to become peacemakers?
2. Which of the communities that you belong to foster the peaceable virtues that the bishops wish to nurture?
3. What is the bishops' definition of peace?
4. How do they define the "global common good"? How must governments go about achieving it? What must the global community do if a sovereign nation fails to work for the common good?
5. What do the bishops mean by "development"? How can such development lead to peace?
6. How would you define "solidarity"? The bishops indicate categories of actions to achieve solidarity. Provide examples of actions for each category.

Questions about the Argument

1. Why do the bishops use verses from the Hebrew Bible and the New Testament? How might such use contribute to their ethos as arguers? What impact might citing the Bible have on their audience?
2. To what extent are the bishops making a traditional argumentative case? For example, do they propose a thesis and support it? To what extent might the purpose of a pastoral letter differ from that of an argument?
3. The bishops use many words that have religious associations or meanings. List as many of these words as you can find. Does the use of these charged words contribute to the persuasive power of the piece?
4. Look ahead to *The Declaration of Independence* (p. 183). How do these American bishops draw on its premises and echo its language?

Douglas P. Lackey, "Varieties of Pacifism"

Douglas Lackey (1945–) was educated at Michigan State University and Yale University. He has taught for over thirty years at Baruch College of the City University of New York, where he won the Distinguished Teaching Award in 2002. Lackey is the author of five books, including *Moral Principles and Nuclear Weapons* (1984), *Ethics and Strategic Defense: American Philosophers Debate Star Wars and the Future of Nuclear Deterrence* (1989), and *God, Immortality, Ethics: A Concise Introduction to Philosophy* (1990). In 2003, his play protesting the suffering of war in the Israeli/Palestinian conflict, "Kaddish in East Jerusalem," was produced in New York City. The passage below distinguishing types of pacifism comes from *The Ethics of War and Peace* (1989).

1. Varieties of Pacifism

Everyone has a vague idea of what a pacifist is, but few realize that there are many kinds of pacifists. (Sometimes the different kinds quarrel with each other!) One task for the student of international ethics is to distinguish the different types of pacifism and to identify which types represent genuine moral theories.

Most of us at some time or other have run into the "live and let live" pacifist, the person who says, "I am absolutely opposed to killing and violence—but I don't seek to impose my own code on anyone else. If other people want to use violence, so be it. They have their values and I have mine." For such a person, pacifism is one life style among others, a life style committed to gentleness and care, and opposed to belligerence and militarism. Doubtless, many people who express such commitments are sincere and are prepared to live by their beliefs. At the same time, it is important to see why "live and let live" pacifism does not constitute a moral point of view.

When someone judges that a certain action, A, is morally wrong, that judgment entails that no one should do A. Thus, there is no way to have moral values without believing that these values apply to other people. If a person says that A is morally wrong but that it doesn't matter if other people do A, than that person either is being inconsistent or doesn't know what the word "moral" means. If a person believes that killing, in certain circumstances, is morally wrong, that belief implies that no one should kill, at least in those circumstances. If a pacifist claims that killing is wrong in all circumstances, but that it is permissible for other people to kill on occasion, then he has not understood the universal character of genuine moral principles. If pacifism is to be a moral theory, it must be prescribed for all or prescribed for none.

Once one recognizes this "universalizing" character of genuine moral beliefs, one will take moral commitments more seriously than those who treat a moral code as a personal lifestyle. Since moral principles apply to everyone, we must take care that our moral principles are correct, checking that they are not inconsistent with each other, developing and adjusting them so that they are detailed and subtle enough to deal with a variety of circumstances, and making sure that they are defensible against the objections of those who do not accept them. Of course many pacifists do take the business of morality seriously and advance pacifism as a genuine moral position, not as a mere life-style. All such serious pacifists believe that *everyone* ought to be a pacifist, and that those who reject pacifism are deluded or wicked. Moreover, they do not simply endorse pacifism; they offer arguments in its defense.

We will consider four types of pacifist moral theory. First, there are pacifists who maintain that the central idea of pacifism is the immorality of killing. Second, there are pacifists who maintain that the essence of pacifism is the immorality of violence, whether this be violence in personal relations or

5

violence in relations between nation-states. Third, there are pacifists who argue that personal violence is always morally wrong but that political violence is sometimes morally right: for example, that it is sometimes morally permissible for a nation to go to war. Fourth and finally, there are pacifists who believe that personal violence is sometimes permissible but that war is always morally wrong.

Albert Schweitzer, who opposed all killing on the grounds that life is sacred, was the first sort of pacifist. Mohandas Gandhi and Leo Tolstoy, who opposed not only killing but every kind of coercion and violence, were pacifists of the second sort: I will call such pacifists "universal pacifists." St. Augustine, who condemned self-defense but endorsed wars against heretics, was a pacifist of the third sort. Let us call him a "private pacifist," since he condemned only violence in the private sphere. Pacifists of the fourth sort, increasingly common in the modern era of nuclear and total war, I will call "antiwar pacifists."

2. The Prohibition against Killing
The Biblical Prohibition

One simple and common argument for pacifism is the argument that the Bible, God's revealed word, says to all people "Thou shalt not kill" (Exod. 20:13). Some pacifists interpret this sentence as implying that no one should kill under any circumstances, unless God indicates that this command is suspended, as He did when He commanded Abraham to slay Isaac. The justification for this interpretation is the words themselves, "Thou shalt not kill," which are presented in the Bible bluntly and without qualification, not only in Exodus but also in Deuteronomy (5:17).

This argument, however, is subject to a great many criticisms. The original language of Exodus and Deuteronomy is Hebrew, and the consensus of scholarship says that the Hebrew sentence at Exodus 20:23, "Lo Tirzach," is best translated as "Thou shalt do no murder," not as "Thou shalt not kill." If this translation is correct, then Exodus 20:13 does not forbid all killing but only those killings that happen to be murders. Furthermore, there are many places in the Bible where God commands human beings to kill in specified circumstances. God announces 613 commandments in all, and these include "Thou shalt not suffer a witch to live" (Exod. 22:18); "He that blasphemeth the name of the Lord . . . shall surely be put to death, and all the congregation shall stone him" (Lev. 24:16); "He that killeth any man shall surely be put to death" (Lev. 24:17); and so forth. It is difficult to argue that these instructions are like God's specific instructions to Abraham to slay Isaac: these are general commandments to be applied by many people, to many people, day in and day out. They are at least as general and as divinely sanctioned as the commandment translated "Thou shalt not kill."

There are other difficulties for pacifists who pin their hopes on prohibitions in the Hebrew Bible. Even if the commandment "Thou shalt not kill," properly interpreted, did prohibit all types of killing, the skeptics can ask whether this, by itself, proves that all killing is immoral. First, how do we know that statements in the Hebrew Bible really are God's word, and not just the guesses of ancient scribes? Second, even if the commandments in the Bible do express God's views, why are we morally bound to obey divine commands? (To say that we will be punished if we do not obey is to appeal to fear and self-interest, not to moral sentiments). Third, are the commandments in the Old Testament laws for all people, or just laws for the children of Israel? If they are laws for all people, then all people who do not eat unleavened bread for Passover are either deluded or wicked. If they are laws only for the children of Israel, they are religious laws and not moral laws, since they lack the universality that all moral laws must have.

Finally, the argument assumes the existence of God, and philosophers report that the existence of God is not easy to demonstrate. Even many religious believers are more confident of the truth of basic moral judgments, such as "Small children should not be tortured to death for purposes of amusement," than they are confident of the existence of God. For such people, it would seem odd to try to justify moral principles by appeals to religious principles, since the evidence for those religious principles is weaker than the evidence for the moral principles they are supposed to justify. . . .

10

3. Universal Pacifism
Christian Pacifism

Universal pacifists are morally opposed to all violence, not just to killing. Many universal pacifists derive their views from the Christian Gospels. In the Sermon on the Mount, Christ taught:

> Ye have heard that it hath been said, An eye for an eye, a tooth for a tooth: But I say unto you, that ye resist not evil: but whosoever shall smite thee on the right cheek, turn to him the other also. . . .
>
> Ye have heard it said, thou shalt love thy neighbor, and hate thine enemy. But I say unto you, Love your enemies, bless them that curse you, do good to them that hate you. . . . that ye may be the children of your father which is in heaven: for he maketh the sun to rise on the evil and on the good, and sendeth the rain on the just and the unjust. (Matt. 5:38–45)

In the early centuries of the Christian era, it was widely assumed that to follow Christ and to obey His teaching meant that one should reject violence and refuse service in the Roman army. But by the fifth century, after the Roman Empire had become Christian and after barbarian Goths in 410 sacked Rome itself, Church Fathers debated whether Christ really intended that the Empire and its Church should remain undefended. The Church Fathers noticed passages in the Gospels that seem to contradict pacifism:

> Think not that I am come to send peace on earth: I came not
> to send peace, but a sword.
>
> For I am come to set a man at variance against his father,
> and the daughter against her mother, and the daughter-in-law
> against her mother-in-law. (Matt. 10:34–35)

15

And there are several instances in the Gospels (for instance, Matt. 8:5–10) in which Jesus encounters soldiers and does not rebuke them for engaging in an occupation that is essentially committed to violence. Rather, he argues, "Render unto Caesar the things which are Caesar's; and unto God the things that are God's" (Matt. 22:21). This would seem to include military service, or at least taxes to pay for the army.

A thorough analysis of whether the Gospels command pacifism is beyond the scope of this book. The passages in the Sermon on the Mount seem to be clearly pacifist; yet many eminent scholars have denied the pacifist message. A more interesting question, for philosophy, if not for biblical scholarship, is this: If Jesus did preach pacifism in the Sermon on the Mount, did He preach it as a moral doctrine?

Jesus did not view his teaching as replacing the moral law as he knew it:

> Think not that I am come to destroy the law, or the prophets: I am come not to destroy, but to fulfill. . . .
>
> Till heaven and earth pass, one jot or one tittle shall in no wise pass from the law, till all be fulfilled (Matt. 5:17–18)

Perhaps, then, the prescriptions of the Sermon on the Mount should be interpreted as rules that one must obey in order to follow Christ, or rules that one must follow in order to obtain salvation. But it does not follow from this alone that everyone has an obligation to follow Christ, and it does not follow from this alone that everyone has an obligation to seek salvation. Even Christians will admit that some people have refused to become Christians and have led morally admirable lives nonetheless; and if salvation is a good, one can nevertheless choose to reject it, just as a citizen can neglect to hand in a winning lottery ticket without breaking the law. If so, the prescriptions of the Sermon on the Mount apply only to Christians seeking a Christian salvation. They are not universally binding rules and do not qualify as moral principles. . . .

Gandhian Pacifism

Certainly the most interesting and effective pacifist of the twentieth century was Mohandas Gandhi (1869–1948). Though a devout Hindu, Gandhi developed his doctrine of nonviolence from elementary metaphysical concepts that are by no means special to Hinduism: 20

> Man as an animal is violent but as spirit is nonviolent. The moment he awakes to the spirit he cannot remain violent. Either he progresses towards *ahimsa* [nonviolence] or rushes to his doom. *(Nonviolence in Peace and War, I*, p. 311)

The requirement not to be violent seems wholly negative; sleeping people achieve it with ease. But for Gandhi the essential moral task is not merely to be nonviolent but to use the force of the soul *(satyagraha,* "truth grasping") in a continual struggle for justice. The methods of applied *satyagraha* developed by Gandhi—the weaponless marches, the sit-downs and sit-ins, strikes and boycotts, fasts and prayers—captured the admiration of the world and have been widely copied, most notably by Martin Luther King, Jr., in his campaigns against racial discrimination. According to Gandhi, each person, by engaging in *satyagraha* and experiencing suffering on behalf of justice, purifies the soul from pollution emanating from man's animal nature:

> A *satyagrahi* is dead to his body even before his enemy attempts to kill him, i.e. he is free from the attachments of his body and lives only in the victory of his soul. *(Nonviolence in Peace and War, I,* p. 318) Nonviolence implies as complete self-purification as is humanly possible. *(Nonviolence in Peace and War, I,* p. 111)

By acting nonviolently, pacifists not only purify their own souls but also transform the souls of their opponents: "A nonviolent revolution is not a program of seizure of power. It is a program of transformation of relationships, ending in peaceful transfer of power" *(Nonviolence in Peace and War, II,* p. 8).

Though in most places Gandhi emphasizes the personal   25
redemption that is possible only through nonviolent resistance to evil, the spiritually positive effect of nonviolence on evil opponents is perhaps equally important, since "The soul of the *satyagrahi* is love" *(Nonviolence in Peace and War, II,* p. 59).

Gandhi, then, is far from preaching the sacredness of biological life. What matters is not biological life but the condition of the soul, the natural and proper state of which is *ahimsa.* The evil of violence is that it distorts and disrupts this natural condition of the soul. The basic moral law *(dharma)* for all people is to seek the restoration of their souls to the harmony of *ahimsa.* This spiritual restoration cannot be achieved by violence, but only by the application of *satyagraha.* Disharmony cannot produce harmony; violence cannot produce spiritual peace.

The "sacredness of life" defense of pacifism ran into difficulties analyzing situations in which taking one life could save many lives. For Gandhi, this is no problem at all: taking one life may save many biological lives, but it will not save souls. On the contrary, the soul of the killer will be perverted by the act, and that perversion—not the loss of life—is what matters morally.

The system of values professed by Gandhi—that the highest human good is a harmonious condition of soul—must be kept in mind when considering the frequent accusation that Gandhi's method of nonviolent resistance "does not work," that nonviolence alone did not and could not force the British to leave India, and that nonviolent resistance to murderous tyrants like Hitler will only provoke the mass murder of the innocent. Perhaps the practice of nonviolence could not "defeat" the British or "defeat" Hitler, but by Gandhi's standard the use of military force would only produce a greater defeat, perverting the souls of thousands engaged in war and intensifying the will to violence on the opposing side. On the other hand, the soul of the *satyagrahi* will be strengthened and purified by nonviolent struggle against British imperialism or German Nazism, and in this purification the Gandhian pacifist can obtain spiritual victory even in the face of political defeat.

India did not adopt the creed of nonviolence after the British left in 1948, and it is hardly likely that any modern nation-state will organize its international affairs along Gandhian lines. But none of this affects the validity of Gandhi's arguments, which indicate how things ought to be, not how they are. We have seen that Gandhi's principles do not falter in the face of situations in which taking one life can save lives on balance. But what of situations in which the sacrifice of spiritual purity by one will prevent the corruption of many souls? Suppose, for example, that a Gandhian believes (on good evidence) that a well-timed commando raid will prevent a nation from embarking on an aggressive war, a war that would inflame whole populations with hatred for the enemy. Wouldn't a concern with one's own spiritual purity in such a situation show an immoral lack of concern for the souls of one's fellow men?

Another problem for Gandhi concerns the relationship   30
between violence and coercion. To coerce people is to make them act against their will, for fear of the consequences they will suffer if they do not obey. Coercion, then, is a kind of spiritual violence, directed against the imagination and will of the victim. The "violence" most conspicuously rejected by Gandhi—pushing, shoving, striking with hands, the use of weapons, the placing of bombs and explosives—is essentially physical violence, directed against the bodies of opponents. But if physical violence against bodies is spiritually corrupting,

psychological violence directed at the will of opponents must be even more corrupting.

In his writings Gandhi condemned coercion. Yet in practice he can hardly be said to have renounced *psychological* coercion. Obviously he would have preferred to have the British depart from India of their own free will, deciding that it was in their own best interest, or at least morally necessary, to leave. But if the British had decided, in the absence of coercion, to stay, Gandhi was prepared to exert every kind of nonviolent pressure to make them go. And when Gandhi on occasion attempted to achieve political objectives by a "fast unto death," his threat of self-starvation brought enormous psychological pressure on the authorities, who, among other things, feared the riots would ensue should Gandhi die.

The Gandhian pacifist, then, must explain why psychological pressure is permissible if physical pressure is forbidden. One possible answer is that physical pressure cannot transform the soul of the opponents, but psychological pressure, since it operates on the mind, can effect a spiritual transformation. Indeed, Gandhi characterized his terrifying fasts as acts of education, not coercion. But the claim that these fasts were not coercive confuses the noncoercive intention behind the act with its predictable coercive effects; and if education is the name of the game, the nonpacifists will remark that violence has been known to teach a few good lessons in its day. In many spiritual traditions, what matters essentially is not the kind of pressure but that the right pressure be applied at the right time and in the right way. Zen masters have brought students to enlightenment by clouting them on the ears, and God helped St. Paul to see the light by knocking him off his horse.

In addition to these technical problems, many people will be inclined to reject the system of values from which Gandhi's deductions flow. Many will concede that good character is important and that helping others to develop moral virtues is an important task. But few agree with Gandhi that the development of moral purity is the supreme human good, and that other goods, like the preservation of human life, or progress in the arts and sciences, have little or no value in comparison. If even a little value is conceded to these other things, then on occasion it will be necessary to put aside the project of developing spiritual purity in order to preserve other values. These acts of preservation may require physical violence, and those who use violence to defend life or beauty or liberty may indeed be corrupting their souls. But it is hard to believe that an occasional and necessary act of violence on behalf of these values will totally and permanently corrupt the soul, and those who use violence judiciously may be right in thinking that the saving of life or beauty or liberty may be worth a small or temporary spiritual loss.

4. Private Pacifism

Perhaps the rarest form of pacifist is the pacifist who renounces violence in personal relations but condones the use of force in the political sphere. Such a pacifist will not use violence for self-defense but believes that it is permissible for the state to use judicial force against criminals and military force against foreign enemies. A private pacifist renounces self-defense but supports national defense.

Augustine's Limited Pacifism

Historically, private pacifism developed as an attempt to rec-   35
oncile the demands of the Sermon on the Mount with the Christian duty to charity. The Sermon on the Mount requires Christians to "resist not evil"; the duty of charity requires pity for the weak who suffer the injustice of the strong. For St. Augustine (354–430), one essential message of the Gospels is the good news that this present life is as nothing compared with the life to come. The person who tries to hold on to earthly possessions is deluded as to what is truly valuable: "If any man will sue thee at the law, and take away thy coat, let him have thy cloak also" (Matt. 5:40). What goes for earthly coats should go for earthly life as well, so if any man seeks to take a Christian life, the Christian should let him have it. On this view, the doctrine "resist no evil" is just an expression of contempt for earthly possessions.

But according to Augustine there are some things in this world that do have value: justice, for example, the relief of suffering, and the preservation of the Church, which Augustine equated with civilization itself. To defend these things with necessary force is not to fall prey to delusions about the good. For Augustine, then, service in the armed forces is not inconsistent with Christian values.

One difficulty for theories like Augustine's is that they seem to justify military service only when military force is used in a just cause. Unfortunately, once in the service, the man in the ranks is not in a position to evaluate the justice of his nation's cause; indeed, in many modern nations, the principle of military subordination to civilian rule prevents even generals from evaluating the purposes of war declared by political leaders. But Augustine argues that the cause of justice cannot be served without armies, and armies cannot function unless subordinates follow orders without questioning the purposes of the conflict. The necessary conditions for justice and charity require that some men put themselves in positions in which they might be required to fight for injustice.

The Problem of Self-Defense

Many will agree with Augustine that most violence at the personal level—the violence of crime, vendetta, and domestic brutality, for example—goes contrary to moral principles. But most are prepared to draw the line at personal and collective self-defense. Can the obligation to be charitable justify participation in military service but stop short of justifying the use of force by private citizens, if that force is exercised to protect the weak from the oppression of the strong? Furthermore, the obligation to be charitable does not exclude acts of charity toward oneself. For Augustine, violence was a dangerous tool, best kept out of the hands of the citizens and best left strictly at the disposal of the state. Beset with fears of crime in the streets, the contemporary American is less inclined to worry about the anarchic effects of private uses of defensive force and more inclined to worry about the protection the police seem unable to provide.

For these worried people, the existence of a right to self-defense is self-evident. But the existence of this right is not self-evident to universal or private pacifists; and it was not self-evident to St. Augustine. In the Christian tradition, no right to self-defense was recognized until its existence was certified by Thomas Aquinas in the thirteenth century. Aquinas derived the right to self-defense from the universal tendency to self-preservation, assuming (contrary to Augustine) that a natural tendency must be morally right. As for the Christian duty to love one's enemy, Aquinas argued that acts of self-defense have two effects—the saving of life and the taking of life—and that self-defensive uses of force intend primarily the saving of life. This makes the use of force in self-defense a morally permissible act of charity. The right to self-defense is now generally recognized in Catholic moral theology and in Western legal systems. But it can hardly be said that Aquinas' arguments, which rely heavily on assumptions from Greek philosophy, succeed in reconciling the claims of self-defense with the prescriptions of the Sermon on the Mount.

5. Antiwar Pacifism

Most people who believe in the right to personal self-defense   40
also believe that some wars are morally justified. In fact, the notion of self-defense and the notion of just war are commonly linked; just wars are said to be defensive wars, and the justice of defensive war is inferred from the right of personal self-defense, projected from the individual to the national level. But some people reject this projection: they endorse the validity of personal self-defense, but they deny that war can be justified by appeal to self-defense or any other right. On the contrary, they argue that war always involves an inexcusable violation of rights. For such antiwar pacifists, all participation in war is morally wrong.

The Killing of Soldiers

One universal and necessary feature of wars is that soldiers get killed in them. Most people accept such killings as a necessary evil, and judge the killing of soldiers in war to be morally acceptable. If the war is fought for the just cause, the killing of enemy soldiers is justified as necessary to the triumph of right. If the war is fought for an unjust cause, the killing of enemy soldiers is acceptable because it is considered an honorable thing to fight for one's country, right or wrong, provided that one fights well and cleanly. But the antiwar pacifist does not take the killing of soldiers for granted. Everyone has a right to life, and the killing of soldiers in war is intentional killing, a deliberate violation of the right to life. According to the standard interpretation of basic rights, it is never morally justifiable to violate a basic right in order to produce some good; the end, in such cases, does not justify the means. How, then, can the killing of soldiers in war be morally justified—or even excused?

Perhaps the commonest reply to the challenge of antiwar pacifism is that killing in war is a matter of self-defense, *personal* self-defense, the right to which is freely acknowledged by the antiwar pacifist. In war, the argument goes, it is either kill or be killed—and that type of killing is killing in self-defense. But though the appeal to self-defense is natural, antiwar pacifists believe that it is not successful. First of all, on the usual understanding of "self-defense," those who kill can claim the justification of self-defense only if (a) they had no other way to save their lives or preserve themselves from physical harm except by killing, and (b) they did nothing to provoke the attack to which they are subjected. Antiwar pacifists point out that soldiers on the battlefield do have a way of saving themselves from death or harm without killing anyone: they can surrender. Furthermore, for soldiers fighting for an unjust cause—for example, German soldiers fighting in the invasion of Russia in 1941—it is difficult to argue that they "did nothing to provoke" the deadly force directed at them. But if the German army provoked the Russians to stand and fight on Russian soil, German soldiers cannot legitimately claim self-defense as a moral justification for killing Russian soldiers.

To the nonpacifist, these points might seem like legalistic quibbles. But the antiwar pacifist has an even stronger argument against killing soldiers in war. The vast majority of soldiers who die in war do not die in "kill or be killed" situations. They are killed by bullets, shells, or bombs directed from safe launching points "safe" in the sense that those who shoot the bullets or fire the shells or drop the bombs are in no immediate danger of death. Since those who kill are not in immediate danger of death, they cannot invoke "self-defense" to justify the deaths they cause.

Some other argument besides self-defense, then, must explain why the killing of soldiers in war should not be classified as murder. Frequently, nonpacifists argue that the explanation is found in the doctrine of "assumption of risk," the idea, common in civil law, that persons who freely assume a risk have only themselves to blame if the risk is realized. When a soldier goes to war, he is well aware that one risk of his trade is getting killed on the battlefield. If he dies on the field, the responsibility for his death lies with himself, not with the man who shot him. By assuming the risk—so the argument goes—he waived his right to life, at least on the battlefield.

One does not have to be a pacifist to see difficulties in this argument. First of all, in all substantial modern wars, most of the men on the line are not volunteers, but draftees. Only a wealthy nation like the United States can afford an all-volunteer army, and most experts believe that the American volunteer ranks will have to be supplemented by draftees should the United States become involved in another conflict on the scale of Korea or Vietnam.

Second, in many cases in which a risk is realized, responsibility for the bad outcome lies not with the person who assumed the risk but with the person who created it. If an arsonist sets fire to a house and a parent rushes in to save the children, dying in the rescue attempt, responsibility for the parent's death lies not with the parent who assumed the risk, but with the arsonist who created it. So if German armies invade Russia, posing the risk of death in battle, and if Russian soldiers assume this risk and fight back, the deaths of Russians are the fault of German invaders, not the fault of the defenders who assumed the risk.

These criticisms of German foot soldiers will irritate many who served in the armed forces and who know how little political and military decision making is left to the men on the front lines, who seem to be the special target of these pacifist arguments. But antiwar pacifists will deny that their aim is to condemn the men on the battlefield. Most antiwar pacifists feel that soldiers in war act under considerable compulsion and are excused for that reason from responsibility for the killing they do. But to say that battlefield killings are *excusable* is not to say that they are morally *justified*. On the contrary, if such killings are excusable, it must be that there is some immorality to be excused.

45

The Killing of Civilians

In the chronicles of ancient wars, conflict was total and loss in battle was frequently followed by general slaughter of men, women, and children on the losing side. It has always been considered part of the trend toward civilization to confine the destruction of war to the personnel and instruments of war, sparing civilians and their property as much as possible. This civilizing trend was conspicuously reversed in World War II, in which the ratio of civilian deaths to total war deaths was perhaps the highest it had been since the wars of religion in the seventeenth century. A very high ratio of civilian deaths to total deaths was also characteristic of the war in Vietnam. Given the immense firepower of modern weapons and the great distances between the discharges of weapons and the explosions of bullets or shells near the targets, substantial civilian casualties are an inevitable part of modern land war. But it is immoral to kill civilians, the antiwar pacifist argues, and from this it follows that modern land warfare is necessarily immoral.

Few nonpacifists will argue that killing enemy civilians is justifiable when such killings are avoidable. Few will argue that killing enemy civilians is justifiable when such killings are the *primary* objective of a military operation. But what about the deaths of civilians that are the unavoidable results of military operations directed to some *other* result? The pacifist classifies such killings as immoral, whereas most nonpacifists call them regrettable but unavoidable deaths, not murders. But why are they not murder, if the civilians are innocent, and if it is known in advance that some civilians will be killed? Isn't this an intentional killing of the innocent, which is the traditional definition of murder?

The sophisticated nonpacifist may try to parry this thrust   50
with analogies to policies outside the arena of war, There are, after all, many morally acceptable policies that, when adopted, have the effect of killing innocent persons. If the Congress decides to set a speed limit of 55 miles per hour on federal highways, more people will die than if Congress sets the speed limit at 45 miles per hour. Since many people who die on the highway are innocent, the Congress has chosen a policy that knowingly brings death to the innocent, but no

one calls it murder. Or suppose, for example, that a public health officer is considering a national vaccination program to forestall a flu epidemic. He knows that if he does not implement the vaccination program, many people will die from the flu. On the other hand, if the program is implemented, a certain number of people will die of allergic reactions to the vaccine. Most of the people who die from allergic reactions will be people who would not have died of the flu if the vaccination program had not been implemented. So the vaccination program will kill innocent people who would otherwise be saved if the program were abandoned. If the public health officer implements such a program, we do *not* think that he is a murderer.

Nonpacifists argue that what makes the action of Congress and the action of the public health officer morally permissible in these cases is that the deaths of the innocent, although foreseen, are not the intended goal of these policies. Congress does not want people to die on the highways; every highway death is a regrettable death. The purpose of setting the speed limit at 55 miles per hour is not to kill people but to provide a reasonable balance between safety and convenience. Likewise, it is not the purpose of the public health officer to kill people by giving them vaccine. His goal is to save lives on balance, and every death from the vaccine is a regrettable death. Likewise, in war, when civilians are killed as a result of necessary military operations, the deaths of the civilians are not the intended goal of the military operation. They are foreseen, but they are always regretted. If we do not accuse Congress of murder and the Public Health Service of murder in these cases, consistency requires that we not accuse military forces of murder when they cause civilian deaths in war, especially if every attempt is made to keep civilian deaths to a minimum.

Antiwar pacifists do not condemn the Congress and the Public Health Service in cases like these. But they assert that the case of war is different in a morally relevant way. To demonstrate the difference, antiwar pacifists provide an entirely different analysis of the moral justification for speed limits and vaccination programs. In their opinion, the facts that highway deaths and vaccination deaths are "unintended" and "regretted" is morally irrelevant. The real justification lies in

the factor of consent. In the case of federal highway regula-
tions, the rules are decided by Congress, which is elected by
the people, the same people who use the highways. If Congress
decides on a 55-mile-an-hour limit, this is a regulation that, in
some sense, highway drivers have imposed upon themselves.
Those people who die on the highway because of a higher
speed limit have, in a double sense, assumed the risks generated by that speed limit: they have, through the Congress, created the risk, and by venturing onto the highway, have freely
exposed themselves to the risk. The responsibility for these
highway deaths, then, lies either on the drivers themselves or
on the people who crashed into them—not on the Congress.

Likewise, in the case of the vaccination program, if people
are warned in advance of the risks of vaccination, and if they
nevertheless choose to be vaccinated, they are responsible for
their own deaths should the risks be realized. According to
the antiwar pacifist, it is this consent given by drivers and
vaccination volunteers that justifies these policies, and it is
precisely this element of consent that is absent in the case of
the risks inflicted on enemy civilians in time of war.

Consider the standard textbook example of allegedly justifiable killing of civilians in time of war. Suppose that the
destruction of a certain bridge is an important military objective, but if the bridge is bombed, it is very likely that civilians
living close by mill be killed. (The civilians cannot be warned
without alerting the enemy to reinforce the bridge.) If the
bridge is bombed and some civilians are killed, the bombing
victims are not in the same moral category as highway victims
or victims of vaccination. The bombing victims did not order
the bombing of themselves through some set of elected representatives. Nor did the bombing victims freely consent to the
bombing of their bridge. Nor was the bombing in any way
undertaken as a calculated risk in the interest of the victims.
For all these reasons, the moral conclusions regarding highway legislation and vaccination programs do not carry over to
bombing of the bridge.

Nonpacifists who recognize that it will be very difficult to
fight wars without bombing bridges may argue that the victims
of this bombing in some sense assumed the risks of bombardment by choosing to live close to a potential military target.

55

Indeed, it is occasionally claimed that all the civilians in a nation at war have assumed the risks of war, since they could avoid the risks of war simply by moving to a neutral country. But such arguments are strained and uncharitable, even for those rare warring nations that permit freedom of emigration. Most people consider it a major sacrifice to give up their homes, and an option that requires such a sacrifice cannot be considered an option open for free choice. The analogy between the unintended victims of vaccination and the unintended civilian victims of war seems to have broken down.

The Balance of Good and Evil in War

It is left to the nonpacifist to argue that the killing of soldiers and civilians in war is in the end justifiable in order to obtain great moral goods that can be obtained only by fighting for them. Civilians have rights to life, but those rights can be outweighed by the national objectives, provided those objectives are morally acceptable and overwhelmingly important. Admittedly, this argument for killing civilians is available only to the just side in a war, but if the argument is valid, it proves that there can *be* a just side, contrary to the arguments of antiwar pacifism.

Antiwar pacifists have two lines of defense. First, they can continue to maintain that the end does not justify the means, if the means be murderous. Second, they can, and will, go on to argue that it is a tragic mistake to believe that there are great moral goods that can be obtained only by war. According to antiwar pacifists, the amount of moral good produced by war is greatly exaggerated. The Mexican War, for example, resulted in half of Mexico being transferred to American rule. This was a great good for the United States, but not a great moral good, since the United States had little claim to the ceded territory, and no great injustice would have persisted if the war had not been fought at all.

The Revolutionary War in America is widely viewed as a war that produced a great moral good; but if the war had not been fought, the history of the United States would be similar to the history of Canada (which remained loyal) and no one feels that the Canadians have suffered or are suffering great injustices that the American colonies avoided by war. Likewise, it is difficult to establish the goods produced by World War I or the moral losses that would have ensued if the winning side, "our side," had lost. Bertrand Russell imagined the results of a British loss in World War I as follows:

> The greatest sum that foreigners could possibly exact would be the total economic rent of the land and natural resources of England. [But] the working classes, the shopkeepers, manufacturers, and merchants, the literary men and men of science—all the people that make England of any account in the world—have at most an infinitesimal and accidental share in the rental of England. The men who have a share use their rents in luxury, political corruption, taking the lives of birds, and depopulating and enslaving the rural districts. It is this life of the idle rich that would be curtailed if the Germans exacted tribute from England. (*Justice in War Time*, pp. 48–49)

But multiplying examples of wars that did little moral good will not establish the pacifist case. The pacifist must show that *no* war has done enough good to justify the killing of soldiers and the killing of civilians that occurred in the war. A single war that produces moral goods sufficient to justify its killings will refute the pacifist claim that *all* wars are morally unjustifiable. Obviously this brings the antiwar pacifist head to head with World War II.

60

It is commonly estimated that 35 million people died as a result of World War II. It is difficult to imagine that any cause could justify so much death, but fortunately the Allies need only justify their share of these killings. Between 1939 and 1945 Allied forces killed about 5.5 million Axis soldiers and about 1 million civilians in Axis countries. Suppose that Britain and the United States had chosen to stay out of World War II and suppose Stalin had, like Lenin, surrendered to Germany shortly after the invasion. Does avoiding the world that would have resulted from these decisions justify killing 6.5 million people? If Hitler and Tojo had won the war, doubtless they would have killed a great many people both before and after victory, but it is quite likely that the total of *additional* victims, beyond those they killed in the war that *was* fought, would have been less than 6.5 million and, at any rate, the responsibility for those deaths would fall on Hitler and Tojo, not on Allied nations. If Hitler and Tojo had won the war, large portions of the world would have fallen under foreign domination, perhaps for a very long time. But the antiwar pacifist will point out that the main areas of Axis foreign domination—China and Russia— were not places in which the citizens enjoyed a high level of freedom *before the war began*. Perhaps the majority of people in the conquered areas would have worked out a *modus vivendi* with their new rulers, as did the majority of French citizens during the German occupation. Nor can it be argued that World War II was necessary to save six million Jews from annihilation in the Holocaust, since in fact the war did *not* save them.

The ultimate aims of Axis leaders are a matter for historical debate. Clearly the Japanese had no intention of conquering the United States, and some historians suggest that Hitler hoped to avoid war with England and America, declaring war with England reluctantly, and only after the English declared it against him. Nevertheless, popular opinion holds that Hitler intended to conquer the world, and if preventing the conquest of Russia and China could not justify six and one-half million killings, most Americans are quite confident that preventing the conquest of England and the United States does justify killing on this scale.

The antiwar pacifist disagrees. Certainly German rule of England and the United States would have been a very bad thing. At the same time, hatred of such German rule would be particularly fueled by hatred of foreigners, and hatred of foreigners, as such, is an irrational and morally unjustifiable passion. After all, if rule by foreigners were, by itself, a great moral wrong, the British, with their great colonial empire, could hardly consider themselves the morally superior side in World War II.

No one denies that a Nazi victory in World War II would have had morally frightful results. But, according to antiwar pacifism, killing six and one-half million people is also morally frightful, and preventing one moral wrong does not obviously outweigh committing the other. Very few people today share the pacifists' condemnation of World War II, but perhaps that is because the dead killed by the Allies cannot speak up and make sure that their losses are properly counted on the moral scales. Antiwar pacifists speak on behalf of the enemy dead, and on behalf of all those millions who would have lived if the war had not been fought. On this silent constituency they rest their moral case.

Questions about the Passage

1. Distinguish the position of the "live and let live" pacifist from the pacifism based on a moral point of view.
2. What are the obstacles to using the prohibition against killing in the Hebrew Bible as a basis for pacifism?
3. Define *ahimsa* as Gandhi uses the term. How is this concept crucial to his philosophy of pacifism?
4. What is the literal definition of *satyagraha*? How should the person who applies it behave in the face of violence?
5. What is "private pacifism," and how is it rooted in the Sermon on the Mount? How does Augustine distinguish between an individual acting violently to protect earthly possessions and a soldier defending, with force if necessary, the cause of justice?
6. Explain Aquinas' argument that self-defense is "a morally permissible act of charity."
7. Why do antiwar pacifists reject the argument that killing in war can be seen as self-defense?
8. Why does the pacifist consider even unavoidable civilian deaths in war to be immoral?
9. How do antiwar pacifists answer the challenge that war is sometimes necessary to achieve a great moral good or end a great moral evil?

Questions about the Argument

1. Consider Lackey's credibility, reliability, and authority. How would you evaluate his ethos?
2. Describe the audience Lackey is addressing in this piece. What strategies does he use to meet their needs?
3. Much of Lackey's writing is expository: he explains, defines, and categorizes. How does he move beyond this to make an argument?
4. As an arguer, Lackey does not take the easy way out by creating "straw man" cases (see p. 33). The examples of wars in Part 5 of the passage present tough challenges to pacifism. In paragraphs 60–64 he deals with World War II. How convincing is his case for antiwar pacifism there? Explain.
5. Lackey establishes a pattern of discourse in Parts 2, 3, and 4 of the passage. What is it? Hint: How does he present each position? How does he analyze each? Does he take issue with any of

these positions? How does this pattern change in Part 5? What does this change signal about his viewpoint?

6. Do you think Lackey is a pacifist? If so, what sort?

Confession of Faith in a Mennonite Perspective: Peace, Justice, and Nonresistance

The Mennonite Church descends from the Dutch and Swiss evangelical Anabaptist (re-baptism, that is, adult baptism) Protestants of the sixteenth century. Their name derives from the Dutch founder of early congregations, Menno Simons (c. 1496–1561). Mennonites have a number of different branches in Canada, the U.S., Europe, and Central and South America. All Mennonites generally agree on certain points of faith, including the baptism of believers only, repentance and conversion as necessities for salvation, pacifism and the refusal to take oaths, and simplicity of habits and clothing. Mennonites from Germany, Holland, and other European countries settled in the U.S. beginning in the late seventeenth century, and today mostly live in Pennsylvania, Ohio, and the Middle West. The movement today includes the Mennonite Church ("Old Mennonites"), the largest body, the General Conference of the Mennonite Church of North America, and the Amish Church, one of the most conservative branches and itself divided into the Old Order Amish and the Conservative Amish. Worldwide, there are about one million Mennonites.

Mennonites have issued statements of belief, or confessions of faith, since their beginnings in order to interpret Scripture, guide belief and practice, build unity among the congregations of the church, and respond to current world events. *The Confession of Faith in a Mennonite Perspective* is a statement issued in 1995 by the two major North American branches, the Mennonite Church and the General Conference of the Mennonite Church. The 1995 *Confession* is divided into four sets of articles. Article 22, reprinted below, comes from the third set, which deals with discipleship.

> We believe that peace is the will of God. God created the world in peace, and God's peace is most fully revealed in Jesus Christ, who is our peace and the peace of the whole world. Led by the Holy Spirit, we follow Christ in the way of peace, doing justice, bringing reconciliation, and practicing nonresistance even in the face of violence and warfare. Although God created a peaceable world, humanity chose the way of unrighteousness and violence.[1] The spirit of revenge

increased, and violence multiplied, yet the original vision of peace and justice did not die.[2] Prophets and other messengers of God continued to point the people of Israel toward trust in God rather than in weapons and military force.[3]

The peace God intends for humanity and creation was revealed most fully in Jesus Christ. A joyous song of peace announced Jesus' birth.[4] Jesus taught love of enemies, forgave wrongdoers, and called for right relationships.[5] When threatened, he chose not to resist, but gave his life freely.[6] By his death and resurrection, he has removed the dominion of death and given us peace with God.[7] Thus he has reconciled us to God and has entrusted to us the ministry of reconciliation.[8] As followers of Jesus, we participate in his ministry of peace and justice. He has called us to find our blessing in making peace and seeking justice. We do so in a spirit of gentleness, willing to be persecuted for righteousness' sake.[9] As disciples of Christ, we do not prepare for war, or participate in war or military service. The same Spirit that empowered Jesus also empowers us to love enemies, to forgive rather than to seek revenge, to practice right relationships, to rely on the community of faith to settle disputes, and to resist evil without violence.[10]

Led by the Spirit, and beginning in the church, we witness to all people that violence is not the will of God. We witness against all forms of violence, including war among nations, hostility among races and classes, abuse of children and women, violence between men and women, abortion, and capital punishment.

We give our ultimate loyalty to the God of grace and peace, who guides the church daily in overcoming evil with good, who empowers us to do justice, and who sustains us in the glorious hope of the peaceable reign of God.[11]

Notes

1. Gen. 1–11
2. Isa. 2:2–4
3. Lev. 26:6; Isa. 31:1; Hos. 2:18
4. Luke 2:14
5. Matt. 5:44; 6:14–15
6. Matt. 26:52–53; 1 Pet. 2:21–24
7. 1 Cor. 15:54–55; Rom. 5:10–11; Eph. 2:11–18

8. 2 Cor. 5:18–21
9. Matt. 5:3–12
10. Matt. 5:39; 1 Cor. 6:1–16; Rom. 12:14–21
11. Isa. 11:1–9

Questions about the Passage

1. How are Mennonites supposed to act in our world of violence?
2. Give a descriptive title to each paragraph of this text. Convert these titles into an outline of the steps needed to achieve peace.
3. The Mennonites include Article 22 in the section of their Confession devoted to discipleship. Look up "discipleship" in a good dictionary. Why does the section on peace belong here?
4. Look up "ministry" and "witness" as well. How does an understanding of the connotations of these words clarify your grasp of the Mennonite position?

Questions about the Argument

1. This Article relies heavily on scriptural sources. Select several of these verses and look them up in a Bible. You may instead go online to http://www.mennolink.org/doc/cof/art.22.html and follow the footnote links. Why does the Confession not include the verses verbatim? Are they using the sources to make a case? If so, how?
2. What characteristics does a Confession share with an argument? How does it differ from an argument?
3. How does a Confession differ from a pastoral letter? Does each have the same purpose?
4. Does a Confession have to be persuasive? Why or why not?

Mohandas K. Gandhi, "The Doctrine of Ahimsa"

Mohandas Karamchand Gandhi (1869–1948), called the Mahatma ("Great Soul"), is widely considered one of the great leaders of the twentieth century. Not only did he successfully lead the nonviolent struggle to end Britain's imperial rule of his native India, but he developed a philosophy of nonviolent resistance and civil disobedience campaigns that continues to be used to protest and change the unjust exercise of authority throughout the world. In addition, the example of his own life of devotion to his people and country, to truth, to nonviolence, and to self-sacrifice in these causes made him millions of admirers.

An English-trained lawyer, Gandhi moved to Natal, South Africa early in his career. To protest the country's policies of racial discrimination, he founded the Natal Indian Congress in 1894 and then began to develop his concept of *satyagraha*, nonviolent, but sometimes illegal, resistance to illegitimate authority. *Satyagraha* was first put into practice in mass civil disobedience in South Africa, and Gandhi brought it back to India when he returned there in 1914. In 1915 he founded his first religious community, called the Satyagraha Ashram, in his native district of Gujarat. After World War I ended, Gandhi began organizing mass nonviolent demonstrations and other acts of civil disobedience aimed at repressive colonial laws and, ultimately, at forcing the British to grant Indian Home Rule. Gandhi was arrested, convicted, and imprisoned for seditious conspiracy in 1922. He continued to speak, write, and lead the movement for Home Rule in the 1920s, 1930s, and 1940s. In the 1947 Partition, India and Pakistan were created as independent states, dividing the Hindu and Muslim majority populations. During the violence that broke out between the two populations at Partition, Gandhi, who had opposed the two-state model, began a fast to protest the bloodshed and to work for peace and understanding. During this fast, a Hindu fanatic, enraged by Gandhi's words of brotherhood, assassinated him on January 30, 1948.

The passage reprinted below comes from Gandhi's description of his Satyagraha Ashram, in which he describes the principles the members should follow. Additional information about Gandhi's philosophy of nonviolence can be found in Douglas Lackey's "Varieties of Pacifism" in this chapter (p. 159).

The Doctrine of *Ahimsa*

Literally speaking, *Ahimsa* means "non-killing." But to me it has a world of meaning, and takes me into realms much higher, infinitely higher. It really means that you may not offend anybody; you may not harbor an uncharitable thought, even in connection with one who may consider himself to be your enemy. To one who follows this doctrine there is no room for an enemy. But there may be people who consider themselves to be his enemies. So it is held that we may not harbor an evil thought even in connection with such persons. If we return blow for blow we depart from the doctrine of *Ahimsa*. But I go farther. If we resent a friend's action, or the so-called enemy's action, we still fall short of this doctrine. But when I say we should not resent, I do not say that we should acquiesce: by the word "resenting" I mean wishing that some harm should be done to the enemy; or that he should be put out of the way, not even by any action of ours, but by the action of somebody else, or, say, by divine agency. If we harbor even this thought we depart from this doctrine of Non-Violence. Those who join the Ashram have literally to accept that meaning.

This does not mean that we practice that doctrine in its entirety. Far from it. It is an ideal which we have to reach, and it is an ideal to be reached even at this very moment, if we are capable of doing so. But it is not a proposition in Geometry; it is not even like solving difficult problems in higher mathematics—it is infinitely more difficult. Many of us have burnt the midnight oil in solving those problems. But if you want to follow out this doctrine you will have to do much more than burn the midnight oil. You will have to pass many a sleepless night, and go through many a mental torture, before you can even be within measurable distance of this goal. It is the goal, and nothing less than that, which you and I have to reach, if we want to understand what a religious life means.

A man who believes in the efficacy of this doctrine finds it the ultimate stage, when he is about to reach the goal, the whole world at his feet. If you express your love—*Ahimsa*—in such manner that it impresses itself indelibly upon your so-called enemy, he must return that love. Under this rule there is no room for organized assassinations, or for murders openly committed, or for any violence for the sake of your country, and even for guarding the honor of precious ones that may be under your charge. After all, that would be a poor defense of their honor. This doctrine tells us that we may guard the honor of those under our charge by delivering our own lives into the hands of the man who would commit the sacrilege. And that requires far greater courage than delivering of blows. If you do not retaliate, but stand your ground between your charge and the opponent, simply receiving the blows without retaliating. What happens? I give you my promise that the whole of his violence will be expended on you, and your friend will be left unscathed. Under this plan of life there is no conception of patriotism which justifies such wars as you witness today in Europe.

Questions about the Passage

1. How does Gandhi extend the definition of *Ahimsa* beyond its denotative meaning of "non-killing"? What examples does he use to clarify his meaning?
2. What does Gandhi say one will have to go through in order to reach the goal of *Ahimsa*? What will one have to repudiate?
3. What does Gandhi teach is the way to respond to a violent threat against those "under our charge"? How does this response translate to a national level in a war?

Questions about the Argument

1. This text is clearly an extended definition of *Ahimsa*. Is it also an argument? Why or why not?
2. What is the source of Gandhi's moral authority as a writer? Consider his life and actions as well as the text.
3. Compare the form of this text to the bishops' pastoral letter and to the Mennonite Confession. What qualities and purposes does it share with either or both? Is it closer to one or the other, or is it something altogether different?

Writing Assignments

Conversations

1. You are participating in an inter-faith group planning a Rainbow Covenant observance (review Waskow's suggestion for a Rainbow Covenant liturgy in Chapter 5, p. 141) and need to plan the liturgy. Alternatively, you are part of a group planning a secular peace celebration. Describe what you would include in such a liturgy or celebration, drawing upon the peace readings in this chapter and your own knowledge and experience. You might consider, for example, including poetry, songs, and philosophical writings as well as religious texts.
2. Research what liturgies have been created for the Rainbow Covenant or for secular peace observations. See church, synagogue, and mosque Web sites, peace church materials, Waskow's Shalom Center, and other peace organizations' publications for help. What would you select from the actual liturgies or observances you discovered?

Writing Sequence: Exploring a Pacifist Position

In June 1940, just after the fall of France to Nazi Germany, Gandhi wrote about resisting the violence of what was known as Hitlerism, which he defined as "naked, ruthless force reduced to an exact science and worked with scientific precision." He believed that "Hitlerism will never be defeated by counter-Hitlerism. It can only breed superior Hitlerism raised to nth degree." Gandhi contemplated a continent-wide nonviolent resistance *(satyagraha)* to Hitlerism:

> [I]magine the state of Europe today if the Czechs, the Poles, the Norwegians, the French and the English had all said to Hitler: "You need not make your scientific preparation for destruction. We will meet your violence with non-violence. You will, therefore, be able to destroy our non-violent army without tanks, battleships and airships." It may be retorted that the only difference would be that Hitler would have got without fighting what he has gained after a bloody fight. Exactly. The history of Europe would then have been written differently. Possession might (but only might) have been then taken under non-violent resistance, as it has been taken now after perpetration of untold barbarities. Under non-violence only those would have been killed who had trained themselves to be killed, if need be, but without killing anyone and without bearing malice towards anybody. I dare say that in that case Europe would have added several inches to its moral stature. And in the end I expect it is the moral worth that will count. All else is dross. (M. K. Gandhi, "How to Combat Hitlerism," [June 22, 1940] *The Gandhi Reader,* ed. Homer A. Jack. New York: Grove Press, 1994. 337, 338.)

1. What is Gandhi saying? Explore your response to Gandhi's words. Do you agree with his ideas? Why or why not? What more do you need to know to mount a defense of or attack on his view?

2. Read Gandhi's essay "How to Combat Hitlerism" cited above, found both in *The Gandhi Reader* and in M. K. Gandhi, *Non-Violence in Peace and War* (Ahmedabad: Navajivan, 1942, Vol. I, pp. 310–12). Summarize his argument. What evidence does Gandhi supply that would either support or undermine the position that you took in question 1?

3. Drawing upon the readings in this text, critique or defend Gandhi's position. Writers you should use to support your view are Lackey and the U.S. Catholic Bishops, and at least one other of your choice.

7

Just War Traditions in Practice

C hapter 7 reminds us that the history of ideas is not merely an arid intellectual exercise. Ideas like those underpinning Just War theory still count, and they figure today in our thinking about war. In the section entitled "American Just Wars?" we look at a famous document by Thomas Jefferson and speeches by Presidents Franklin Roosevelt and Ronald Reagan that justify three American conflicts, at least two of which most would call just. The address by Reagan is an attempt to justify the American military response to the Libyan-backed bombing of a Berlin disco as both self-defense and preemptive action to prevent the export of terrorism. This situation presages later arguments by President George W. Bush that have been used to justify preemptive action against future terrorist attacks.

The second section focuses on the recent conflicts in Afghanistan and Iraq. Here we present writers and cartoons that express different viewpoints, but see Just War doctrine as vital and relevant and useful in helping us make the difficult decision to go to war.

As citizens ourselves, well-informed about Just War thinking, we are now prepared to take our place in the conversation.

American "Just Wars"?

Thomas Jefferson, The Declaration of Independence

The Declaration of Independence, approved July 4, 1776 as "The Unanimous Declaration of the Thirteen United States of America" by the Second Continental Congress, announced the formal separation of the colonies from Great Britain. Thomas Jefferson (1743–1826), John Adams, Benjamin Franklin, Roger Sherman, and Robert R. Livingston made up the drafting committee, but Jefferson wrote the initial draft, which was revised once by Franklin, Adams, and Jefferson before it went to Congress and a second time in Congress.

The document established the new revolutionary government and allowed it to seek aid from foreign countries in its war with Great Britain. *The Declaration* draws on ideas of the Enlightenment, especially those of John Locke, and puts them into political practice as well as justifying, through a series of grievances, the break with British rule. Since its proclamation, *The Declaration* has influenced and inspired revolutionary movements throughout the world.

> In Congress, July 4, 1776.
>
> The unanimous Declaration of the thirteen united States of America,
>
> When in the Course of human events, it becomes necessary for one people to dissolve the political bands which have connected them with another, and to assume among the powers of the earth, the separate and equal station to which the Laws of Nature and of Nature's God entitle them, a decent respect to the opinions of mankind requires that they should declare the causes which impel them to the separation.
>
> We hold these truths to be self-evident, that all men are created equal, that they are endowed by their Creator with certain unalienable Rights, that among these are Life, Liberty and the pursuit of Happiness—That to secure these rights, Governments are instituted among Men, deriving their just powers from the consent of the governed—That whenever any Form of Government becomes destructive of these ends, it is the Right of the People to alter or to abolish it, and to institute new Government, laying its foundation on such principles and organizing its powers in such form, as to them shall seem most likely to effect their Safety and Happiness. Prudence, indeed, will dictate that Governments long established should not be changed for light and transient causes; and accordingly all experience hath shewn, that mankind are more disposed to suffer, while evils are sufferable, than to right themselves by abolishing the forms to which they are accustomed. But when a long train of abuses and usurpations, pursuing invariably

the same Object evinces a design to reduce them under absolute Despotism, it is their right, it is their duty, to throw off such Government, and to provide new Guards for their future security—Such has been the patient sufferance of these Colonies; and such is now the necessity which constrains them to alter their former Systems of Government. The history of the present King of Great Britain is a history of repeated injuries and usurpations, all having in direct object the establishment of an absolute Tyranny over these States. To prove this, let Facts be submitted to a candid world.

He has refused his Assent to Laws, the most wholesome and necessary for the public good.

He has forbidden his Governors to pass Laws of immediate and pressing importance, unless suspended in their operation till his Assent should be obtained; and when so suspended, he has utterly neglected to attend to them.

He has refused to pass other Laws for the accommodation of large districts of people, unless those people would relinquish the right of Representation in the Legislature, a right inestimable to them and formidable to tyrants only.

He has called together legislative bodies at places unusual, uncomfortable, and distant from the depository of their public Records, for the sole purpose of fatiguing them into compliance with his measures.

He has dissolved Representative Houses repeatedly, for opposing with manly firmness his invasions on the rights of the people.

He has refused for a long time, after such dissolutions, to cause others to be elected; whereby the Legislative powers, incapable of Annihilation, have returned to the People at large for their exercise; the State remaining in the mean time exposed to all the dangers of invasion from without, and convulsions within.

He has endeavoured to prevent the population of these States; for that purpose obstructing the Laws for Naturalization of Foreigners; refusing to pass others to encourage their migrations hither, and raising the conditions of new Appropriations of Lands.

He has obstructed the Administration of Justice, by refusing his Assent to Laws for establishing Judiciary powers.

He has made Judges dependent on his Will alone, for the tenure of their offices, and the amount and payment of their salaries.

He has erected a multitude of New Offices, and sent hither swarms of Officers to harass our people, and eat out their substance.

He has kept among us, in times of peace, Standing Armies without the Consent of our legislatures.

He has affected to render the Military independent of and superior to the Civil power.

He has combined with others to subject us to a jurisdiction foreign to our constitution, and unacknowledged by our laws; giving his Assent to their Acts of pretended Legislation:

For Quartering large bodies of armed troops among us:

For protecting them, by a mock Trial, from punishment for any Murders which they should commit on the Inhabitants of these States:

For cutting off our Trade with all parts of the world:

For imposing Taxes on us without our Consent:

For depriving us in many cases, of the benefits of Trial by Jury:

For transporting us beyond Seas to be tried for pretended offences:

For abolishing the free System of English Laws in a neighbouring Province, establishing therein an Arbitrary government, and enlarging its Boundaries so as to render it at once an example and fit instrument for introducing the same absolute rule into these Colonies:

For taking away our Charters, abolishing our most valuable Laws, and altering fundamentally the Forms of our Governments:

For suspending our own Legislatures, and declaring themselves invested with power to legislate for us in all cases whatsoever.

He has abdicated Government here, by declaring us out of his Protection and waging War against us.

He has plundered our seas, ravaged our Coasts, burnt our towns, and destroyed the lives of our people.

He is at this time transporting large Armies of foreign Mercenaries to compleat the works of death, desolation and tyranny, already begun with circumstances of Cruelty &

perfidy scarcely paralleled in the most barbarous ages, and totally unworthy the Head of a civilized nation.

He has constrained our fellow Citizens taken Captive on the high Seas to bear Arms against their Country, to become the executioners of their friends and Brethren, or to fall themselves by their Hands.

He has excited domestic insurrections amongst us, and has endeavoured to bring on the inhabitants of our frontiers, the merciless Indian Savages, whose known rule of warfare, is an undistinguished destruction of all ages, sexes and conditions.

In every stage of these Oppressions We have Petitioned for Redress in the most humble terms: Our repeated Petitions have been answered only by repeated injury. A Prince whose character is thus marked by every act which may define a Tyrant, is unfit to be the ruler of a free people.

Nor have We been wanting in attentions to our Brittish brethren. We have warned them from time to time of attempts by their legislature to extend an unwarrantable jurisdiction over us. We have reminded them of the circumstances of our emigration and settlement here. We have appealed to their native justice and magnanimity, and we have conjured them by the ties of our common kindred to disavow these usurpations, which, would inevitably interrupt our connections and correspondence. They too have been deaf to the voice of justice and of consanguinity. We must, therefore, acquiesce in the necessity, which denounces our Separation, and hold them, as we hold the rest of mankind, Enemies in War, in Peace Friends.

We, therefore, the Representatives of the united States of America, in General Congress, Assembled, appealing to the Supreme Judge of the world for the rectitude of our intentions, do, in the Name, and by Authority of the good People of these Colonies, solemnly publish and declare, That these United Colonies are, and of Right ought to be Free and Independent States; that they are Absolved from all Allegiance to the British Crown, and that all political connection between them and the State of Great Britain, is and ought to be totally dissolved; and that as Free and Independent States, they have full Power to levy War, conclude Peace, contract Alliances, establish Commerce, and to do all other

Acts and Things which Independent States may of right do. And for the support of this Declaration, with a firm reliance on the protection of divine Providence, we mutually pledge to each other our Lives, our Fortunes and our sacred Honor.

Questions about the Passage

1. Outline the passage. What are the major sections into which you would divide it? What principles of classification have you used to make your divisions?
2. Jefferson includes a long, undivided list of grievances. Into what subcategories might they be divided? Look at the verbs he uses; consider the types of grievances he lists. Defend your decision.
3. Thinking of this document as a kind of template for other societies to use, what grievances against Milosevic might the Serbians make, or the Afghanis against the Taliban, or the Iraqis against Saddam Hussein and the Baath party? Following the logic of *The Declaration*, are the grievances sufficient to justify a change of government?

Questions about the Argument

1. Do you think the truths that Jefferson enunciates in his second paragraph are indeed "self-evident"? Might his immediate audience have seen them differently?
2. Throughout *The Declaration*, identify words that carry emotional weight. To which emotions do they appeal?
3. *The Declaration* is often used as an example of effective argument. Make a case for its efficacy. How does Jefferson use appeals to ethos, audience, logos, and pathos to defend his position?
4. Why does this document belong in a casebook on Just War?

Franklin Delano Roosevelt, Address to Congress Requesting a Declaration of War with Japan, *December 8, 1941*

Probably most Americans know what Pearl Harbor Day is—December 7, 1941, "a date which will live in infamy," as President Franklin D. Roosevelt (1882–1945) memorably called it. Early in the morning of December 7th, the Japanese attacked the Pacific Fleet anchored in Pearl Harbor, Oahu, Hawaii. The U.S. forces were taken completely by surprise. The Japanese sank or severely damaged nineteen naval vessels, including eight battleships, and 188 U.S. aircraft were destroyed. Over 2000 servicemen were killed and over 1100 wounded; 68 civilians also died. As FDR notes in his address, the United States and Japan were engaged in diplomatic negotiations in Washington at the time; the United States had instituted an oil embargo and frozen Japanese assets that summer in response to Japanese aggression in China and Southeast Asia. With the attack on Pearl Harbor, the United States entered World War II, which had begun in Europe in September 1939.

You can hear Roosevelt deliver the address and hear the applause and cheers of his first audience, Congress, as it was broadcast to the nation at a number of World Wide Web sites, including http://www.historychannel.com/speeches.

> To the Congress of the United States:
> Yesterday, Dec. 7, 1941—a date which will live in infamy—the United States of America was suddenly and deliberately attacked by naval and air forces of the Empire of Japan. The United States was at peace with that nation and, at the solicitation of Japan, was still in conversation with the government and its emperor looking toward the maintenance of peace in the Pacific. Indeed, one hour after Japanese air squadrons had commenced bombing in Oahu, the Japanese ambassador to the United States and his colleagues delivered to the Secretary of State a formal reply to a recent American message. While this reply stated that it seemed useless to continue the existing diplomatic negotiations, it contained no threat or hint of war or armed attack.
>
> It will be recorded that the distance of Hawaii from Japan makes it obvious that the attack was deliberately planned many days or even weeks ago. During the intervening time, the Japanese government has deliberately sought to deceive the United States by false statements and expressions of hope for continued peace.
>
> The attack yesterday on the Hawaiian Islands has caused severe damage to American naval and military forces. Very many American lives have been lost. In addition, American ships have been reported torpedoed on the high seas between San Francisco and Honolulu.
>
> Yesterday, the Japanese government also launched an attack against Malaya.
>
> Last night, Japanese forces attacked Hong Kong.
>
> Last night, Japanese forces attacked Guam.

Last night, Japanese forces attacked the Philippine Islands.

Last night, the Japanese attacked Wake Island.

This morning, the Japanese attacked Midway Island.

Japan has, therefore, undertaken a surprise offensive extending throughout the Pacific area. The facts of yesterday speak for themselves. The people of the United States have already formed their opinions and well understand the implications to the very life and safety of our nation.

As commander in chief of the Army and Navy, I have   5
directed that all measures be taken for our defense.

But always will our whole Nation remember the character of the onslaught against us. No matter how long it may take us to overcome this premeditated invasion, the American people in their righteous might will win through to absolute victory. I believe I interpret the will of the Congress and of the people when I assert that we will not only defend ourselves to the uttermost, but will make very certain that this form of treachery shall never endanger us again.

Hostilities exist. There is no blinking at the fact that our people, our territory and our interests are in grave danger.

With confidence in our armed forces—with the unbounding determination of our people—we will gain the inevitable triumph—so help us God.

I ask that the Congress declare that since the unprovoked and dastardly attack by Japan on Sunday, December 7, 1941, a state of war has existed between the United States and the Japanese Empire.

Questions about the Passage

1. Listen to the speech and notice where the audience cheers. Why do they cheer at those places?
2. Look up both the denotative and connotative meanings of the following words: "infamy," "onslaught," "treachery," "dastardly." Why do you think Roosevelt selected these words rather than more common synonyms?
3. Note the verbs and adverbs Roosevelt uses to describe the actions of the Japanese: "suddenly and deliberately planned," "deliberately sought to deceive," "premeditated invasion," "unprovoked and dastardly attack." Note also the outcomes he

envisions for Americans: "righteous might," "absolute victory," "inevitable triumph," "unbounding determination." Why do you think he selects these phrases? What effect does he achieve?

4. Why does Roosevelt say, "so help us God," in the next to last paragraph? What other similar use of this phrase does it recall?

5. Does this speech fit within the framework of Just War theory? If so, how?

Questions about the Argument

1. What gives Roosevelt authority to make his request of Congress?
2. Who, in addition to Congress, is his audience?
3. What evidence does Roosevelt cite to justify his argument that we should declare that a state of war exists?
4. The events Roosevelt notes are prefaced by time signals, "yesterday," "last night," and "this morning." What inference might he wish his audience to make about what will follow? How does the conclusion Roosevelt reaches in the final paragraph depend upon inductive reasoning?
5. How does Roosevelt use both the meanings of the words you investigated above and repetition and parallelism (in paragraph 3) to persuade his audience? Are these legitimate uses of emotional appeal?

Ronald Reagan, Address to the Nation on the United States Air Strike against Libya, *April 14, 1986*

President Reagan (1911–) went before the nation and much of the world to speak even as military aircraft were in the air on their mission called Operation El Dorado Canyon, against Libya. As he states, the strike was in direct response to Libyan involvement in the April 5th bombing of the La Belle discothèque in Berlin that injured 200 and killed an American soldier and a civilian. The U.S. government had intelligence that indicated that Col. Muammar Qadhafi, the military ruler of Libya since 1969, had ordered the bombing. The U.S. government was determined to destroy Qadhafi's ability to aid international terrorism. As early as 1982, the United States banned Libyan oil imports. In March 1986, the situation became more serious, as Libyan missiles were launched, without hitting their targets, against U.S. aircraft of the Sixth Fleet assembled off the Libyan coast for maneuvers. Four of the five targets of the April 15–16 strike were terrorist bases or directly supported terrorist activity, according to the Reagan Administration. The strike also seems to have been an attempt to kill Qadhafi himself, which failed. The Libyan air strike, like later actions of the United States, were undertaken unilaterally without complete international consensus and were opposed by some allies, including France and Germany.

> My fellow Americans:
> At 7 o'clock this evening eastern time air and naval forces of the United States launched a series of strikes against the headquarters, terrorist facilities, and military assets that support Mu'ammar Qadhafi's subversive activities. The attacks were concentrated and carefully targeted to minimize casualties among the Libyan people with whom we have no quarrel. From initial reports, our forces have succeeded in their mission.
> Several weeks ago in New Orleans, I warned Colonel Qadhafi we would hold his regime accountable for any new terrorist attacks launched against American citizens. More recently I made it clear we would respond as soon as we determined conclusively who was responsible for such attacks. On April 5th in West Berlin a terrorist bomb exploded in a nightclub frequented by American servicemen. Sergeant Kenneth Ford and a young Turkish woman were killed and 230 others were wounded, among them some 50 American military personnel. This monstrous brutality is but the latest act in Colonel Qadhafi's reign of terror. The evidence is now conclusive that the terrorist bombing of La Belle discothèque was planned and executed under the direct orders of the Libyan regime. On March 25th, more than a week before the attack, orders were sent from Tripoli to the Libyan People's Bureau in East Berlin to conduct a terrorist attack against Americans to cause maximum and indiscriminate casualties. Libya's agents then planted the bomb. On April 4th the People's Bureau alerted Tripoli that the attack would be carried out the following morning. The next day they reported back to Tripoli on the great success of their mission.
> Our evidence is direct; it is precise; it is irrefutable. We have solid evidence about other attacks Qadhafi has planned against the U.S. installations and diplomats and even American tourists. Thanks to close cooperation with our friends, some of

these have been prevented. With the help of French authorities, we recently aborted one such attack: a planned massacre, using grenades and small arms, of civilians waiting in line for visas at an American Embassy.

Colonel Qadhafi is not only an enemy of the United States. His record of subversion and aggression against the neighboring States in Africa is well documented and well known. He has ordered the murder of fellow Libyans in countless countries. He has sanctioned acts of terror in Africa, Europe, and the Middle East, as well as the Western Hemisphere. Today we have done what we had to do. If necessary, we shall do it again. It gives me no pleasure to say that, and I wish it were otherwise. Before Qadhafi seized power in 1969, the people of Libya had been friends of the United States. And I'm sure that today most Libyans are ashamed and disgusted that this man has made their country a synonym for barbarism around the world. The Libyan people are a decent people caught in the grip of a tyrant.

To our friends and allies in Europe who cooperated in   5
today's mission, I would only say you have the permanent gratitude of the American people. Europeans who remember history understand better than most that there is no security, no safety, in the appeasement of evil. It must be the core of Western policy that there be no sanctuary for terror. And to sustain such a policy, free men and free nations must unite and work together. Sometimes it is said that by imposing sanctions against Colonel Qadhafi or by striking at his terrorist installations we only magnify the man's importance, that the proper way to deal with him is to ignore him. I do not agree.

Long before I came into this office, Colonel Qadhafi had engaged in acts of international terror, acts that put him outside the company of civilized men. For years, however, he suffered no economic or political or military sanction; and the atrocities mounted in number, as did the innocent dead and wounded. And for us to ignore by inaction the slaughter of American civilians and American soldiers, whether in nightclubs or airline terminals, is simply not in the American tradition. When our citizens are abused or attacked anywhere in the world on the direct orders of a hostile regime, we will respond so long as I'm in this Oval Office. Self-defense is not only our right, it is our duty. It is the purpose behind the mission undertaken tonight, a mission fully consistent with Article 51 of the United Nations Charter.

We believe that this preemptive action against his terrorist installations will not only diminish Colonel Qadhafi's capacity to export terror, it will provide him with incentives and reasons to alter his criminal behavior. I have no illusion that tonight's action will ring down the curtain on Qadhafi's reign of terror. But this mission, violent though it was, can bring closer a safer and more secure world for decent men and women. We will persevere. This afternoon we consulted with the leaders of Congress regarding what we were about to do and why. Tonight I salute the skill and professionalism of the men and women of our Armed Forces who carried out this mission. It's an honor to be your Commander in Chief. We Americans are slow to anger. We always seek peaceful avenues before resorting to the use of force—and we did. We tried quiet diplomacy, public condemnation, economic sanctions, and demonstrations of military force. None succeeded. Despite our repeated warnings, Qadhafi continued his reckless policy of intimidation, his relentless pursuit of terror. He counted on America to be passive. He counted wrong. I warned that there should be no place on Earth where terrorists can rest and train and practice their deadly skills. I meant it. I said that we would act with others, if possible, and alone if necessary to ensure that terrorists have no sanctuary anywhere. Tonight, we have.

Thank you, and God bless you.

Note: The President spoke at 9 P.M. from the Oval Office at the White House. The address was broadcast live on nationwide radio and television.

Questions about the Passage

1. What does Reagan say occurred at 7 P.M., April 14, 1986?
2. What action did Qadhafi take after the warning he was given? What had he done prior to this warning?
3. How did the United States try to deal with Qadhafi before April 14th?
4. Reagan calls the action taken on April 14th both "self-defense" and "preemptive." How does he distinguish between these terms?

1. How does Reagan make his case against Qadhafi? Who is his audience? Why does Reagan specifically salute the armed forces? What evidence that Reagan provides do you find the most persuasive?
2. To what extent do Reagan's actions fit into Just War categories? Where, if anywhere, might they diverge from Just War principles?
3. Has Reagan made his case? Why or why not?

Response to Recent Conflicts

Afghanistan

Richard Falk, "Defining a Just War"

Richard Falk (1930–) has been the Albert G. Milbank Professor of International Law and Practice, Princeton University, since 1965. Educated at the University of Pennsylvania, and Yale and Harvard Law Schools, Falk has had a distinguished career as a professor, an advocate before the International Court of Justice, and a legal theorist about international relations, institutions, and the pursuit of peace through such institutions. He is the author of over forty books, including *This Endangered Planet: Prospects and Proposals for Human Survival* (1971), *Explorations at the Edge of Time: The Prospects for World Order* (1992), *Human Rights Horizons: The Pursuit of Justice in a Globalizing World* (2000), and *The Great Terror War* (2003) as well as many articles. He has argued that four main threats face the world: nuclear war, overpopulation, loss of natural resources, and the contamination of the earth's environment. Falk has been described as a peace theorist and even has been accused of being a utopian; he looks to restructured international bodies to prevent war and to economic globalization to make possible improved lives throughout the world. In the context of his work, Falk's acceptance of a limited "just war" in Afghanistan in October 2001 is a significant statement. He strongly opposed the March 2003 invasion of Iraq.

> I have never since my childhood supported a shooting war in which the United States was involved, although in retrospect I think the NATO war in Kosovo achieved beneficial results. The war in Afghanistan against apocalyptic terrorism qualifies in my understanding as the first truly just war since World War II. But the justice of the cause and of the limited ends is in danger

of being negated by the injustice of improper means and excessive ends. Unlike World War II and prior just wars, this one can be won only if tactics adhere to legal and moral constraints on the means used to conduct it, and to limited ends.

The perpetrators of the September 11 attack cannot be reliably neutralized by nonviolent or diplomatic means; a response that includes military action is essential to diminish the threat of repetition, to inflict punishment and to restore a sense of security at home and abroad. The extremist political vision held by Osama bin Laden, which can usefully be labeled "apocalyptic terrorism," places this persisting threat well outside any framework of potential reconciliation or even negotiation for several reasons: Its genocidal intent is directed generically against Americans and Jews; its proclaimed goal is waging an unconditional civilizational war—Islam against the West—without drawing any distinction between civilian and military targets; it has demonstrated a capacity and willingness to inflict massive and traumatizing damage on our country and a tactical ingenuity and ability to carry out its missions of destruction by reliance on the suicidal devotion of its adherents.

There are three types of responses to the attack, each of which contains some merit and enjoys some support. None of them are adequate, however.

I. Antiwar/Pacifist Approach

The pacifist position opposing even limited military action overlooks the nature of the threat and is thus irrelevant to meeting the central challenge of restoring some sense of security among our citizenry and in the world generally.

Also, in the current setting, unlike in the civil rights movement and the interventionist conflicts of the cold war era (especially Vietnam), antiwar and pacifist stands possess little or no cultural resonance with the overwhelming majority of Americans. It may be that at later stages of the war this assessment will prove to have been premature, and even now Quaker, Christian, Gandhian and Buddhist forms of pacifism offer a profound critique of wars. These critiques should be seriously heeded, since they lend weight to the view that the use of force should be marginal and kept to an absolute minimum. Certainly the spiritually motivated pacifist witness can

5

be both inspirational and instructive, and help to mitigate and interrogate militarist postures.

Another form of antiwar advocacy rests on a critique of the United States as an imperialist superpower or empire. This view also seems dangerously inappropriate in addressing the challenge posed by the massive crime against humanity committed on September 11. Whatever the global role of the United States—and it is certainly responsible for much global suffering and injustice, giving rise to widespread resentment that at its inner core fuels the terrorist impulse—it cannot be addressed so long as this movement of global terrorism is at large and prepared to carry on with its demonic work. These longer-term concerns—which include finding ways to promote Palestinian self-determination, the internationalization of Jerusalem and a more equitable distribution of the benefits of global economic growth and development—must be addressed. Of course, much of the responsibility for the failure to do so lies with the corruption and repressive policies of governments, especially in the Middle East, outside the orbit of U.S. influence. A distinction needs to be drawn as persuasively as possible between inherently desirable lines of foreign policy reform and retreating in the face of terrorism.

II. Legalist/UN Approach

International treaties that deal with terrorism on civil aircraft call for cooperation in apprehending suspects and allow for their subsequent indictment and prosecution by national courts. Such laws could in theory be invoked to capture Osama bin Laden and his leading associates and charge them with international crimes, including crimes against humanity. A tribunal could be constituted under the authority of the United Nations, and a fair trial could then be held that would avoid war and the ensuing pain, destruction and associated costs. The narrative of apocalyptic terrorism could be laid before the world as the crimes of Nazism were bared at Nuremberg.

But this course is unlikely to deal effectively with the overall threat. A public prosecution would give bin Laden and associates a platform to rally further support among a large constituency of sympathizers, and conviction and punishment would certainly be viewed as a kind of legal martyrdom. It would be impossible to persuade the United States government to empower such a tribunal unless it was authorized to impose capital punishment, and it is doubtful that several of the permanent members of the Security Council could be persuaded to allow death sentences. Beyond this, the evidence linking bin Laden to the September 11 attacks and other instances of global terrorism may well be insufficient to produce an assured conviction in an impartial legal tribunal, particularly if conspiracy was not among the criminal offenses that could be charged. European and other foreign governments are unlikely to be willing to treat conspiracy as a capital crime. And it strains the imagination to suppose that the Bush Administration would relinquish control over bin Laden to an international tribunal. On a more general level, it also seems highly improbable that the U.S. government can be persuaded to rely on the collective security mechanisms of the UN even to the unsatisfactory degree permitted during the Gulf War.

To be sure, the UN Security Council has provided a vague antiterrorist mandate as well as an endorsement of a U.S. right of response, but such legitimizing gestures are no more than that. For better and worse, the United States is relying on its claimed right of self-defense, and Washington seems certain to insist on full operational control over the means and ends of the war that is now under way. Such a reliance is worrisome, given past U.S. behavior and the somewhat militaristic character of both the leadership in Washington and the broader societal orientation in America toward the use of overwhelming force against the nation's enemies.

Yet at this stage it is unreasonable to expect the U.S. government to rely on the UN to fulfill its defensive needs. The UN lacks the capability, authority and will to respond to the kind of threat to global security posed by this new form of terrorist world war. The UN was established to deal with wars among states, while a transnational actor that cannot be definitively linked to a state is behind the attacks on the United States. Al Qaeda's relationship to the Taliban regime in Afghanistan is contingent, with Al Qaeda being more the sponsor of the state rather than the other way around.

Undoubtedly, the world would be safer and more secure with a stronger UN that had the support of the leading states in the world. The United States has for years acted more to obstruct than to foster such a transformation. Surely the long-term effects of this crisis should involve a new surge of support for a reformed UN that would have independent means of financing its operations, with its own peacekeeping and enforcement capabilities backed up by an international criminal court. Such a transformed UN would generate confidence that it could and would uphold its charter in an evenhanded manner that treats people equally. But it would be foolish to pretend that the UN today, even if it were to enjoy a far higher level of U.S. support than it does, could mount an effective response to the September 11 attacks.

III. Militarist Approach

Unlike pacifism and legalism, militarism poses a practical danger of immense proportions. Excessive reliance on the military will backfire badly, further imperiling the security of Americans and others, spreading war and destruction far afield, as well as emboldening the government to act at home in ways that weaken U.S. democracy. So far the Bush Administration has shown some understanding of these dangers, going slowly in its reliance on military action and moving relatively cautiously to bolster its powers over those it views as suspicious or dangerous, so as to avoid the perception of waging a cultural war against Islam. The White House has itself repeatedly stressed that this conflict is unlike previous wars, that nonmilitary means are also important, that victory will come in a different way and that major battlefield encounters are unlikely to occur.

Such reassurances, however, are not altogether convincing. The President's current rhetoric seems to reflect Secretary of State Colin Powell's more prudent approach, which emphasizes diplomacy and nonmilitary tactics, and restricts military action to Al Qaeda and the Taliban regime. Even here, there is room for dangerous expansion, depending on how the Al Qaeda network is defined. Some maximalists implicate twenty or more countries as supporters of terrorism. Defense Secretary Donald Rumsfeld, his deputy Paul Wolfowitz and others are definitely beating the drums for a far wider war; they seem to regard the attacks as an occasion to implement their own vision of a new world, one that proposes to rid the world of "evil" and advances its own apocalyptic vision. This vision seeks the destruction of such organizations as Hezbollah and Hamas, which have only minimal links to Al Qaeda and transnational terror, and which have agendas limited mainly to Palestinian rights of self-determination and the future of Jerusalem. These organizations, while legally responsible for terrorist operations within their sphere of concerns, but also subject to terrorist provocations, have not shown any intention of pursuing bin Laden's apocalyptic undertaking. Including such groups on the U.S. target list will surely undermine the depth and breadth of international support and engender dangerous reactions throughout the Islamic world, and possibly in the West as well.

Beyond this, there is speculation that there will be a second stage of response that will include a series of countries regarded as hostile to the United States, who are in possession of weapons of mass destruction but are not currently related to global terrorism in any significant fashion. These include Iraq, Libya and possibly even Syria, Iran and Sudan. To expand war objectives in this way would be full of risks, require massive military strikes inflicting much destruction and suffering, and would create a new wave of retaliatory violence directed against the United States and Americans throughout the world. If military goals overshoot, either by becoming part of a design to destroy Israel's enemies or to solve the problem of proliferation of weapons of mass destruction, the war against global terrorism will be lost, and badly.

Just as the pacifist fallacy involves unrealistic exclusion of military force from an acceptable response, the militarist fallacy involves an excessive reliance on military force in a manner that magnifies the threat it is trying to diminish or eliminate. It also expands the zone of violence in particularly dangerous ways that are almost certain to intensify and inflame anti-Americanism. It should be kept in mind that war occasions deep suffering, and recourse to international force should be both a last resort and on as limited a scale as possible. 15

But there is a fourth response, which has gained support among foreign policy analysts and probably a majority of Americans.

IV. Limiting Means and Ends

Unlike in major wars of the past, the response to this challenge of apocalyptic terrorism can be effective only if it is also widely perceived as legitimate. And legitimacy can be attained only if the role of military force is marginal to the overall conduct of the war and the relevant frameworks of moral, legal and religious restraint are scrupulously respected.

Excessive use of force in pursuing the perpetrators of September 11 will fan the flames of Islamic militancy and give credence to calls for holy war. What lent the WTC/Pentagon attack its quality of sinister originality was the ability of a fanatical political movement to take advantage of the complex fragility and vulnerability of advanced technology. Now that this vulnerability has been exposed to the world, it is impossible to insure that other extremists will not commit similar acts—even if Osama bin Laden is eliminated.

The only way to wage this war effectively is to make sure that force is used within relevant frameworks of restraint. Excessive force can take several forms, like the pursuit of political movements remote from the WTC attack, especially if such military action is seen as indirectly doing the dirty work of eliminating threats to Israel's occupation of Palestinian territories and Jerusalem. Excessiveness would also be attributed to efforts to destroy and restructure regimes, other than the Taliban, that are hostile to the United States but not significantly connected with either the attack or Al Qaeda.

The second, closely related problem of successfully framing a response is related to the U.S. manner of waging war: The U.S. temperament has tended to approach war as a matter of confronting evil. In such a view, victory can be achieved only by the total defeat of the other, and with it, the triumph of good.

In the current setting, goals have not been clarified, and U.S. leaders have used grandiose language about ending terrorism and destroying the global terrorist network. The idea of good against evil has been a consistent part of the process of public mobilization, with the implicit message that nothing less than a total victory is acceptable. What are realistic ends? Or put differently, what ends can be reconciled with a commitment to achieve an effective response? What is needed is extremely selective uses of force, especially in relation to the

20

Taliban, combined with criminal law enforcement operations—cutting off sources of finance, destroying terrorist cells,
using policing techniques abetted, to the extent necessary, by
paramilitary capabilities.

Also troubling is the Bush Administration's ingrained dis-
dain for multilateralism and its determination to achieve security for the United States by military means—particularly missile defense and space weaponization. This unilateralism has
so far been masked by a frantic effort to forge a global coalition, but there is every indication that the U.S. government
will insist on complete operational control over the war and
will not be willing to accept procedures of accountability
within the UN framework.

The Administration has often said that many of the actions
in this war will not be made known to the public. But an
excessive emphasis on secrecy in the conduct of military operations is likely to make the uses of force more difficult to justify to those who are skeptical about U.S. motives and goals,
thus undercutting the legitimacy of the war.

In building a global coalition for cooperative action, especially with respect to law enforcement in countries where Al
Qaeda operates, the U.S. government has struck a number of
Faustian bargains. It may be necessary to enter into arrange-
ments with governments that are themselves responsible for
terrorist policies and brutal repression, such as Russia in
Chechnya and India in Kashmir. But the cost of doing so is to
weaken claims that a common antiterrorist front is the foundation of this alliance. For some governments the war against
apocalyptic terrorism is an opportunity to proceed with their
own repressive policies free from censure and interference.
The U.S. government should weigh the cost of writing blank
checks against the importance of distinguishing its means and
ends from the megaterrorist ethos that animated the September 11 attacks. There are some difficult choices ahead, including the extent to which Afghan opposition forces, particularly
the Northern Alliance, should be supported in view of their
own dubious human rights record.

How, then, should legitimacy be pursued in the current
context? The first set of requirements is essentially political: to
disclose goals that seem reasonably connected with the attack

25

and with the threat posed by those who planned, funded and carried it out. In this regard, the destruction of both the Taliban regime and the Al Qaeda network, including the apprehension and prosecution of Osama bin Laden and any associates connected with this and past terrorist crimes, are appropriate goals. In each instance, further specification is necessary. With respect to the Taliban, its relation to Al Qaeda is established and intimate enough to attribute primary responsibility, and the case is strengthened to the degree that its governing policies are so oppressive as to give the international community the strongest possible grounds for humanitarian intervention. We must make a distinction between those individuals and entities that have been actively engaged in the perpetration of the visionary program of international, apocalyptic terrorism uniquely Al Qaeda's and those who have used funds or training to advance more traditional goals relating to grievances associated with the governance of a particular country and have limited their targets largely to the authorities in their countries, like the ETA in Spain and the IRA in Ireland and Britain.

Legitimacy with respect to the use of force in international settings derives from the mutually reinforcing traditions of the "just war" doctrine, international law and the ideas of restraint embedded in the great religions of the world. The essential norms are rather abstract in character, and lend themselves to debate and diverse interpretation. The most important ideas are:

- the principle of discrimination: force must be directed at a military target, with damage to civilians and civilian society being incidental;
- the principle of proportionality: force must not be greater than that needed to achieve an acceptable military result and must not be greater than the provoking cause;
- the principle of humanity: force must not be directed even against enemy personnel if they are subject to capture, wounded or under control (as with prisoners of war);
- the principle of necessity: force should be used only if nonviolent means to achieve military goals are unavailable.

These abstract guidelines for the use of force do not give much operational direction. In each situation we must ask: Do the claims to use force seem reasonable in terms of the ends being pursued, including the obligation to confine civilian damage as much as possible? Such assessments depend on interpretation, but they allow for debate and justification, and clear instances of violative behavior could be quickly identified. The justice of the cause and of the limited ends will be negated by the injustice of improper means and excessive ends. Only the vigilance of an active citizenry, alert to this delicate balance, has much hope of helping this new war to end in a true victory.

Questions about the Passage

1. Summarize each type of argument against the war in Afghanistan that Falk includes: the antiwar/pacifist approach, the legalist/ UN approach, and the militarist approach. Why does he find each approach lacking?
2. Summarize the "limiting means and ends" approach that he favors. What problems does it resolve? What questions does it leave unanswered? What does this approach have in common with Just War theory?

Questions about the Argument

1. What are Falk's credentials for arguing a prowar case for Afghanistan?
2. What is Falk's claim? How does he qualify it?
3. Is Falk's primary audience, the readership of *The Nation,* likely to be sympathetic to his argument? Research the demographics of this audience. How does he try to answer objections they might raise?
4. Falk's main strategy is to raise other possibilities and then refute them before exploring the position he favors. Is it an effective strategy? What are the assets and risks of this approach? Do you think he has fairly described each position? Has he answered any questions you have? Do you agree with him?
5. To what extent does Falk use emotion to enhance his argument? Pay particular attention to language choices he makes.
6. Do you think Falk would see the same difficulties with the anti-war, legalist, and pacifist approaches to a war with Iraq, with Iran, or with North Korea? Would he favor using limited means and ends in any of these cases? Trying to answer these questions may lead to a worthwhile research project.

Stephen R. Shalom, "A 'Just War'? A Critique of Richard Falk"

Stephen Shalom (1948–) is Professor of Political Science at William Paterson University, Wayne, New Jersey, where he has taught since 1977. He was educated at the Massachusetts Institute of Technology, Northeastern University, and Boston University and is the author or editor of nine books, including *The United States and the Philippines: A Study of Neocolonialism* (1981); *Imperial Alibis: Rationalizing U.S. Intervention After the Cold War* (1993); *Bitter Flowers, Sweet Flowers: East Timor, Indonesia, and the World Community* (2000); and *Which Side Are You On? An Introduction to Politics* (2002). A member of the editorial boards of *New Politics* and *Critical Asian Studies,* Shalom also writes for *Z Magazine.* The essay reprinted below initially appeared on Prof. Shalom's Web page when Falk's "Defining a Just War" was published in *The Nation* in October 2001. His essay can also be found on-line in *Z Magazine.*

> In an article entitled "Defining A Just War" in the October 29 issue of *The Nation,* Richard Falk declares that "The war in Afghanistan . . . qualifies in my understanding as the first truly just war since World War II." Falk goes on to warn that the justice of the cause may be "negated by the injustice of improper means and excessive ends," but this caveat doesn't take away from his initial declaration. He didn't say that a unilateral U.S. military response to the events of September 11 could be just, but that "the war" is just. This sentence, coming as it does from one of the country's most prominent and respected advocates of international peace and justice, will have, I'm afraid, profoundly deleterious consequences. "This is a just war," people will say; "even Richard Falk says so." And his later points about the need for following the legal and moral principles of necessity, proportionality, discrimination, and humanity will be largely ignored.
>
> But even if we interpret Falk's position as saying that a U.S. war could be just, as long as it follows the principles he elaborates, his argument is still terribly wrong. First, because his principles were violated from day one of the war, and, second, because he dismisses the alternative of acting through the United Nations.
>
> One doesn't know exactly when Falk finalized his article. Perhaps by now—as UN officials and aid agencies are pleading for a halt in the bombing so that food can get to literally millions of Afghans at risk of starvation—he has come to believe

that the war has crossed the line from just to unjust. But there were warnings about the impact of bombing on desperate Afghan civilians well before the first bomb fell. (For example, the *New York Times* reported [30 Sept. 2001] that "the threat of American-led military attacks turns" the Afghan people's "long-running misery into a potential catastrophe.") That a great humanitarian crisis was likely in the event of bombing was known, and thus the war never met Falk's criteria of discrimination (don't harm civilians), proportionality (force must not be greater than the provoking cause), and humanity.

Moreover, the war never met Falk's criterion of necessity (force should not be used when non-violent means are available). On October 5—two days before the onset of the bombing—the Taliban ambassador to Pakistan stated: "We are prepared to try him if America provides solid evidence of Osama bin Laden's involvement in the attacks on New York and Washington." Asked if bin Laden could be tried in another country, the ambassador said, "We are willing to talk about that, but . . . we must be given the evidence." Indeed, said the ambassador, legal proceedings could begin even before the United States offered any evidence: "Under Islamic law, we can put him on trial according to allegations raised against him and then the evidence would be provided to the court." Washington dismissed the ambassador's remarks, refused to provide evidence, declared that its demands were non-negotiable, and initiated its bombardment of Afghanistan. Was the Taliban offer serious? Could it have been the basis for further concessions? Who knows? Washington never pursued it. Surely, however, going to war in such circumstances does not meet the criterion of necessity.

Falk rejects a pacifist response to the events of September 11, and I think he's right: on a hijacked plane heading into a skyscraper, force may be needed to stop the slaughter; and if terrorists who direct these hijackings refuse to voluntarily turn themselves in, then force may be necessary to apprehend them and bring them to justice. Falk rejects as well a response of excessive militarism, and again I think he's correct (though he fails to see how the excessive militarism he rejects shares many features with the actual war being waged, the war he terms "truly just").

Another approach Falk rejects is one which emphasizes the role of the United States in the world. Falk agrees with proponents of this approach that Washington is "certainly responsible for much global suffering and injustice, giving rise to wide-spread resentment that at its inner core fuels the terrorist impulse." Falk agrees too that longer-term concerns must be addressed, including "finding ways to promote Palestinian self-determination, the internationalization of Jerusalem and a more equitable distribution of the benefits of global economic growth and development"—though he oddly adds that "of course, much of the responsibility" for failing to address these concerns "lies with the corruption and repressive policies of governments, especially in the Middle East, outside the orbit of U.S. influence." But while regimes outside the U.S. orbit, such as Iraq, Syria, and Libya, are no doubt vile, it is hard to see what responsibility they bear for preventing Palestinian self-determination. The obstruction there would seem to come from Washington itself and from a country very much within the U.S. sphere: namely, Israel. Nor do Iraq, Syria, and Libya have nearly as much to do with global inequality as those nations closely tied to the United States—Saudi Arabia and the Gulf oil sheikdoms.

Palestinian self-determination is not simply a "longer-term concern." True, its impact on anti-U.S. terrorism will not be immediate. An Israeli withdrawal from the occupied territories tomorrow would not erase decades of deep anti-Americanism from the minds of many Middle Easterners. But peace in Palestine would immediately end the terrorism being experienced on a daily basis by Palestinians (as well as Israelis).

Still, Falk is right that all people are entitled to security, and Americans are not wrong to be concerned about their well-being as long as the people responsible for the horrific attack of September 11 remain at large.

So how might the culprits be brought to justice? One option is to use the UN or international law (which—unlike the pacifist position—does not preclude the use of force) to apprehend the suspects in order to place them on trial for crimes against humanity. Such an approach, says Falk, would not "deal effectively with the overall threat." But Falk's arguments here are extremely weak.

Falk says first that there are problems with a public trial. I'll   10
consider whether these problems are as serious as Falk suggests, but notice first the implication of Falk's position. The United States issued an ultimatum to the Taliban to turn over bin Laden and his Al Qaeda associates. Let's say they did so.

What would Falk have had the United States do with them then? Execute them without a trial? Hold a secret trial and then execute them? If you object on principle to publicly trying bin Laden and company then you are objecting to Washington's public position. (I say Washington's "public" position, because the United States' dismissal of the Taliban's October 5 offer shows it was never interested in a turn-over.) To say that bin Laden should not be tried is saying that the United States should not even have demanded that bin Laden be turned over, but instead simply begun bombing.

What are the problems with public prosecution, according to Falk?

> It would be impossible to persuade the United States government to empower such a tribunal unless it was authorized to impose capital punishment, and it is doubtful that several of the permanent members of the Security Council could be persuaded to allow death sentences.

What is Falk saying? That this is a just war because the alternative would be a policy which the United States wouldn't accept? Since when do we judge whether a country's policy is right by reference to whether the country likes alternative policies? Iraq invaded Kuwait in 1990 in part because Kuwait was violating its oil production quotas to Iraq's detriment. Would anyone think of justifying the Iraqi invasion by noting that it would be impossible to persuade Baghdad to pursue the alternative course of action—negotiation?

Now perhaps what Falk really means is that a trial would be wrong because he, Falk, would not accept any punishment short of the death penalty. If so, he ought to say this, and not put it on the U.S. government. Some progressives may feel that they could make an exception to their usual opposition to capital punishment in this case, but in fact the argument against the death penalty is stronger, rather than weaker, in cases of terrorism. As terrorism experts note, while executing a lone murderer may not propel very many people to become murderers, executing a terrorist leader with many followers creates a martyr and builds support for the terrorist cause. In any event, to justify the U.S. war on the grounds that "several permanent members of the Security Council" (that is, Britain and France) oppose the death penalty is bizarre to say the least.

Falk goes on to spell out what he sees as the problems with   15
a public trial:

> the evidence linking bin Laden to the September 11 attacks and
> other instances of global terrorism may well be insufficient to
> produce an assured conviction in an impartial legal tribunal,
> particularly if conspiracy was not among the criminal offenses
> that could be charged. European and other foreign governments
> are unlikely to be willing to treat conspiracy as a capital crime.

We should reject a trial because the evidence may not be sufficient to convict? But yet the evidence is good enough to wage
war, with all its horrendous consequences? And then there's
that capital punishment argument again: the evidence may be
sufficient only if conspiracy can be charged—which of course it
can be—but this may preclude execution. So instead we follow
a course that will knowingly lead to a huge number of deaths.

Falk goes on to note that "it strains the imagination to suppose that the Bush Administration would relinquish control
over bin Laden to an international tribunal." But, again, is it the
job of the Left to support wars—and deem them "truly just"—
whenever the nation waging the war is unwilling to act in a just
and reasonable way? It no doubt strained the imagination to
suppose that the United States government would have allowed
elections in Vietnam in 1956 which would probably have been
won by Ho Chi Minh. But would anyone conclude that therefore Washington was justified in waging war on Vietnam?

Falk continues with more in the same vein: "it also seems
highly improbable that the U.S. government can be persuaded
to rely on the collective security mechanisms of the UN. . . ."
It was also highly improbably that Al Capone could have
been persuaded to rely on legal methods of earning a living.
That doesn't make his criminal activities "truly just."

> For better and worse, the United States is relying on its   20
> claimed right of self-defense, and Washington seems certain
> to insist on full operational control over the means and ends
> of the war that is now under way.

Yes, indeed, Washington is insisting on full operation control.
But the Left is not supposed to merely note Washington's
insistence, but criticize it when that insistence is wrong.

Falk then declares that

> . . . at this stage it is unreasonable to expect the U.S. govern-
> ment to rely on the UN to fulfill its defensive needs. The UN
> lacks the capability, authority and will to respond to the kind
> of threat to global security posed by this new form of terrorist
> world war.

The first sentence is somewhat ambiguous. Is Falk saying only
that it is unreasonable to expect Washington to rely on the
UN? (This is true. It is unreasonable to expect the United
States to act lawfully in general, given its long record of ignoring international law, thumbing its nose at the UN, and choosing military solutions to problems that might have been
solved peacefully.) Or is he saying that it is unreasonable for
the U.S. government to rely on the UN, the interpretation suggested by the second sentence in the quotation above?

Why does the UN lack the "capability, authority, and will" to
respond to terrorism? In terms of authority, the UN has the legal
right to take any measures that it deems necessary to deal with
terrorism, while the U.S. right to act is legally constrained—yes,
it may act in self-defense to an armed attack, but self-defense
applies only to cases where (in the words of the Caroline precedent) "necessity of that self-defense is instant, overwhelming,
and leaving no choice of means, and no moment for delibera-
tion." So self-defense would permit the United States to shoot
down attacking enemy planes, but not to wage a war half way
around the globe a month after a terrorist attack, a war that U.S.
officials say might go on for years.

What about the UN's capability? The UN is an extremely   25
weak institution and has no military units of its own. To be
sure, one reason the UN is so weak is because major powers,
not least the United States, have determined to keep it ineffec-
tive. So Washington has been delinquent in paying its UN dues,
has refused to establish a Military Staff Committee that could
coordinate a UN military response, has failed to provide the
UN with military contingents (as called for in Chapter VII of the
UN Charter), and has flouted international law (ignoring, for
example, the ruling of the World Court demanding that the U.S.
cease what were essentially terrorist acts against Nicaragua).
But despite these past failings of the United States, there is no

reason the UN would be incapable of action today if the United States allowed it to do so. The Security Council could call for the turn-over of those responsible for the September 11 attacks and if force were needed to get them, it could request the loan of appropriate forces from member states, including the United States, that would operate under the direction and control of the Security Council. The only obstacle to this happening is the cooperation of the United States government. So once again we meet Falk's strange moral logic: the U.S. war in Afghanistan is "truly just" because the UN is incapable of acting by virtue of the U.S. unwillingness to go to the UN.

Why does all this matter? Why should we care whether the United States goes to war on its own or instead goes through the United Nations, which may employ force? It matters to us for precisely the reasons it matters—from the other side—to the U.S. government. Why has Washington avoided going to the UN? First, because doing so would establish the precedent that the United States is bound by law and can't do just whatever it feels like. The Bush administration doesn't want this precedent and, correspondingly, we should want it. We should want a world where—as much as possible—law, not vigilantism, prevails.

Second, the U.S. resists going to the UN because it will then not have full freedom of action. Once it is determined that "something" should be done about the September 11 perpetrators, there are countless decisions to be made and the question is: who is to make them? Should these decisions be made by Washington or by some international body? The Bush administration wants to keep all decision-making in its own hands. We should want—as much as possible—to minimize unilateral decision-making by the United States. Is there a guarantee that the UN would make better decisions than Washington? No. But if one considers the crucial decisions, there is good reason to believe that the UN would have decided better. And many of these decisions involve precisely the sorts of concerns that Falk raised when he described the problems with the militarist approach.

The UN would have been likely to demand evidence, rather than just taking George Bush's word for bin Laden's guilt. The UN would have been more likely to pursue the Taliban's offer to turn over bin Laden. Perhaps the UN would have determined that the offer was just a stalling tactic. But shouldn't this determination be made by an international body rather than by one country alone? Consider: there was a terrorist bombing of the legislature in Indian-held Kashmir on October 1, killing dozens of civilians. India suspected Pakistani involvement. Would we want India to issue an ultimatum to Pakistan and then decide whether Pakistan has complied, and then, if New Delhi decides no, it launches a war? This is a prescription for disaster. Would anyone consider such a war "truly just"?

Another reason why we shouldn't want individual nations deciding on their own to launch a war to combat terrorism is that any war involves serious negative human consequences. Pacifists believe that these adverse consequences outweigh any conceivable justification for war. Non-pacifists believe that sometimes war is the only way to prevent even more horrible outcomes, but surely the most careful moral consideration must precede any decision for war. So who should make this moral determination? In Afghanistan, it is excruciatingly clear that the harm to the civilian population is immense. The United States might believe that these civilian deaths will be "worth it" (to use Madeleine Albright's response when she was asked about the half million dead from sanctions on Iraq), but is this really something to be decided by the Bush administration alone? By saying that it is "just" for the United States to be waging this war outside the confines of the United Nations, Falk has removed the one potential check on unilateral U.S. action. The well-being of millions of people in Afghanistan are on the line, and it can't possibly be right that their fate—and the value of their lives—should be determined unilaterally by Washington. Of course, actions that kill large numbers of civilians should be condemned whether or not there is the UN imprimatur. But a decision by the UN is likely to be more just than one made alone by the United States.

Nor can it be right that the judgment regarding which targets   30
are appropriate to hit or which weapons are appropriate to use (such as cluster bombs, condemned by the Red Cross) be simply made in the United States. Nor the choice of countries to attack (something currently being debated within the Bush administration). Falk wants "force to be used within relevant

frameworks of restraint," but then dismisses UN oversight, the one restraint that might actually have an effect. If you approve of the unleashing of a tiger, you can't very well complain that the tiger is now destroying more than humanity, necessity, proportionality, and discrimination permit.

Moreover, the war on Afghanistan threatens to destabilize Pakistan (a country with nuclear weapons), and much of the Arab and Islamic world. One would expect the international community to be more sensitive to this danger than the United States government has been, as it conducts what George Bush called its "crusade" against terrorism. To U.S. policy-makers, over-reaction has certain benefits: it creates (as the Cold War did) an atmosphere conducive to military spending and restrictions on civil liberties, and it facilitates the acquisition of world-wide military bases and ties to reprehensible regimes. For the rest of us, though, the international dangers from over-reaction are substantial. And we might note that the prospect of destabilization is far greater in the face of a U.S. war than an international operation: Iran, for example, which condemned the U.S. bombing, indicated that it would have been willing to support a UN action. More importantly, many nations—including U.S. allies in the Middle East and Europe—have urged due caution, warning that a massive assault will play into bin Laden's hands, a caution that would likely be given more weight in an international, than a U.S., response.

An international response will not always be possible. In some situations, one can imagine China or Russia—or the United States—using their veto power in the Security Council to block a UN action that would have been warranted on the basis of justice. But there is no reason to think that that would have been the case regarding September 11. Both China and Russia for their own reasons, both good and bad, support strong action against terrorism. Security Council action would have been forthcoming, though—one hopes—it would not have been all that the United States wanted.

The problem with the United Nations was not that it would have blocked appropriate action, but that it might have given the United States a blank check—which would hardly be an improvement over unilateral U.S. action. This is what the UN did during the Gulf War, when it permitted the U.S. to unilaterally decide whether Saddam Hussein's offers were worth considering, when to start bombing, which targets to hit (including civilian infrastructure), and on which terms to end the war. Then Washington used its veto power to prevent the Council from lifting the sanctions imposed before the war, so that hundreds of thousands of civilians have died over the past decade, while Saddam Hussein has been strengthened.

This seems to be the only circumstance under which the United States is willing to go to the UN: when it thinks it can get a blank check. We should call instead for real UN control over any military action and more generally real UN determination of the appropriate response—short range and long range—to the events of September 11. We should further push for this control to lodge in the General Assembly, rather than the Security Council—something permitted by the Uniting for Peace Resolution—where there is no big power veto. This is by no means an ideal solution. But it is far better—from the point of view of humanitarianism and justice—than unilateral U.S. action. And it offers a serious response to our fellow citizens who are rightly concerned about their security.

Questions about the Passage

1. Why does Shalom think it important to critique Falk's argument?
2. According to Shalom, where, specifically, is Falk wrong? Where is he also right?
3. In what ways does the war in Afghanistan not meet Shalom's principles of Just War?

Questions about the Argument

1. Does Stephen Shalom have the same level of credentials and reputation as does Richard Falk? If not, what does he do to gain authority to write this piece?
2. Where are his assumptions the same as Falk's? How do they differ?
3. What inferences can you make about the audience he has in mind? How does he accommodate their needs?
4. Why does Shalom think it important to provide a detailed critique of Falk's argument? Does Shalom present the argument fairly? What is the counter claim that Shalom makes?

5. Shalom avoids a blanket condemnation of Falk's points, admitting when Falk is right. Locate where Shalom does this. Is this strategy rhetorically effective? Why or why not?

6. What are the steps of Shalom's method of refutation? Try them out to critique another argument you have been asked to read. How useful are they?

7. Compare and contrast Aquinas' method of refutation with Shalom's. Which do you think is more successful? Why?

Howard Zinn, "A Just Cause, Not a Just War"

Howard Zinn (1922–), historian, playwright, and political activist, was educated at New York University and Columbia University. During World War II, he served in the U.S. Army Air Forces as a bombardier, which gave him an understanding of the terror of war, and caused him to examine war as a historian. He taught history from 1956–1963 at Spelman College in Atlanta, a historic Black college, where he was very active in the Civil Rights Movement. In 1964, he became a professor of political science at Boston University (Emeritus since 1988), where he continued to be a progressive activist, opposing the Vietnam War. He is the author of many essays and over twenty books, including three plays and his autobiography, *You Can't Be Neutral on a Moving Train: A Personal History of Our Times* (1994); his best known work is *A People's History of the United States* (1980, 1984, 1999) which has sold over 400,000 copies. *A People's History* follows the New History school of thought that writes history from the point of view of the powerless and unknown, the working classes and minority groups. Zinn continues to speak and write about social issues, and he writes regularly for *The Progressive,* where the essay below was published in December 2001.

> I believe two moral judgments can be made about the present "war": The September 11 attack constitutes a crime against humanity and cannot be justified, and the bombing of Afghanistan is also a crime, which cannot be justified.
>
> And yet, voices across the political spectrum, including many on the left, have described this as a "just war." One longtime advocate of peace, Richard Falk, wrote in *The Nation* that this is "the first truly just war since World War II." Robert Kuttner, another consistent supporter of social justice, declared in *The American Prospect* that only people on the extreme left could believe this is not a just war.

I have puzzled over this. How can a war be truly just when it involves the daily killing of civilians, when it causes hundreds of thousands of men, women, and children to leave their homes to escape the bombs, when it may not find those who planned the September 11 attacks, and when it will multiply the ranks of people who are angry enough at this country to become terrorists themselves?

This war amounts to a gross violation of human rights, and it will produce the exact opposite of what is wanted: It will not end terrorism; it will proliferate terrorism.

I believe that the progressive supporters of the war have   5
confused a "just cause" with a "just war." There are unjust causes, such as the attempt of the United States to establish its power in Vietnam, or to dominate Panama or Grenada, or to subvert the government of Nicaragua. And a cause may be just—getting North Korea to withdraw from South Korea, getting Saddam Hussein to withdraw from Kuwait, or ending terrorism—but it does not follow that going to war on behalf of that cause, with the inevitable mayhem that follows, is just.

The stories of the effects of our bombing are beginning to come through, in bits and pieces. Just eighteen days into the bombing, *The New York Times* reported: "American forces have mistakenly hit a residential area in Kabul." Twice, U.S. planes bombed Red Cross warehouses, and a Red Cross spokesman said: "Now we've got 55,000 people without that food or blankets, with nothing at all."

An Afghan elementary school-teacher told a *Washington Post* reporter at the Pakistan border: "When the bombs fell near my house and my babies started crying, I had no choice but to run away."

A *New York Times* report: "The Pentagon acknowledged that a Navy F/A-18 dropped a 1,000-pound bomb on Sunday near what officials called a center for the elderly. . . . The United Nations said the building was a military hospital. . . . Several hours later, a Navy F-14 dropped two 500-pound bombs on a residential area northwest of Kabul." A U.N. official told a *New York Times* reporter that an American bombing raid on the city of Herat had used cluster bombs, which spread deadly "bomblets" over an area of twenty football fields. This, the *Times* reporter wrote, "was the latest of a growing number of accounts of American bombs going astray and causing civilian casualties."

An A.P. reporter was brought to Karam, a small mountain village hit by American bombs, and saw houses reduced to rubble. "In the hospital in Jalalabad, twenty-five miles to the east, doctors treated what they said were twenty-three victims of bombing at Karam, one a child barely two months old, swathed in bloody bandages," according to the account. "Another child, neighbors said, was in the hospital because the bombing raid had killed her entire family. At least eighteen fresh graves were scattered around the village."

The city of Kandahar, attacked for seventeen straight days,   10
was reported to be a ghost town, with more than half of its 500,000 people fleeing the bombs. The city's electrical grid had been knocked out. The city was deprived of water, since the electrical pumps could not operate. A sixty-year-old farmer told the A.P. reporter, "We left in fear of our lives. Every day and every night, we hear the roaring and roaring of planes, we see the smoke, the fire. . . . I curse them both—the Taliban and America."

A *New York Times* report from Pakistan two weeks into the bombing campaign told of wounded civilians coming across the border. "Every half-hour or so throughout the day, someone was brought across on a stretcher. . . . Most were bomb victims, missing limbs or punctured by shrapnel. . . . A young boy, his head and one leg wrapped in bloodied bandages, clung to his father's back as the old man trudged back to Afghanistan."

That was only a few weeks into the bombing, and the result had already been to frighten hundreds of thousands of Afghans into abandoning their homes and taking to the dangerous, mine-strewn roads. The "war against terrorism" has become a war against innocent men, women, and children, who are in no way responsible for the terrorist attack on New York.

And yet there are those who say this is a "just war."

Terrorism and war have something in common. They both involve the killing of innocent people to achieve what the killers believe is a good end. I can see an immediate objection to this equation: They (the terrorists) deliberately kill innocent people; we (the war makers) aim at "military targets," and civilians are killed by accident, as "collateral damage."

Is it really an accident when civilians die under our bombs?   15
Even if you grant that the intention is not to kill civilians, if

they nevertheless become victims, again and again and again, can that be called an accident? If the deaths of civilians are inevitable in bombing, it may not be deliberate, but it is not an accident, and the bombers cannot be considered innocent. They are committing murder as surely as are the terrorists.

The absurdity of claiming innocence in such cases becomes apparent when the death tolls from "collateral damage" reach figures far greater than the lists of the dead from even the most awful act of terrorism. Thus, the "collateral damage" in the Gulf War caused more people to die—hundreds of thousands, if you include the victims of our sanctions policy—than the very deliberate terrorist attack of September 11. The total of those who have died in Israel from Palestinian terrorist bombs is somewhere under 1,000. The number of dead from "collateral damage" in the bombing of Beirut during Israel's invasion of Lebanon in 1982 was roughly 6,000.

We must not match the death lists—it is an ugly exercise—as if one atrocity is worse than another. No killing of innocents, whether deliberate or "accidental," can be justified. My argument is that when children die at the hands of terrorists, or—whether intended or not—as a result of bombs dropped from airplanes, terrorism and war become equally unpardonable.

Let's talk about "military targets." The phrase is so loose that President Truman, after the nuclear bomb obliterated the population of Hiroshima, could say: "The world will note that the first atomic bomb was dropped on Hiroshima, a military base. That was because we wished in this first attack to avoid, insofar as possible, the killing of civilians."

What we are hearing now from our political leaders is, "We are targeting military objectives. We are trying to avoid killing civilians. But that will happen, and we regret it." Shall the American people take moral comfort from the thought that we are bombing only "military targets"?

The reality is that the term "military" covers all sorts of targets that include civilian populations. When our bombers deliberately destroy, as they did in the war against Iraq, the electrical infrastructure, thus making water purification and sewage treatment plants inoperable and leading to epidemic waterborne diseases, the deaths of children and other civilians cannot be called accidental.

20

Recall that in the midst of the Gulf War, the U.S. military bombed an air raid shelter, killing 400 to 500 men, women, and children who were huddled to escape bombs. The claim was that it was a military target, housing a communications center, but reporters going through the ruins immediately afterward said there was no sign of anything like that.

I suggest that the history of bombing—and no one has bombed more than this nation—is a history of endless atrocities, all calmly explained by deceptive and deadly language like "accident," "military targets," and "collateral damage."

Indeed, in both World War II and in Vietnam, the historical record shows that there was a deliberate decision to target civilians in order to destroy the morale of the enemy—hence the firebombing of Dresden, Hamburg, Tokyo, the B-52s over Hanoi, the jet bombers over peaceful villages in the Vietnam countryside. When some argue that we can engage in "limited military action" without "an excessive use of force," they are ignoring the history of bombing. The momentum of war rides roughshod over limits.

The moral equation in Afghanistan is clear. Civilian casualties are certain. The outcome is uncertain. No one knows what this bombing will accomplish—whether it will lead to the capture of Osama bin Laden (perhaps), or the end of the Taliban (possibly), or a democratic Afghanistan (very unlikely), or an end to terrorism (almost certainly not).

And meanwhile, we are terrorizing the population (not the terrorists, they are not easily terrorized). Hundreds of thousands are packing their belongings and their children onto carts and leaving their homes to make dangerous journeys to places they think might be more safe.

25

Not one human life should be expended in this reckless violence called a "war against terrorism."

We might examine the idea of pacifism in the light of what is going on right now. I have never used the word "pacifist" to describe myself, because it suggests something absolute, and I am suspicious of absolutes. I want to leave openings for unpredictable possibilities. There might be situations (and even such strong pacifists as Gandhi and Martin Luther King believed this) when a small, focused act of violence against a monstrous, immediate evil would be justified.

In war, however, the proportion of means to ends is very, very different. War, by its nature, is unfocused, indiscriminate, and especially in our time when the technology is so murderous, inevitably involves the deaths of large numbers of people and the suffering of even more. Even in the "small wars" (Iran vs. Iraq, the Nigerian war, the Afghan war), a million people die. Even in a "tiny" war like the one we waged in Panama, a thousand or more die.

Scott Simon of NPR wrote a commentary in *The Wall Street Journal* on October 11 entitled, "Even Pacifists Must Support This War." He tried to use the pacifist acceptance of self-defense, which approves a focused resistance to an immediate attacker, to justify this war, which he claims is "self-defense." But the term "self-defense" does not apply when you drop bombs all over a country and kill lots of people other than your attacker. And it doesn't apply when there is no likelihood that it will achieve its desired end.

Pacifism, which I define as a rejection of war, rests on a very powerful logic. In war, the means—indiscriminate killing—are immediate and certain; the ends, however desirable, are distant and uncertain.   30

Pacifism does not mean "appeasement." That word is often hurled at those who condemn the present war on Afghanistan, and it is accompanied by references to Churchill, Chamberlain, Munich. World War II analogies are conveniently summoned forth when there is a need to justify a war, however irrelevant to a particular situation. At the suggestion that we withdraw from Vietnam, or not make war on Iraq, the word "appeasement" was bandied about. The glow of the "good war" has repeatedly been used to obscure the nature of all the bad wars we have fought since 1945.

Let's examine that analogy. Czechoslovakia was handed to the voracious Hitler to "appease" him. Germany was an aggressive nation expanding its power, and to help it in its expansion was not wise. But today we do not face an expansionist power that demands to be appeased. We ourselves are the expansionist power—troops in Saudi Arabia, bombings of Iraq, military bases all over the world, naval vessels on every sea—and that, along with Israel's expansion into the West Bank and Gaza Strip, has aroused anger.

It was wrong to give up Czechoslovakia to appease Hitler. It is not wrong to withdraw our military from the Middle East, or for Israel to withdraw from the occupied territories, because there is no right to be there. That is not appeasement. That is justice.

Opposing the bombing of Afghanistan does not constitute "giving in to terrorism" or "appeasement." It asks that other means be found than war to solve the problems that confront us. King and Gandhi both believed in action—nonviolent direct action, which is more powerful and certainly more morally defensible than war.

To reject war is not to "turn the other cheek," as pacifism   35
has been caricatured. It is, in the present instance, to act in ways that do not imitate the terrorists.

The United States could have treated the September 11 attack as a horrific criminal act that calls for apprehending the culprits, using every device of intelligence and investigation possible. It could have gone to the United Nations to enlist the aid of other countries in the pursuit and apprehension of the terrorists.

There was also the avenue of negotiations. (And let's not hear: "What? Negotiate with those monsters?" The United States negotiated with—indeed, brought into power and kept in power—some of the most monstrous governments in the world.) Before Bush ordered in the bombers, the Taliban offered to put bin Laden on trial. This was ignored. After ten days of air attacks, when the Taliban called for a halt to the bombing and said they would be willing to talk about handing bin Laden to a third country for trial, the headline the next day in *The New York Times* read: "President Rejects Offer by Taliban for Negotiations," and Bush was quoted as saying: "When I said no negotiations, I meant no negotiations."

That is the behavior of someone hellbent on war. There were similar rejections of negotiating possibilities at the start of the Korean War, the war in Vietnam, the Gulf War, and the bombing of Yugoslavia. The result was an immense loss of life and incalculable human suffering.

International police work and negotiations were—still are— alternatives to war. But let's not deceive ourselves; even if we succeeded in apprehending bin Laden or, as is unlikely, destroying the entire Al Qaeda network, that would not end the threat of terrorism, which has potential recruits far beyond Al Qaeda.

To get at the roots of terrorism is complicated. Dropping   40
bombs is simple. It is an old response to what everyone
acknowledges is a very new situation. At the core of unspeak-
able and unjustifiable acts of terrorism are justified grievances
felt by millions of people who would not themselves engage
in terrorism but from whose ranks terrorists spring.

Those grievances are of two kinds: the existence of profound
misery—hunger, illness—in much of the world, contrasted to
the wealth and luxury of the West, especially the United
States; and the presence of American military power everywhere in the world, propping up oppressive regimes and
repeatedly intervening with force to maintain U.S. hegemony.

This suggests actions that not only deal with the long-term
problem of terrorism but are in themselves just.

Instead of using two planes a day to drop food on
Afghanistan and 100 planes to drop bombs (which have been
making it difficult for the trucks of the international agencies
to bring in food), use 102 planes to bring food.

Take the money allocated for our huge military machine
and use it to combat starvation and disease around the world.
One-third of our military budget would annually provide
clean water and sanitation facilities for the billion people in
the world who have none.

Withdraw troops from Saudi Arabia, because their presence   45
near the holy shrines of Mecca and Medina angers not just bin
Laden (we need not care about angering him) but huge numbers of Arabs who are not terrorists.

Stop the cruel sanctions on Iraq, which are killing more than
a thousand children every week without doing anything to
weaken Saddam Hussein's tyrannical hold over the country.

Insist that Israel withdraw from the occupied territories,
something that many Israelis also think is right, and which
will make Israel more secure than it is now.

In short, let us pull back from being a military superpower,
and become a humanitarian superpower.

Let us be a more modest nation. We will then be more
secure. The modest nations of the world don't face the threat
of terrorism.

Such a fundamental change in foreign policy is hardly to be   50
expected. It would threaten too many interests: the power of

political leaders, the ambitions of the military, the corporations that profit from the nation's enormous military commitments.

Change will come, as at other times in our history, only when American citizens—becoming better informed, having second thoughts after the first instinctive support for official policy—demand it. That change in citizen opinion, especially if it coincides with a pragmatic decision by the government that its violence isn't working, could bring about a retreat from the military solution.

It might also be a first step in the rethinking of our nation's role in the world. Such a rethinking contains the promise, for Americans, of genuine security, and for people elsewhere, the beginning of hope.

Questions about the Passage

1. What reasons does Zinn give to demonstrate that the war in Afghanistan is not a just war?
2. Zinn says he is not a pacifist. What reasons does he give? How does he define pacifism?
3. How does Zinn distinguish between a just cause and a just war? Why is this an important distinction?

Questions about the Argument

1. What are Zinn's credentials? Is his forum, *The Progressive,* appropriate for his argument? Find out what you can about the editorial policy of this journal.
2. Given the widespread support for the war in Afghanistan, coming as it did right after September 11, what strategies does Zinn adopt to bring readers to his side or at least to get them to hear him out?
3. How does he use specific examples to build his case? Do these lists of killing and destruction work more powerfully as inductive logic leading to his statement, "And yet there are those who say this is a just war," or as emotional appeals?
4. Zinn uses an analogy between war and terrorism to help make his case. Do you think the analogy is valid? To what extent? How crucial is this analogy to his case?
5. Are you persuaded by this argument as a whole? Why or why not?

Iraq

George W. Bush, Remarks at the United Nations General Assembly, *September 12, 2002*

After months of discussion about invading Iraq, President George W. Bush (1946–) spoke to the United Nations General Assembly. The administration's apparent unilateral intentions had been criticized both at home and abroad, so the president's speech urging U.N. unity against Saddam Hussein's regime marked an important moment in the move towards war in Iraq. Prior to the speech, the White House portrayed it as one of the most important in Bush's presidency. *The New York Times* reported the next day: "Foreign leaders and delegates applauded politely and expressed relief that the president had turned to the United Nations for another Security Council resolution to press his case against Iraq. But some said they were concerned that the world body would, in effect, be used to oust the leader of a member nation." By September 21, the U.N. had responded to the speech; Secretary General Kofi Annan announced that Iraq would allow U.N. weapons inspectors to return, which they did. After two months of American negotiations with U.N. Security Council members, the Security Council voted unanimously on November 8, 2002 to approve the U.S.-sponsored resolution giving Iraq an ultimatum to open itself to complete weapons inspection and to turn over weapons information or face "serious consequences." Ultimately, the United States invaded Iraq on March 19, 2003 with a few allies, the "coalition of the willing," but without the backing of the United Nations.

> Mr. Secretary General, Mr. President, distinguished delegates, and ladies and gentlemen: We meet one year and one day after a terrorist attack brought grief to my country, and brought grief to many citizens of our world. Yesterday, we remembered the innocent lives taken that terrible morning. Today, we turn to the urgent duty of protecting other lives, without illusion and without fear.
>
> We've accomplished much in the last year—in Afghanistan and beyond. We have much yet to do—in Afghanistan and beyond. Many nations represented here have joined in the fight against global terror, and the people of the United States are grateful.
>
> The United Nations was born in the hope that survived a world war—the hope of a world moving toward justice,

escaping old patterns of conflict and fear. The founding members resolved that the peace of the world must never again be destroyed by the will and wickedness of any man. We created the United Nations Security Council, so that, unlike the League of Nations, our deliberations would be more than talk, our resolutions would be more than wishes. After generations of deceitful dictators and broken treaties and squandered lives, we dedicated ourselves to standards of human dignity shared by all, and to a system of security defended by all.

Today, these standards, and this security, are challenged. Our commitment to human dignity is challenged by persistent poverty and raging disease. The suffering is great, and our responsibilities are clear. The United States is joining with the world to supply aid where it reaches people and lifts up lives, to extend trade and the prosperity it brings, and to bring medical care where it is desperately needed.

As a symbol of our commitment to human dignity, the United   5
States will return to UNESCO. (Applause.) This organization has been reformed and America will participate fully in its mission to advance human rights and tolerance and learning.

Our common security is challenged by regional conflicts— ethnic and religious strife that is ancient, but not inevitable. In the Middle East, there can be no peace for either side without freedom for both sides. America stands committed to an independent and democratic Palestine, living side by side with Israel in peace and security. Like all other people, Palestinians deserve a government that serves their interests and listens to their voices. My nation will continue to encourage all parties to step up to their responsibilities as we seek a just and comprehensive settlement to the conflict.

Above all, our principles and our security are challenged today by outlaw groups and regimes that accept no law of morality and have no limit to their violent ambitions. In the attacks on America a year ago, we saw the destructive intentions of our enemies. This threat hides within many nations, including my own. In cells and camps, terrorists are plotting further destruction, and building new bases for their war against civilization. And our greatest fear is that terrorists will find a shortcut to their mad ambitions when an outlaw regime supplies them with the technologies to kill on a massive scale. In one place—in one regime—we find all these dangers, in their most lethal and aggressive forms, exactly the kind of aggressive threat the United Nations was born to confront.

Twelve years ago, Iraq invaded Kuwait without provocation. And the regime's forces were poised to continue their march to seize other countries and their resources. Had Saddam Hussein been appeased instead of stopped, he would have endangered the peace and stability of the world. Yet this aggression was stopped—by the might of coalition forces and the will of the United Nations.

To suspend hostilities, to spare himself, Iraq's dictator accepted a series of commitments. The terms were clear, to him and to all. And he agreed to prove he is complying with every one of those obligations.

He has proven instead only his contempt for the United   10
Nations, and for all his pledges. By breaking every pledge—by his deceptions, and by his cruelties—Saddam Hussein has made the case against himself.

In 1991, Security Council Resolution 688 demanded that the Iraqi regime cease at once the repression of its own people, including the systematic repression of minorities—which the Council said, threatened international peace and security in the region. This demand goes ignored.

Last year, the U.N. Commission on Human Rights found that Iraq continues to commit extremely grave violations of human rights, and that the regime's repression is all pervasive. Tens of thousands of political opponents and ordinary citizens have been subjected to arbitrary arrest and imprisonment, summary execution, and torture by beating and burning, electric shock, starvation, mutilation, and rape. Wives are tortured in front of their husbands, children in the presence of their parents—and all of these horrors concealed from the world by the apparatus of a totalitarian state.

In 1991, the U.N. Security Council, through Resolutions 686 and 687, demanded that Iraq return all prisoners from Kuwait and other lands. Iraq's regime agreed. It broke its promise. Last year the Secretary General's high-level coordinator for this issue reported that Kuwait, Saudi, Indian, Syrian, Lebanese, Iranian, Egyptian, Bahraini, and Omani nationals remain unaccounted for—more than 600 people. One American pilot is among them.

In 1991, the U.N. Security Council, through Resolution 687, demanded that Iraq renounce all involvement with terrorism, and permit no terrorist organizations to operate in Iraq. Iraq's regime agreed. It broke this promise. In violation of Security Council Resolution 1373, Iraq continues to shelter and support terrorist organizations that direct violence against Iran, Israel, and Western governments. Iraqi dissidents abroad are targeted for murder. In 1993, Iraq attempted to assassinate the Emir of Kuwait and a former American President. Iraq's government openly praised the attacks of September the 11th. And al Qaeda terrorists escaped from Afghanistan and are known to be in Iraq.

In 1991, the Iraqi regime agreed to destroy and stop devel-   15
oping all weapons of mass destruction and long-range mis-siles, and to prove to the world it has done so by complying with rigorous inspections. Iraq has broken every aspect of this fundamental pledge.

From 1991 to 1995, the Iraqi regime said it had no biological weapons. After a senior official in its weapons program defected and exposed this lie, the regime admitted to producing tens of thousands of liters of anthrax and other deadly biologi-cal agents for use with Scud warheads, aerial bombs, and air-craft spray tanks. U.N. inspectors believe Iraq has produced two to four times the amount of biological agents it declared, and has failed to account for more than three metric tons of material that could be used to produce biological weapons. Right now, Iraq is expanding and improving facilities that were used for the production of biological weapons.

United Nations' inspections also revealed that Iraq likely maintains stockpiles of VX, mustard and other chemical agents, and that the regime is rebuilding and expanding facili-ties capable of producing chemical weapons.

And in 1995, after four years of deception, Iraq finally admitted it had a crash nuclear weapons program prior to the Gulf War. We know now, were it not for that war, the regime in Iraq would likely have possessed a nuclear weapon no later than 1993.

Today, Iraq continues to withhold important information about its nuclear program—weapons design, procurement logs, experiment data, an accounting of nuclear materials and docu-mentation of foreign assistance. Iraq employs capable nuclear scientists and technicians. It retains physical infrastructure needed to build a nuclear weapon. Iraq has made several attempts to buy high-strength aluminum tubes used to enrich uranium for a nuclear weapon. Should Iraq acquire fissile material, it would be able to build a nuclear weapon within a year. And Iraq's state-controlled media has reported numerous meetings between Saddam Hussein and his nuclear scientists, leaving little doubt about his continued appetite for these weapons.

Iraq also possesses a force of Scud-type missiles with ranges   20
beyond the 150 kilometers permitted by the U.N. Work at testing and production facilities shows that Iraq is building more long-range missiles that it can inflict mass death throughout the region.

In 1990, after Iraq's invasion of Kuwait, the world imposed economic sanctions on Iraq. Those sanctions were maintained after the war to compel the regime's compliance with Security Council resolutions. In time, Iraq was allowed to use oil revenues to buy food. Saddam Hussein has subverted this program, working around the sanctions to buy missile technology and military materials. He blames the suffering of Iraq's people on the United Nations, even as he uses his oil wealth to build lavish palaces for himself, and to buy arms for his country. By refusing to comply with his own agreements, he bears full guilt for the hunger and misery of innocent Iraqi citizens.

In 1991, Iraq promised U.N. inspectors immediate and unrestricted access to verify Iraq's commitment to rid itself of weapons of mass destruction and long-range missiles. Iraq broke this promise, spending seven years deceiving, evading, and harassing U.N. inspectors before ceasing cooperation entirely. Just months after the 1991 cease-fire, the Security Council twice renewed its demand that the Iraqi regime cooperate fully with inspectors, condemning Iraq's serious violations of its obligations. The Security Council again renewed that demand in 1994, and twice more in 1996, deploring Iraq's clear violations of its obligations. The Security Council renewed its demand three more times in 1997, citing flagrant violations; and three more times in 1998, calling Iraq's behavior totally unacceptable. And in 1999, the demand was renewed yet again.

As we meet today, it's been almost four years since the last U.N. inspectors set foot in Iraq, four years for the Iraqi regime to plan, and to build, and to test behind the cloak of secrecy. We know that Saddam Hussein pursued weapons of mass murder even when inspectors were in his country. Are we to assume that he stopped when they left? The history, the logic, and the facts lead to one conclusion: Saddam Hussein's regime is a grave and gathering danger. To suggest otherwise is to hope against the evidence. To assume this regime's good faith is to bet the lives of millions and the peace of the world in a reckless gamble. And this is a risk we must not take.

Delegates to the General Assembly, we have been more than patient. We've tried sanctions. We've tried the carrot of oil for food, and the stick of coalition military strikes. But Saddam Hussein has defied all these efforts and continues to develop weapons of mass destruction. The first time we may be completely certain he has a—nuclear weapons is when, God forbid, he uses one. We owe it to all our citizens to do everything in our power to prevent that day from coming.

The conduct of the Iraqi regime is a threat to the authority   25
of the United Nations, and a threat to peace. Iraq has answered a decade of U.N. demands with a decade of defiance. All the world now faces a test, and the United Nations a difficult and defining moment. Are Security Council resolutions to be honored and enforced, or cast aside without consequence? Will the United Nations serve the purpose of its founding, or will it be irrelevant?

The United States helped found the United Nations. We want the United Nations to be effective, and respectful, and successful. We want the resolutions of the world's most important multilateral body to be enforced. And right now those resolutions are being unilaterally subverted by the Iraqi regime. Our partnership of nations can meet the test before us, by making clear what we now expect of the Iraqi regime.

If the Iraqi regime wishes peace, it will immediately and unconditionally forswear, disclose, and remove or destroy all weapons of mass destruction, long-range missiles, and all related material.

If the Iraqi regime wishes peace, it will immediately end all support for terrorism and act to suppress it, as all states are required to do by U.N. Security Council resolutions.

If the Iraqi regime wishes peace, it will cease persecution of its civilian population, including Shi'a, Sunnis, Kurds, Turkomans, and others, again as required by Security Council resolutions.

If the Iraqi regime wishes peace, it will release or account for   30
all Gulf War personnel whose fate is still unknown. It will return the remains of any who are deceased, return stolen prop-

erty, accept liability for losses resulting from the invasion of Kuwait, and fully cooperate with international efforts to resolve these issues, as required by Security Council resolutions.

If the Iraqi regime wishes peace, it will immediately end all illicit trade outside the oil-for-food program. It will accept U.N. administration of funds from that program, to ensure that the money is used fairly and promptly for the benefit of the Iraqi people.

If all these steps are taken, it will signal a new openness and accountability in Iraq. And it could open the prospect of the United Nations helping to build a government that represents all Iraqis—a government based on respect for human rights, economic liberty, and internationally supervised elections.

The United States has no quarrel with the Iraqi people; they've suffered too long in silent captivity. Liberty for the Iraqi people is a great moral cause, and a great strategic goal. The people of Iraq deserve it; the security of all nations requires it. Free societies do not intimidate through cruelty and conquest, and open societies do not threaten the world with mass murder. The United States supports political and economic liberty in a unified Iraq.

We can harbor no illusions—and that's important today to remember. Saddam Hussein attacked Iran in 1980 and Kuwait in 1990. He's fired ballistic missiles at Iran and Saudi Arabia, Bahrain, and Israel. His regime once ordered the killing of every person between the ages of 15 and 70 in certain Kurdish villages in northern Iraq. He has gassed many Iranians, and 40 Iraqi villages.

My nation will work with the U.N. Security Council to meet   35
our common challenge. If Iraq's regime defies us again, the world must move deliberately, decisively to hold Iraq to account. We will work with the U.N. Security Council for the necessary resolutions. But the purposes of the United States should not be doubted. The Security Council resolutions will be enforced—the just demands of peace and security will be met—or action will be unavoidable. And a regime that has lost its legitimacy will also lose its power.

Events can turn in one of two ways: If we fail to act in the face of danger, the people of Iraq will continue to live in brutal submission. The regime will have new power to bully and dominate and conquer its neighbors, condemning the

Middle East to more years of bloodshed and fear. The regime will remain unstable—the region will remain unstable, with little hope of freedom, and isolated from the progress of our times. With every step the Iraqi regime takes toward gaining and deploying the most terrible weapons, our own options to confront that regime will narrow. And if an emboldened regime were to supply these weapons to terrorist allies, then the attacks of September the 11th would be a prelude to far greater horrors.

If we meet our responsibilities, if we overcome this danger, we can arrive at a very different future. The people of Iraq can shake off their captivity. They can one day join a democratic Afghanistan and a democratic Palestine, inspiring reforms throughout the Muslim world. These nations can show by their example that honest government, and respect for women, and the great Islamic tradition of learning can triumph in the Middle East and beyond. And we will show that the promise of the United Nations can be fulfilled in our time.

Neither of these outcomes is certain. Both have been set before us. We must choose between a world of fear and a world of progress. We cannot stand by and do nothing while dangers gather. We must stand up for our security, and for the permanent rights and the hopes of mankind. By heritage and by choice, the United States of America will make that stand. And, delegates to the United Nations, you have the power to make that stand, as well.

Thank you very much. (Applause.)

Questions about the Passage

1. How does President Bush view the U.N.: its initial mission, its current role, and the role of the U.N. Security Council? What is the threat to its relevance? How does Bush view the U.S. relationship to the U.N.? Does he want to work with the U.N.?

2. Bush gives at least three reasons for enforcing U.N. resolutions against Iraq. What are they? What support does Bush provide for these reasons? Can you find any other reasons for enforcement, perhaps ones not stated overtly?

3. What must Iraq do if it wants peace? Do you agree that these are steps Iraq must take?

Questions about the Argument

1. What do you know about President Bush's background, education, and experience? What authority does he have to give this speech? How credible is his authority?
2. How do Americans, Europeans, and people of the Middle East view President Bush? How important is one's political position in assessing Bush?
3. Who is Bush's primary audience? His extended audience? How does he appeal to each audience? Which of their concerns does he address? How does he tailor his language to each audience?
4. Does Bush make his case that Iraq has failed to comply with U.N. resolutions? If so, how?
5. How does he use deduction and induction in his speech? Look for specific examples.
6. To which emotions does Bush appeal in Paragraphs 36 and 38? Elsewhere in the speech, do you find uses of language and example that have emotional impact? What are they?
7. Is this a rhetorically effective speech? Was it effective in achieving its purpose? Why or why not? Think here of such aims of argument as informing, convincing, persuading, and moving to action.

Susan Thistlethwaite, "'Just War' or Is It Just a War?"

Susan Thistlethwaite (1948–), a theologian, is the president of the Chicago Theological Seminary, where she has been a faculty member since 1982. She has also taught at Mount Holyoke College, Wesley Theological Seminary, and Boston University. Educated at Smith College and Duke University, Thistlethwaite is an ordained minister of the United Church of Christ, a liberal Protestant denomination that has identified itself as a "Just Peace Church" since 1985. Rev. Thistlethwaite is the author or editor of seven books, including *A Just Peace Church* (1986). The piece reprinted below appeared as a "Voice of the People" letter to the editor of the *Chicago Tribune* on October 15, 2002.

> President Bush has gotten his congressional mandate to launch a war on Iraq. America will, for the first time in its modern history, attack someone who has not attacked us or our allies first. We will exercise a first-strike option, something the United States did not do even at the height of the Cold War.

We now abandon any pretense that this proposed war against Iraq is just. It cannot be justified.

We will strike not because Iraq has attacked us, not because there is any direct proof Iraq harbors those who have attacked us, not because Iraq has attacked one of our allies, but because we think maybe, just maybe, Iraq might do something we really won't like in the next couple of years.

Studs Terkel called World War II "the last good war." And perhaps it was.

But that hasn't kept presidents from arguing that wars they   5
wanted to wage since then are good and are justified. The first President George Bush went to great lengths in 1991 to argue before religious broadcasters that his proposed Gulf War fulfilled every tenet of the long-standing Just War theory.

Why did he bother?

He bothered because war is horrific. War wreaks havoc on societies, destabilizes fragile balances of power, provokes others to join the violence and sears itself into the memory of those who survive. It takes a lot to justify going to war. Presidents before George W. Bush seemed to know that.

Ethicists and theologians, military strategists and politicians have spent almost 2,000 years working out a theory of how you can justify war when it is so horrific. It is called, aptly enough, Just War theory. Taught at the War College in Washington, D.C., in Christian seminaries and political science departments, Just War theory is the major thinking of most religious traditions and military strategists on how to justify war.

Just War theory first began with the agonizing reflections of a saint. St. Augustine looked at the horrors barbarian invaders were inflicting on the Roman citizens and he asked himself if a Christian could ever justify going to war. He answered a very qualified "yes." A Christian can go to war if it is to "defend the vulnerable other." His version didn't even include self-defense. Self-defense was added about 500 years later by another saint, Thomas Aquinas. You have a just cause, said Aquinas, when you are defending yourself. You have to have right authority (be a government), you need to have a right intention (not just love violence), you need to have a good outcome (more good should result than the evil of violence), you need to be proportional (not use more force than necessary), you need to have a reasonable hope for success (peace should result), and it must be the very last resort (all diplomacy must be exhausted).

We can see that no part of Just War theory supports a first-   10
strike option.

To have a just cause, you have to be defending yourself (or defending someone else from attack). Not in this proposed war with Iraq. We just think somebody sometime might get attacked by Iraq. Vice President Dick Cheney's 1992 white paper calls this "anticipatory action to defend ourselves." That means, "hit 'em first and then hit 'em back." That way you cover all the bases. It is immoral.

And we sure haven't exhausted every diplomatic measure. As retired Marine Gen. Anthony Zinni, former head of Central Command, was quoted as saying in the Oct. 11 *Chicago Tribune,* "I believe he [Saddam Hussein] is . . . containable at this moment. War and violence are a very last resort." Clearly the general has studied his Just War theory.

St. Augustine wanted to know if Christians could resist barbarians. If the United States strikes first against Iraq, then it is Americans who have become the barbarians. We have learned nothing in more than 1,500 years of moral reasoning.

Questions about the Passage

1. According to Thistlethwaite, why cannot the war against Iraq be justified?
2. Why did the first President Bush argue in 1991 that his proposed Gulf War was in line with Just War theory?
3. Does Thistlewaite think that Just War theory can be used to justify war with Iraq?

Questions about the Argument

1. Investigate Thistlethwaite's credentials and reputation. How do her qualifications compare to those of Colson (p. 234)?
2. Examine Thistlethwaite's claim and the reasons with which she supports it. How convincing are her reasons?
3. What is the analogy with which Thistlethwaite ends her article? Do you think it is a valid analogy? Tease out the basis for comparison within the analogy. Have you changed your opinion? What kind of effect on the reader do you think she intends to have?

Charles Colson, "Just War in Iraq"

Charles Colson (1931–) has followed an unusual and highly public career path. Educated at Brown University and George Washington University, where he received a J.D. in 1959, he served in the office of the Assistant Secretary of the Navy and worked as an administrative assistant to Senator Leverett Saltonstall (Republican of Massachusetts) from 1956–1961.

From 1969–1973, Colson was special counsel to the president, the famously loyal "hatchet man" of President Richard Nixon. In 1974 Colson was convicted of several Watergate crimes—covering up the break-in of Democratic Party headquarters and burglarizing the office of Daniel Ellsberg's psychiatrist in search of damaging personal information about the man who had released the "Pentagon Papers"—and he served seven months of a three-year prison sentence. While awaiting trial, Colson became a born-again Christian, and after his release from prison he founded Prison Fellowship Ministries, one of the largest organizations of its kind to minister to prisoners, ex-prisoners, and their children. He has dedicated himself to this ministry for almost thirty years. Colson is a prolific writer, having published thirty books of theology, autobiography, and Christian fiction, including his autobiography *Born Again* (1976), which popularized the title phrase describing a new or renewed Christian faith. Since 1983, Colson has been a contributing editor to *Christianity Today*, where the essay printed below appeared in December 2002.

> When the war began in Afghanistan, Defense Secretary Donald Rumsfeld asked a handful of religious leaders to brief him on just-war doctrine. Most of us gave high marks to the administration's efforts to meet just-war standards. I asked, however, the one discordant question: "How would the administration justify a preemptive strike on Iraq?" Without hesitation, Rumsfeld cited the precedent of Israel's attack on an Iraqi nuclear plant in 1981.
>
> One year later, the question is no longer hypothetical. As I write, U.S. forces are massing for war with Iraq. By the time you read this, troops may be in Baghdad. But whatever happens, the morality of a preemptive strike will continue as a hot debate. Last September, the President drew the battle line, boldly declaring preemption as a national policy.
>
> The issue is of particular concern to Christians since we are the heirs of the just-war tradition formulated by Augustine 1,600 years ago. Historically, the doctrine's requirement of just cause has been defined as responding to an attack.

But has terrorism changed the rules? Should the doctrine be "stretched," as just-war expert George Weigel argues? Can a preemptive strike be morally justified?

The first response from the church was negative. U.S.   5
Catholic bishops oppose an attack unless Iraq can be linked to the September 11 terror strikes. One hundred Christian ethicists announced opposition; so did the general secretary of the Middle East Council of Churches. The new Archbishop of Canterbury and Pope John Paul II both expressed reservations.

But I think this reflects too narrow an understanding of just war. Our attitudes may be unduly influenced by Cold War memories. For four decades, the world was kept in relative peace—at least from nuclear holocaust—by nuclear checkmate. The West and the U.S.S.R. embraced the policy of Mutual Assured Destruction, in which both sides targeted the other's cities. Neither side dared attack, fearing a hugely destructive retaliatory strike; with civilians deliberately targeted, preemption was unthinkable.

But this was not the case before the Cold War. Proponents of "anticipatory self-defense" frequently cite a famous precedent of the British attacking across Niagara to prevent an invasion by Irish revolutionaries in Canada. And no less a Christian eminence than Sir Thomas More wrote, "if any foreign prince takes up arms and prepares to invade their land, they immediately attack him in full force outside their own borders."

In the run up to World War II, many argued that Hitler should not be appeased. European leaders engaged in extraordinary—and we now realize counterproductive—diplomatic efforts to avoid war. Had the allies had the weapons, would a preemptive strike against the Nazis have been justified before they overran Poland? In hindsight the answer is clear, as it was to the Christian pastors who were executed for conspiring to kill Hitler.

The question of preemptive strike turns on facts. For 12 years, Saddam Hussein has mocked the United Nations and the world. If he is, as the U.S. and British believe, stockpiling weapons of mass destruction and acting in concert with terrorists, he forfeits claims of sovereign immunity.

Unlike the Cold War, when early warning systems could   10
detect missile launches, terrorists give no warning. If Saddam Hussein were to prepare a missile for launch, the U.S. would certainly be warranted in firing in self-defense. Giving a terrorist

a dirty bomb to be delivered in a suitcase is no different—except for delivery time—from a missile launch.

Of course, all of this presupposes solid intelligence and the goodwill of U.S. and Western leaders. I find it hard to believe that any President, aware of the awesome consequences of his decision and of the swiftness of second-guessing in a liberal democracy, would act recklessly.

Christians should remember that the just-war doctrine is not grounded in revenge, punishment, or even justice.

Thomas Aquinas discussed it in *Summa Theologica*—not in the section on justice but in the section on charity (that is, the love of God). As Christian scholar Darrell Cole writes, "The Christian who fails to use force to aid his neighbor when prudence dictates that force is the best way to render that aid is an uncharitable Christian. Hence Christians who willingly and knowingly refuse to engage in a just war . . . fail to show love towards their neighbor as well as towards God."

Out of love of neighbor, then, Christians can and should support a preemptive strike, if ordered by the appropriate magistrate to prevent an imminent attack.

Questions about the Passage

1. How did the church or church leaders respond to the possibility of a preemptive attack?
2. How might history justify such an attack? Discuss each of Colson's examples.
3. According to Colson, how does the behavior of Saddam Hussein make a case for preemptive attack? With the benefit of hindsight that you as readers have, do you think Colson is right about this case?
4. Where in *Summa Theologica* does Aquinas place his discussion of Just War doctrine? Why does it fit there? Do you think an argument based on charity can justify a preemptive attack?

Questions about the Argument

1. What are Colson's qualifications to make this argument?
2. Spell out the assumptions that underlie his argument. Do you agree with them?
3. What authorities does he use to support his claims? Does Colson use them appropriately to back himself up?
4. Is the conclusion Colson draws in his final paragraph justified by the evidence he presents?

The Cartoonists' Visions: Pro-War and Antiwar Cartoons

Visual images, not just written texts, can also be arguments, especially about current issues being debated. Political cartoons are one voice among many in sometimes heated conversations. Cartoons are topical and time bound. They are very much of the moment. They rely on visual associations, jokes, and allusions. They convey a message economically by careful selection of ideas but with few words. They rely heavily on the use of pathos.

The pro-war and antiwar cartoons presented here range from photographs that have been manipulated to create a new image and message to more typical political cartoons. These cartoons all insist that we see old images and familiar ideas in new ways.

Questions about the Pictures: Cartoon Pair 1 (page 239)

1. Examine carefully this pair of manipulated photographs. How does the StrangeCosmos.com collage of images create humor? What commercial does the image parody? If you block out the images on the right and on the left, how do you respond to the central image?
2. Why is the second manipulated photograph (Fig. 7-2) titled "Bush Inc. War?" What does "Inc." stand for? What does the elephant foot suggest? What does the mouse suggest? Why is it standing up?

Questions about the Argument: Cartoon Pair 1

1. The image in "Can you hear me now" can be viewed as an argument by analogy to the original commercial message. What is the original commercial message? How does the image rephrase this message? Are you persuaded?
2. How does the title "Bush Inc. War" shape our understanding of the image? How does linking "Inc." and "War" constitute an argument? State your answer as a claim. Does the image work as evidence? Why or why not?
3. Each image makes a connection between president Bush and business. What attitude to that connection does each image imply?
4. Are these images prowar or antiwar? Defend your position.

Questions about the Pictures: Cartoon Pair 2 (page 240)

1. In the Ramirez cartoon (Fig. 7-3), what are the concentric circles meant to represent? Who is the figure in the center meant

to represent? Why does he wear striped pants and have a star on his shirt? What answer to the question spoken by this figure does the cartoonist expect? Who is the figure drawing the circle? Characterize the expression on his face. What symbol is on the can of paint?

2. Identify the "talking heads" in the Anderson cartoon. Examine their facial expressions carefully. What do their expressions tell us about who and what they are?

3. Each "head" asks a question. To what issues do these questions refer? How does the final question and answer indicate the cartoonist's perspective?

Questions about the Argument: Cartoon Pair 2

1. Which Just War criteria does this pair of cartoons address?
2. How would you articulate the argument each cartoon makes? Which do you agree with?

Questions about the Pictures: Cartoon Pair 3 (page 241)

1. Payne bases his cartoon (Fig. 7-5) on the cliché of the prisoner in the dungeon. How does he apply this cliché to the prewar Iraq situation? Pay close attention to the details of the picture. What do they tell us? If this were not a cartoon, how might the message in the caption be expanded?

2. Payne and Ramirez both use the idea of the "rush to war." How has the expression been used both in Europe and the U.S.? Are the cartoonists using the term in the same way?

3. In the Rogers cartoon (Fig. 7-6), who is the speaker? How do you know? Why is he wearing military fatigues? Whom does the speaker in the left panel seem to be addressing? In the right panel, what audience is he actually addressing?

Questions about the Argument: Cartoon Pair 3

1. Cartoons usually exaggerate facial and other features to caricature a well-known figure. What is the purpose of caricature? What is the effect of Rogers' exaggerations? Do they create a different effect than those of Kirk Anderson?

2. Which Just War criteria do these cartoons address? What assumptions underlie these cartoons? Spell out what is implied or left out in the argument each cartoon makes.

Cartoon Pair 1

Figure 7-1: *StrangeCosmos.com: "Can you hear me NOW?"*

Figure 7-2: *AllHatNoCattle.com: "Bush Inc.War"*

Cartoon Pair 2

Figure 7-3: *Ramirez: "What's the Rush?"*

Figure 7-4: *Anderson: "Nukes? We don't know . . ."*

Cartoon Pair 3

Figure 7-5: *Payne: "Personally, I'm all for the Rush to War"*

Figure 7-6: *Rogers: " You no longer have to live . . ."*

Writing Assignments

Conversations

1. War in Afghanistan. War in Iraq. Right or wrong? Your college has just sponsored a teach-in on one of these conflicts. Choose one conflict and bring together the experts in a post-teach-in informal debate. This debate may be done as a written assignment or as an in-class activity where students assume the roles of the different participants. For the war in Afghanistan, obvious people to invite would be Falk, Shalom, and Zinn, but you may include other writers from the book who have something pertinent to say. Similarly, the likely candidates to discuss the war in Iraq are Bush, Thistlethwaite, and Colson. But consider other writers and cartoonists as well.

2. Working individually, give a title to each of the six cartoons and be prepared to justify your choice. Then divide into six groups, assigning each group one of the cartoons to consider. Compare your titles for that cartoon and come to an agreement on which is best. Write a paragraph defending the group's choice and present it to the class.

Writing Sequence One: The Presidents' Arguments for War

1. Look back at the Just War texts in Chapter 4. What do they say about just cause, legitimate authority, and right intention? (Hint: start with the U.S. Catholic Bishops but look at earlier texts as well.) What points do you think important for any American president to know?

2. Scrutinize *The Declaration* and the speeches by Roosevelt, Reagan, and Bush. Where do they find the source of authority to wage war? What role do causes for war play in their arguments? How do they make clear their intentions or motives for waging war?

3. Analyze two of the presidents' arguments, evaluating them by the Just War standards for just cause, legitimate authority, and right intention. Choose the argument that makes the strongest case and the argument that makes the weakest case. Be sure that your thesis statement provides the reasons for your decision.

Writing Sequence Two: Preemptive War

1. Explore your thoughts about preemptive attacks. What reasons can you find for them? What concerns do you have about them? Would you always rule them out? What cautions would you give to the president about them?
2. What are the best reasons Colson and Thistlethwaite give for and against such attacks? Where are the arguments weaker?
3. More than likely you knew very little about Thistlethwaite and Colson before reading their articles. Get to know them very well by doing a wide-ranging Internet and reference exploration of their credentials and reputation. Consider how they project their ethos to the audience by the kinds of authorities, language, and argumentative strategies they use.
4. Draw these elements together into a well-developed comparison of the arguments of each writer. Be sure to have an argumentative thesis yourself. Do not merely note the areas of similarity and contrast. Make a claim that is truly argumentative, perhaps one dealing with who makes the better argument and the reasons for it.

Writing Sequence Three: This Argument Really Bugs Me!

1. Choose the one reading from this chapter that you most disagree with. What is it about the argument, position, language, ethos, and/or appeals to emotion that makes you feel and think this way? Does the reading challenge or contradict your values or beliefs?
2. Think about writing a formal response or critique to the reading you selected in assignment 1. You might use Shalom as a model of critique. Be sure to make your own claim—that will differ from the text you are critiquing—or to present an alternative view of the issues raised by the text.

Research Topics and Selected Just War and Peace Bibliography

Suggestions for Research Topics

1. Trace the major changes of Just War theory since its inception. Have these changes reflected the important events of the period in which they occurred? Have these changes been reflected in international law regulating warfare?

2. Do you think Just War criteria must change to respond to development of nuclear and other weapons of mass destruction and to terrorism? Research the debate that has taken place on this issue in order to formulate your own position.

3. The Bush administration's *National Security Strategy* of 2002 (http://www.whitehouse.gov/nsc/nss.html) moves beyond Charles Colson's justification of preemptive strike. Wendell Berry, a well-known environmental writer, examines the *National Security Strategy* in "A Citizen's Response to the National Security Strategy of the United States of America" (*Orion*, March–April 2003, pp. 18–27; see http://www.oriononline.org/pages/om/03-2om/Berry.html). He brings to bear his comprehensive view of human interaction with the environment as well as the close reading skills any good writer must have. In Parts II and III of his cri-

tique, Berry identifies a series of contradictions in the *Strategy*, and at the end of Part III he suggests sources for correcting the policy of preemptive war. Evaluate the fairness of Berry's critique and the soundness of his argument. You may expand this topic by researching other commentaries on the *Strategy* and using them to support your own position on the Bush policy.

4. For those interested in international law: many legal issues are raised in these readings, for example the *Caroline* precedent mentioned by Shalom and the detailed listing of international laws related to Just War. How effective has international law been in preventing wars and, when wars are over, in punishing people and nations that have broken them? You might look at war crimes tribunals, for example.

5. Apply Just War criteria to a war on which you would like to do further research. Determine how the war you have selected meets or fails to meet the criteria both for *jus ad bellum* and *jus in bello*. Do you think a war can be called just if it fails to meet one or two of the criteria?

6. How influential have the so-called peace churches (for example, Quakers, Mennonites, Church of the Brethren) been in shaping the debate about war? Have the secular pacifists been more or less influential?

7. Examine the pacifist position very carefully. What are its strengths and weaknesses? What values might it have even for those who accept that sometimes war is necessary?

8. Since we continue to wage wars, of what use is Just War theory?

9. How effective has pacifism been in preventing war or limiting the effects of war?

10. Not all pacifists are against all wars; there seems to be a kind of selective pacifism like that enunciated by Richard Falk. Which kinds of war or actual wars might this kind of pacifist support? Which would such a pacifist never support?

11. The word jihad has become familiar to Americans because Osama Bin Laden has said he is engaging in jihad or holy war against Americans. Do the kinds of attacks instigated by Bin Laden qualify as jihad? To answer this question, trace the multiple meanings of the term and investigate how it is used in the major branches of Islam.

12. Should wars be waged for humanitarian motives? If so, what kinds of limits should there be on this kind of war? Or you might

set up a debate around the issue or focus on specific wars like Kosovo and Iraq.

13. War always involves some loss of civilian life. How does one determine whether this loss can be tolerated? If it can be, how does one set limits on this loss?

14. Almost sixty years after Hiroshima, the debate still rages over whether dropping the atom bomb was justified to prevent greater loss of life. Take a stand, using the criteria of Just War theory to help you decide your position.

15. Was American involvement in Vietnam ever justified? If not, why? If so, why? Do you think there came a point at which the justification was lost?

16. Examine the rhetoric of other speeches by U.S. presidents as the nation went to war. Do they use Just War language or criteria in their speeches? Look at their purposes and persuasiveness.

Selected Bibliography

These are good places to start your research. The footnotes and bibliographies in these sources will lead you to other pertinent material.

Just War Theory

Bainton, Roland. Christian Attitudes Toward War and Peace: A Historical Survey and Critical Re-evaluation. Nashville: Abingdon P, 1960.

Berg, Sigval M., et al. Peace and the Just War Tradition: Lutheran Perspectives in the Nuclear Age. St. Louis: Concordia, 1986.

Calhoun, Laurie. "Legitimate Authority and 'Just War' in the Modern World." Peace and Change 27.1 (2002): 37–58.

Chesterman, Simon. Just War or Just Peace? Humanitarian Intervention and International Law. Oxford: Oxford UP, 2001.

Elshtain, Jean Bethke, ed. Just War Theory. New York: New York UP, 1992.

Fixdal, Mona, and Dan Smith. "Humanitarian Intervention and Just War." Mershon International Studies Review 42 (1998): 283–312.

Gushee, David. "Just War Divide." Christian Century 14 (Aug. 2002): 26–28.

Hehir, J. Bryan. "Just War Theory in a Post–Cold War World." Journal of Religious Ethics 20.2 (1992): 237–57.

Holmes, Arthur F., ed. War and Christian Ethics. Grand Rapids: Baker Book House, 1975.

Johnson, James Turner. Can Modern War Be Just? New Haven: Yale UP, 1984.

———. Just War Tradition and the Restraint of War: A Moral and Historical Inquiry. Princeton: Princeton UP: 1981.

———. Morality and Contemporary Warfare. New Haven: Yale UP,
1999.

Ramsey, Paul. Force and Political Responsibility. New York: Scribner's,
1968.

Smock, David R. Religious Perspectives on War: Christian, Muslim, and
Jewish Attitudes Toward Force After the Gulf War. Washington,
D.C.: United States Institute of Peace P, 1992.

Thompson, Henry O. World Religions in War and Peace. Jefferson:
McFarland, 1988.

Vaux, Kenneth. Ethics and the War on Terrorism. Eugene: WIPF and
Stock, 2002.

Walters, Leroy Brandt. Five Classic Just-War Theories: A Study in the
Thought of Thomas Aquinas, Vitoria, Suarez, Gentili, and Grotius.
New Haven: Yale UP, 1971.

Walzer, Michael. Just and Unjust Wars: A Moral Argument with Historical Illustrations. 2nd ed. New York: Basic Books, 1992.

———. "The Triumph of Just War Theory (and the Dangers of Success)." Social Research 69.4 (2002): 925–44.

Weigel, George. "The Just War Tradition and the World after September 11." Logos: A Journal of Catholic Thought and Culture
5.3 (2002): 13–44.

Wells, Donald A., ed. An Encyclopedia of War and Ethics. Westport,
CT: Greenwood, 1996.

Pacifism

Bentley, Philip J. "Pacifism: Now More than Ever." Tikkun 17.1
(Jan./Feb. 2002): 15–16.

Brock, Peter, and Nigel Young. Pacifism in the Twentieth Century. Syracuse: Syracuse UP, 1999.

Cady, Duane L. From Warism to Pacifism: A Moral Continuum.
Philadelphia: Temple UP, 1989.

Lutz, Charles P., and Jerry L. Folk. Peace Ways. Minneapolis: Augsburg, 1983.

Murphy, Don. "Can a Christian Be a Pacifist?" Spirituality Today 38
(1986): 100–10.

Miller, Richard B. Interpretations of Conflict: Ethics, Pacifism, and the
Just-War Tradition. Chicago: U of Chicago P, 1991.

Ramachandran, G., and T. K. Mahadevan, eds. Gandhi: His Relevance
for Our Times. Berkeley: World Without War Council, 1971.

Reid, Charles J., ed. Peace in a Nuclear Age: The Bishop's Pastoral Letter in Perspective. Washington, D.C.: Catholic U of America P, 1986.

Waskow, Arthur I. The Limits of Defense. New York: Doubleday, 1961.

Yoder, John Howard. When War is Unjust: Being Honest in Just-War Thinking. 2nd ed. Maryknoll, NY: Orbis Books, 1996.

Jihad

Abou El Fadl, Khaled. Rebellion and Violence in Islamic Law. New York: Cambridge UP, 2001.

———. "The Common and Islamic Law of Duress." Arab Law Quarterly 2 (1991): 121–59.

Espositio, John L. The Islamic Threat: Myth or Reality? 3rd ed. New York: Oxford UP, 1999.

Firestone, Reuven. Jihad: The Origin of Holy War in Islam. Oxford: Oxford UP, 1999.

———. "Conceptions of Holy War in Biblical and Qur'anic Tradition." Journal of Religious Ethics 24:1 (1996): 99–123.

Johnson, James Turner. The Holy War Idea in Western and Islamic Traditions. University Park: Pennsylvania State UP, 1997.

Johnson, James Turner, and John Kelsay, eds. Cross, Crescent, and Sword: The Justification and Limitation of War in Western and Islamic Traditions. Contributions to the Study of Religion 27. Westport: Greenwood P, 1987.

Kelsay, John. "Bin Laden's Reasons: Interpreting Islamic Tradition." Christian Century 27 (Feb. 2002): 26–29.

———. Islam and War: A Study in Comparative Ethics. Louisville: Westminster/John Knox P. 1993.

Keppel, Gilles. Jihad: The Trail of Political Islam. Trans. Anthony F. Roberts. Cambridge: Belknap-Harvard UP, 2002.

Khadduri, Majid. War and Peace in the Law of Islam. Baltimore: Johns Hopkins UP, 1955.

Lawrence, Bruce B. Shattering the Myth: Islam Beyond Violence. Princeton: Princeton UP, 1998.

Partner, Peter. God of Battles: Holy Wars of Christianity and Islam. Princeton: Princeton UP, 1997.

Peters, Rudolph. Jihad in Classical and Modern Islam: A Reader. Princeton: Markus Weiner, 1996.

Sivan, Emmanuel. "The Holy War Tradition in Islam." Orbis 42.2 (1998): 171–94.

Gulf War

DeGosse, David E., ed. But Was It Just? Reflections on the Morality of the Persian Gulf War. New York: Doubleday, 1992.

Sifry, Micah L., and Christopher Cerf, eds. The Gulf War: History, Documents, Opinions. New York: Time Books, 1991.

Iraq and After

Beres, Louis Rene. "The Decision Ahead: Debating a War Against Iraq." Chicago Tribune 16 March 2003, final ed., sec 2: 1+.

Berry, Wendell. "A Citizen's Response to the National Security Strategy of the United States of America." Orion March–April 2003: 18–27.

Carter, Jimmy. "Just War or a Just War?" New York Times 9 March 2003, sec 4: 13.

Grayling, A. C. "Fighting Is a Last Resort." New Statesman 12 August 2002: 10–11.

Kristol, William. "The Imminent War." Weekly Standard 17 March 2003: 9.

Lloyd, John. "The Case for a Just War," New Statesman 16 September 2002: 21–22.

"The National Security Strategy of the United States." September 2002. 3 September 2003 <http://www.whitehouse.gov/nsc/nss.html>.

"Pre-emption, Iraq, and Just War: A Statement of Principles." AmericanValues.org. 14 Nov. 2002. 6 January 2003 <http:// www.americanvalues. org/html/1b___pre-emption.html>.

Stiltner, Brian. "The Justice of War on Iraq." Journal of Lutheran Ethics 3.3 (2003) 3 June 2003 <http://www.elca.org/jle/articles/ contemporary_issues/article.stiltner_brian.html>.

Kosovo

Buckley, William Joseph. Kosovo: Contending Voices on Balkan Interventions. Grand Rapids: William B. Erdmans, 2000.

David, G. Scott, ed. Religion and Justice in the War over Bosnia. New York: Routledge, 1996.

Malcolm, Noel. Kosovo: A Short History. New York: New York UP, 1998.

Mertus, Julie. Kosovo: How Myths and Truths Started a War. Los Angeles: U of California P, 1999.

Orwin, Clifford. "Humanitarian Wars Are a Past Luxury." National Post 15 February 2002: A22.

Parenti, Michael. To Kill a Nation. New York: Verso, 2000.

Vietnam

Arnoldt, Robert P. Vietnam Insights. West Dundee: Visions Unlimited, 1991.

Boyd, Andrew J. The Theory of Just War and its Application to the American War in Vietnam. Chicago: Loyola UP, 1991.

Brown, Robert McAfee, Abraham J. Heschel, and Michael Novak. Vietnam: Crisis of Conscience. New York: Association P, 1967.

Potter, Ralph B. War and Moral Discourse. Richmond: John Knox P, 1969.

White Ralph K. Nobody Wanted War: Misperception, in Vietnam and Other Wars. Garden City: Doubleday, 1968.

World War II

Ferrell, Robert H. Truman and the Bomb: A Documentary History. 2003. Truman Presidential Museum & Library. 3 February 2003 <http://www.trumanlibrary.org/whistlestop/study_collections/bomb/large/ferrell_book.htm>.

Maddox, Robert James. Weapons for Victory: The Hiroshima Decision Fifty Years Later. Columbia: U of Missouri P, 1995.

Sherwin, Martin J. A World Destroyed: Hiroshima and the Origins of the Arms Race. New York: Vintage, 1987.

Takaki, Ronald. Hiroshima: Why America Dropped the Atomic Bomb. New York: Little, 1995.

B

Using Sources in an Argumentative Research Essay

I. Research Resources

Writing an argumentative research essay demands that you learn to do many things—read arguments critically, synthesize other writers' work, and organize and support your own argument. But before you can do any of these things, you must locate relevant, reliable, and thoughtful sources for your essay. The types of critical skills you exercise in reading the texts in this book are also necessary for doing good research. Finding sources may be easy, but finding good sources is often hard because we must be able to distinguish the good from the bad, the thoughtful from the superficial, the reliable from the fly-by-night, and the open-minded from the biased.

Research often begins when you have chosen your research topic but not yet narrowed it or developed a working thesis or claim (see Chapter 3). What you discover about your research topic will help you to narrow your focus and then to take your own position. Students just beginning research in the modern college library have great resources to draw upon. But where should you begin?

There are four types of resources for the research you will likely do for a college argumentative research essay:

1. Field research, such as observations, interviews, surveys, questionnaires

2. Your library (and connected libraries) catalog
3. InfoTrac© College Edition, other databases, and other electronic sources such as CD-ROMs
4. The Internet

Field Research

The information and ideas necessary to understand some current topics can be obtained through research "in the field," direct observation and collection of material in the world. You might, for example, conduct an oral history interview with a veteran to learn how people experienced a particular war. You might email scholars of Just War and ask them their opinions of current world events; they will often respond to thoughtful questions from serious students. It is important to prepare well for field research, so be sure that you have carefully constructed your questions or interview procedure before you begin.

Library Catalogs

Every library maintains a catalog of its holdings of books, periodicals, and electronic publications, normally cataloged according to the Library of Congress or Dewey Decimal System. College and university libraries, as well as many public libraries, are often part of larger library networks that enable you to search the holdings of thousands of other libraries. You should become very familiar with the method to search your own library's catalog and with using the reference materials available in the library. Learn to use the search functions in your online library catalog. Consult the reference librarians; they are extremely knowledgeable and will assist you to do better searches in the library. Remember that most scholarship in the world is still found in the books and journals you can locate through the library catalog.

InfoTrac© College Edition, Databases, and Other Electronic Sources

Libraries subscribe to databases that contain bibliographic information— indexes to publications, citations, and abstracts—and to databases that include full-text services which allow the user to read and download complete sources. Investigate what your library has available and how to access it. Many databases are now available to library patrons from off-campus via the library's Web site.

As part of your purchase of this book, you have access to InfoTrac College Edition. This full-text database, available to you at all times from your computer, includes over 5,000 journals going back in some cases nearly twenty years. You may search InfoTrac College Edition for articles in scholarly publications, journals of opinion, and news magazines. Often you will be able to download a portable document format (PDF) file, which is a true copy of the article as it appeared in print. This type of retrieval enables you to cite page numbers to the original place of publication.

The Internet

The Internet can be a wonderful source for information and ideas for the careful researcher. Government bodies, universities, publishers, individual scholars, and scholarly and professional organizations have published millions of valuable pages on the World Wide Web. Many newspapers and magazines now publish online versions of their current issues, although earlier material may not be accessible or free. Other material available is much more dubious, ranging from personal obsessions to deceptive Web sites that are selling a product or an ideology. It is vital to depend upon the guidance of your librarian or instructor as well as on your own critical analysis in evaluating Web sites. See your library Web site or your librarian for recommended sites when you begin your research.

You will also wish to search directly for your topic on the Internet. You can use keywords and subjects to locate material using search engines such as Google and Yahoo! Evaluate the sites you find this way using the steps below. Remember to record all publication information and the date you accessed the site because you will need these to use and cite the source in your essay.

Internet Site Evaluation Checklist

1. Is the site peer reviewed?

2. Does it give information about how to cite it? Such information is a good indication that the authors see themselves as part of the scholarly conversation.

3. Is there a named author? Who is it? What are his/her credentials? You may have to do research on the author.

4. Check the home page or welcome page. Is there a sponsoring organization? Have you heard of it? Is it reliable? What do the authors say about themselves? Do you have any way to check on them? Are they a recognized authority such as a university or well-known organization? Do not use Web sites where no author or no sponsoring organization is named.

5. Is there any kind of editorial policy or statement of purpose given? Read it carefully so you can judge the intention of the authors.

6. If the site includes text from other sources, can you be sure it is reliably reproduced? If material is scanned in, there is no way to tell if it was correctly and completely added. Look for PDF texts because you can see the original pages and locate the original in the library. You must be able, at the least, to verify the material, so there must be accurate citation of original publication data and/or hyperlinks to original material locations.

7. When was the site last updated? If some years ago, it may no longer be accurate or have been a fly-by-night project to begin with.

8. If it is a commercial site, what sorts of ads appear? Look carefully to see if the site is in fact only an advertisement disguised as information. Ads can also lead you to make critical judgments about the intended audience of the Web site, helping you to evaluate its contents.

9. Finally, there is no substitute for reading critically. You are the judge of the ethos of the Web site. Are you confident that the site is reliable, authoritative, and honest?

Example of Doing Research

Suppose you were interested in exploring whether the Vietnam War could be considered a just war. How would you go about finding adequate and reliable sources?

Look at the four types of research resources above. You would probably not begin with *field research* because you would need to educate yourself before you interviewed or questioned anyone. You should begin with your library catalog.

Library Catalog

Our library catalog at Loyola University Chicago found two books when we entered the keywords *Vietnam* and *just war* in the keyword catalog search:

> Boyd, Andrew J. *The Theory of Just War and its Application to the American War in Vietnam.* Chicago: Loyola UP, 1991.

> McNeal, Patricia F. *Harder than War: Catholic Peacemaking in Twentieth-Century America.* New Brunswick, NJ: Rutgers UP, 1992.

We can print all the publication information and library call number or save it to a file on our computer. We can even email the information to ourselves or to someone else.

Once the books are located in the library, we can see if they lead in an interesting direction. Almost as important, we can use their bibliographies to find the names of other books and articles and can search the catalog for them.

InfoTrac College Edition and Other Databases

A search of InfoTrac College Edition for the keywords *Vietnam* and *just war* together finds three sources. One that looks especially promising is reprinted below as it appears:

> **KERREY'S CULPABILITY: Vietnam & the just-war tradition.** (participation of former senator Bob Kerrey in Vietnam War and moral culpability implied by just-war theory) Gordon Marino.

> *Commonweal* June 1, 2001 v128 i11 p9 Mag.Coll.: 107M0094

Using InfoTrac College Edition assures us that the source has been selected as appropriate for college research. If we need to know more, we can pursue information about both Senator Bob Kerrey and the author, Gordon Marino, in other databases available in the library. Sen. Kerrey is easy to find through many standard biographical reference sources. However, Marino is harder. He is not, for example, in *Who's Who* or *Contemporary Authors*. We can try to see if there is a note about the author in the publication itself, where we learn he is an associate professor of philosophy and director of the Hong/Kirkegaard Library at Saint Olaf College. If further research about him were necessary, we would look for other of his publications and for information about him on Saint Olaf's Web site.

We can also click on the Link button next to his article to find many other sources related to Vietnam. These need to be followed up. *Just war* by itself and *Vietnam* by itself as keywords will locate more sources as well.

The Internet

Using *Vietnam "just war"* to search Google finds 12,700 Web documents. One is a page on a Web site for the 15th Field Artillery Regiment http://www.landscaper.net/peace.htm. There is quite a bit of material on this Web site, but how much can you use? For example, this page includes a definition of Just War that is not credited to an author or source. This is not a particularly reliable source for Just War theory. The writers of the Web site are not authorities and do not claim to be authorities on Just War. What could you use? The regimental history by the regimental historian, who is named, would be authoritative. You can check to see the statement of purpose and the history of the Web site. You can contact the Web master and ask questions. You can follow the links and evaluate them as well. Excerpts from other sources and quotations should not be used unless you can verify them.

Some research topics make evaluation especially difficult. For example, if you were researching World War II, you might use the words *German, WW II, British,* and *Jews* to search in Google. You would then come across the Web site http://www.heretical.com/mkilliam/wwii.html, which seems to have a large number of quotations from primary sources and newspapers. Initially, you might think the site was one you could use in your research.

However, the author's name is given, but not information about the author. And, as you begin to read, if you know anything about the subject, you will see the author is a Hitler supporter and twists facts terribly. If you then turn to the main page and click on some links you will see it is a neo-Nazi site selling anti-Semitic books; there is even a swastika on one page. But if you knew nothing about the subject you might believe this to be objective or at least truthful. Thus the Internet may not be a good place to begin research on a topic you know very little about.

II. Integrating Sources into Your Writing

In general, you will demonstrate your knowledge and credibility as a writer by controlling your use of source material. Remember that you are in charge, not the sources. Certainly utilize the ideas and facts another writer offers, but employ those to support your argument. Do not allow the sources to overshadow your claims.

Avoiding Plagiarism

Plagiarism is a form of fraud or theft in which a writer takes others' words or ideas and presents them as his or her own. Some plagiarism is the result of ignorance or carelessness. More seriously, some is deliberate, such as buying papers to hand in as your own or copying sources and passing them off as your own writing. All kinds of plagiarism violate the basic rules of the conversations we participate in. Inadvertent plagiarism prevents researchers from following up on sources and learning from them directly because sources are not named. Of course, deliberate plagiarism is equivalent to lying to people—never a good basis for a conversation. In addition, plagiarism often leads to severe penalties in both the academic and publishing worlds.

To avoid plagiarism, you must cite your source wherever you paraphrase, summarize, or quote. Both the sources of information—facts, dates, and events—and of ideas must be cited. You must give complete bibliographic data about all sources you use. You must use either the exact words of the source as a quotation or paraphrase or summarize the source's information or ideas in your own words.

Introducing Source Material

There are three ways to use material you have found in your research in your own argument: summary, paraphrase, and quotation. Each has its place. Whether you summarize, paraphrase, or quote, you need to introduce the material in some way. The easiest way is to begin with an attribution:

- According to Richard Falk, . . .
- As John Yoder points out, . . .

Be sure to give the full name of an author you are mentioning for the first time; thereafter you may use the last name only. It can add to your own authority as a writer to identify the authority of your source:

- The Islamic legal scholar Majid Khadduri notes . . .
- University of Chicago Divinity School professor Jean Bethke Elshtain believes that . . .

Give a context or other opening to make sense of a quotation, and be sure that your quotation is part of a grammatical sentence.

Summary

When you wish to state briefly information or an idea from a source, use summary. Use your own words to sum up the main facts or notions; leave out the details. Summary is especially appropriate for information.

Paraphrase

When you want to use information or ideas at greater length from a source, paraphrase it. To paraphrase means to put the passage into your own words, changing the structure as well as the words.

Quotation

Judicious quotation adds authority and credibility to your argumentative research writing. Choose passages that are important to your argument; that are well stated; or that you wish to examine in detail. Avoid using too many quotations. No reader wants to read a patchwork quilt of quotations stitched together by a writer with no words of his or her own. Introduce quotations carefully: do not just plop them in. Quotations longer than four lines should be set off by indenting them ten spaces. If you remove anything from a quoted passage, you must indicate you have done so with ellipses. If you add anything to a quotation, perhaps to clarify a word, place square brackets around the addition.

III. Documenting Sources: MLA and APA Styles

All sources of information and ideas must be cited; you must state what the source is and which part of it you used. The exception is items that are common knowledge, such as, for instance, that the U.S. fought in World War II or that Christianity is the dominant religion of the West.

Both the Modern Language Association (MLA) and the American Psychological Association (APA) have extensive guidelines for preparing papers and publications that include distinct styles of source citation. The styles both require that you keep careful records of your research so that you can accurately cite your sources. Instructors in the humanities generally require students to follow MLA guidelines. In the social sciences, instructors usually require APA format. Use the format your instructor assigns.

Both the MLA and APA formats work by giving a short reference to the source at the end of the passage quoted, paraphrased, or summarized. The reference is keyed to a complete bibliographic entry at the end of the paper, the Works Cited page for MLA, the References or Bibliography for APA.

For more extensive discussions of documentation forms, see the *MLA Handbook for Writers of Research Papers,* 6th Edition and the *APA Publication Manual,* 5th Edition. In addition, both the MLA and the APA have advice about documenting sources, particularly electronic ones, on their respective Web sites, www.mla.org and www.apastyle.org.

Parenthetical Citation

The MLA format requires that you give the author's name and the page number in parentheses following the quotation, summary, or paraphrase. For APA, the author's name, the date or year of publication, and the page numbers are given. In either style, you do not need to repeat the author's name if you give it in the text.

MLA Style

1. Direct Quotation

One major concern is "that America's pre-emptive war will lead directly to the use of the weapons whose mere possession the war is supposed to prevent" (Schell 15).

2. Author Named with Direct Quotation

As Kelsay points out, "with respect to the example of Muhammad, then, it was possible to speak of use of lethal force which was right, in the sense of divinely sanctioned—even, divinely commanded" (45).

3. Summary or Paraphrase

```
After the September 11, 2001 terrorist attacks,
    there were condemnations from almost all
    governments around the world, although in the
    Middle East there was public rejoicing in the
    streets at Americans' suffering (Longworth 19).
```

4. Two or Three Authors

```
The main difference between the assassination of
    John F. Kennedy and that of Abraham Lincoln
    was that Kennedy was "a remembered physical
    presence" while Lincoln was "an image of the
    plastic arts" (Kempton and Ridgeway 63).
```

5. Two Books by the Same Author

To distinguish between two books by the same author that appear in your Works Cited, either include the title in the introduction to the passage or use a short version of the title in the parenthetical citation.

```
Khadduri explains: "The world surrounding the
    Islamic state, composed of all other nations
    and territories that had not been brought under
    its rule, was collectively known as the 'terri-
    tory of war'" (Islamic Law of Nations 12).
```

6. Corporate Author

Some publications are published under the name of an organization or other group. You can use the name of the organization just as you would an author. It is preferable to give the name in the introduction to the cited passage.

```
The Chicago Public Schools Office of School and
    Community Relations notes that Local School
    Councils may set dress code policy (vi).
```

7. Article in an Anthology

If you use an article in a book such as this casebook or any anthology, use the name of the author of the article, not the author or editor of the book.

8. No Author

Use the title in the parenthetical citation if there is no author. You should use a shortened title if possible, starting with the word by which it is alphabetized in the Works Cited.

"We are menaced less by fleets and armies than by
    catastrophic technologies in the hands of the
    embittered few" (<u>National Security Strategy</u> 1).

9. **Indirect Source**

When you wish to use a passage quoted in another source and
cannot locate the original, you may cite the source by naming the
author of the quoted passage and placing the source you found it
in the parenthetical citation.

Burton Leiser describes terrorism as "seemingly
    senseless" (qtd. in Khatchadourian 35).

10. **Scriptures**

References to the names and parts of sacred writings, such as the
Bible, the Qur'an, and the Upanishads are not underlined. Biblical
citations give the book, chapter, and verse, and the standard
abbreviations are preferred.

"They have healed the wound of my people lightly,
    saying, 'Peace, peace,' when there is no
    peace" (Jer. 6:14).

11. **Electronic Sources**

When citing sources from databases and the Internet, follow the
rules for in-text parenthetical citation as much as possible. If there
are no page numbers given, you must cite the entire work. If the
source numbers its paragraphs, then include those as (par. 2) or
(pars. 8–9). It is a good idea to name the source in the text.

Alexander warns that it is easier to list Just
    War principles than to apply them to a
    specific instance.

The Works Cited list gives Alexander's article retrieved through a
full-text database from <u>The Providence Journal-Bulletin</u>.

According to Prados, "There were no significant
    changes in the CIA's intelligence sources on
    Iraq, and in fact there was no real change in
    what the agency was reporting" (29).

This article, from <u>The Bulletin of the Atomic Scientists</u>, was
retrieved as a PDF from InfoTrac College Edition. Therefore, a
page number can be given. If you retrieve it directly from the <u>Bul-
letin's</u> Web site, you will not be able to cite a page number.

The White House Web site's History & Tours sec-
    tion attributes Jefferson's election to the
    vice presidency under John Adams to "a flaw
    in the Constitution."

12. A Television or Radio Program, a Sound Recording, a Film or Video Recording, a Lecture, an Interview, or a Cartoon
These are all cited in the text as entire works. Thus the preferred method is to include the title or the name of the person (such as the director, performer, interviewee, speaker) in the text. The title or name should be the element which begins the entry in your Works Cited.

The Ramirez cartoon expresses a strong pro-war
    position. (The entry in the Works Cited list gives the
    specific cartoon under the cartoonist's name, Mike Ramirez.)

Kathy Kelly inspired the students with her lec-
    ture on working for peace. (The lecture is listed
    under Kelly.)

Mrs. Wayani was married twice and has four chil-
    dren. (The interview with Mrs. Wayani appears under her
    name in the Works Cited list.)

Phillis Wheatley went to England with her mas-
    ter's son, Nathaniel Wheatley, as <u>Africans in
    America</u> explains. (The video recording is listed in the
    Works Cited list by its title.)

APA Style

1. Author with Direct Quotation
    One major concern is "that America's pre-
emptive war will lead directly to the use of the
weapons whose mere possession the war is supposed
to prevent" (Schell, 2003, p. 15).

2. Author Named with Direct Quotation
    As Kelsay (1993) points out, "with respect to
the example of Muhammad, then, it was possible to
speak of use of lethal force which was right, in

the sense of divinely sanctioned—even, divinely commanded" (p. 45).

3. Summary or Paraphrase

After the September 11, 2001 terrorist attacks, there were condemnations from almost all governments around the world, although in the Middle East there was public rejoicing in the streets at Americans' suffering (Longworth, 2001, p. 19).

4. Two or Three Authors

APA uses an ampersand (&) between names in the parenthetical citation but not in the text itself.

The main difference between the assassination of John F. Kennedy and that of Abraham Lincoln was that Kennedy was "a remembered physical presence" while Lincoln was "an image of the plastic arts" (Kempton & Ridgeway, 1968, p. 63).

5. Two Books by the Same Author

In the APA style, the different dates distinguish the different books. Khadduri's other book was published in 1955.

Khadduri (1966) explains: "The world surrounding the Islamic state, composed of all other nations and territories that had not been brought under its rule, was collectively known as the 'territory of war'" (p. 12).

6. Corporate Author

The Chicago Public Schools Office of School and Community Relations (2000) notes that Local School Councils may set dress code policy (p. vi).

7. Article in an Anthology

As with MLA format, use the author of the article in the collection, not the author or editor of the book.

8. No Author

"We are menaced less by fleets and armies than by catastrophic technologies in the hands of the embittered few" (<u>National Security Strategy</u>, 2003, 1).

9. **Indirect Source**

    Burton Leiser (1979) describes terrorism
as "seemingly senseless" (as cited in
Khatchadourian, 2003, p. 35).

10. **Scriptures**
Identical to MLA format, references to the names and parts of
sacred writings, such as the Bible, the Qur'an, and the Upanishads
not underlined. Biblical citations give the book, chapter, and
verse, and the standard abbreviations are preferred.

11. **Electronic Sources**
Give the author's name, the date of publication, and page or paragraph numbers, if they are available, just as you would with a
print source. If no author is given, use a shortened version of the
title. If no date is given, use n.d. to indicate no date.

    Alexander (2003) warns that it is easier to
list Just War principles than to apply them to a
specific instance.

The Works Cited gives Alexander's article retrieved through a
full-text database from *The Providence Journal-Bulletin.*

    According to Prados (2003), "There were no
significant changes in the CIA's intelligence
sources on Iraq, and in fact there was no real
change in what the agency was reporting" (29).

This article, from *The Bulletin of the Atomic Scientists,* was retrieved
as a PDF from InfoTrac College Edition. Therefore, a page number
can be given. If you retrieve it directly from the *Bulletin's* Web site,
you will not be able to cite a page number.

    The White House website's History & Tours
section attributes Jefferson's election to the
vice presidency under John Adams to "a flaw in
the Constitution."

12. **A Television or Radio Program, a Sound Recording, a Film or
Video Recording, a Lecture, an Interview, or a Cartoon**
As in the MLA format, these sources are all cited in the text as
entire works. Thus, the preferred method is to include the title or the
name of the person (such as the director, performer, interviewee,

speaker) in the text. Unlike in MLA format, APA format considers an interview or unpublished lecture unrecoverable data and therefore does not include it in the References list, but it may be cited in the text as a personal communication.

> Mrs. Wayani was married twice and has four children (personal communication, October 17, 2003).

> Phillis Wheatley went to England with her master's son, Nathaniel Wheatley, as *Africans in America* explains.

The video recording is listed in the References list by its title.

The Works Cited and References Lists

All parenthetical citations refer to a work listed on the Works Cited page (MLA) or References list (APA). The reader must be able to find every source named in the body of your essay in the bibliographic listing, which appears at the end of the essay. Therefore the list is alphabetized by the authors' last names or, if no author is given, by the title of the source (excluding *a, an,* and *the* at the beginning of the title).

If you have kept a computer file of all your sources, you can easily arrange them alphabetically. Similarly, if you have kept bibliography notecards, you can alphabetize these. If you have already prepared an annotated bibliography, remove the annotations and attach to the paper.

MLA Style

The Works Cited page is double-spaced. The entries are typed in the "drop-and-hang" style: the first line of the entry is flush against the left margin; each subsequent line of the entry is indented five spaces. A student paper using MLA style is printed at the end of this Appendix.

MLA Form for Books

Author. <u>Title of Book</u>. City: Publisher's Name in Shortened Form, date of publication.

Note that all the important words in the title are capitalized. MLA prefers that titles be underlined rather than italicized, but your instructor might prefer italics for titles. Publishers' names should be abbreviated; use UP for University Press.

1. Book by One Author

Kelsay, John. <u>Islam and War: A Study in Comparative Ethics</u>. Louisville: Westminster/John Knox, 1993.

2. Book by Two or More Authors

If a book has two or three authors, list them in the order they appear on the title page. Reverse only the name of the first author listed and separate the names by commas. If there are more than three authors, use the abbreviation et al. (Latin for *and others*) after the first author, or you may choose to list all the authors.

Hammer, Michael, and James Champy. <u>Reengineering the Corporation: A Manifesto for Business Revolution</u>. New York: HarperBusiness/ HarperCollins, 1993.

Perls, Frederick, Ralph E. Hefferline, and Paul Goodman. <u>Gestalt Therapy: Excitement and Growth in the Human Personality</u>. New York: Dell, 1951.

3. Book with an Editor or Translator

Jack, Homer A., ed. <u>The Gandhi Reader: A Source-book of His Life and Writings</u>. New York: Grove, 1956.

Zohn, Harry, and Karl F. Ross, trans. <u>What If—? Satirical Writings of Kurt Tucholsky</u>. New York: Funk & Wagnalls, 1967.

4. Corporate Author

List the book by the corporate author, such as an association or commission, even if there is an editor listed as well.

Central Conference of American Rabbis. <u>A Passover Haggadah: The New Union Haggadah</u>. Ed. Herbert Bronstein. New York: Central Conference of American Rabbis, 1974.

5. Article or Other Piece in an Anthology

Use the author of the article as the author. Put the title of the article in quotation marks. Give the editor's name after the title of the anthology, which is underlined. Follow the period after the date of the publication with the inclusive pages where the article is found.

Chang, Edward T. "America's First Multiethnic 'Riots.'" <u>The State of Asian America: Activism and Resistance in the 1990s</u>. Ed. Karin Aguilar-San Juan. Boston: South End, 1994. 101–17.

Kempton, Murray, and James Ridgeway. "Romans." <u>The Sense of the Sixties</u>. Ed. Edward Quinn and Paul J. Dolan. New York: Free P, 1968. 63–67.

6. Article in a Reference Book

Cite an article in an encyclopedia or dictionary the way you would one in an anthology (see above) except do not list the editor of the reference work. If the author of the article is given, use the name; otherwise, cite by the title of the article. Common reference books that are published often in new editions do not need full publication data. You need only give the edition (if you can) and the date of publication. You may omit volume and page numbers if the entries are arranged alphabetically.

"Justice." <u>The American Heritage College Dictionary</u>. 3rd ed. 1997.

Kelly, P. M. "Gaia Hypothesis." <u>The Harper Dictionary of Modern Thought</u>. Ed. Alan Bullock and Stephen Trombley. Rev. ed. New York: Harper, 1988.

MLA Form for Articles

Author. "Title of the Article." <u>Journal</u> volume number (year): page numbers.
Author. "Title of the Article." <u>Newspaper</u> date of publication, edition: page numbers.
Author. "Title of the Article." <u>Magazine</u> date of publication: page numbers.

1. Article in a Scholarly Journal

Do not use the issue number unless the journal does not number pages continuously throughout the volume.

Windholz, Anne M. "An Emigrant and a Gentleman: Imperial Masculinity, British Magazines, and the Colony That Got Away." <u>Victorian Studies</u> 42 (1999/2000): 631–58.

```
Flanzbaum, Hilene. "Unprecedented Liberties: Re-
     Reading Phillis Wheatley." MELUS: The Journal
     of the Society for the Study of the Multi-Ethnic
     Literature of the United States 18.3 (1993):
     71-81.
```

2. Article in a Newspaper

```
Schmetzer, Uli. "Spanish, Italian Backers of Iraq
     War Survive Vote." Chicago Tribune 27 May
     2003, late ed., sec 1: 6.
```

3. Article in a Magazine

```
Schell, Jonathan. "The Case against the War." The
     Nation 3 March 2003: 11-23.
```

```
Meyerson, Harold. "The Most Dangerous President
     Ever." American Prospect May 2003: 25-28.
```

MLA Form for Electronic Sources

For electronic sources, you need to collect more information than you do for print sources because there is no uniform publication format as yet for Internet, World Wide Web, and other electronic publications. Be sure to record as much publication data as you can find about electronic sources, including especially the date you accessed the source. Electronic sources can disappear in a way print ones do not, so record your information right away. It is also a good idea to download and save or print a copy of the source.

Publication data you should collect and use to cite electronic sources:

1. Author's name (if given)
2. Title of the document
3. Information about print publication (if published previously or simultaneously in print)
4. Information about electronic publication (title of publication or Internet site)
5. Access information (date of access and URL of the document— but see exceptions below)

The basic Works Cited form is:

Author's name. "Title of the Document." Information about print publication. Information about electronic publication. Access information.

1. Article in a Periodical on the Web

Prados, John. "A Necessary War? Not According to
    U.N. Monitors—or to U.S. Intelligence, Which
    Has Watched the Situation Even More Carefully."
    <u>Bulletin of the Atomic Scientists</u> 59.3 (2003):
    8 pp. 27 May 2003 <http://www.thebulletin.
    org/issues/2003/mj03/mu03prados.html>.

Sometimes the URL becomes so long and complicated that it is difficult to transcribe. In such cases, give the URL of the site's search page instead.

Gonzalez, David. "A Town of Tents and Civil Dis-
    obedience." <u>New York Times on the Web</u>. 1 Aug.
    2001. The New York Times Company. 9 February
    2002 <http://www.nytimes.com>.

2. Article through a Library Subscription Service

Often the URLs from these services are unique to the institution, extremely long, or require access through your institution. In this case access information should include the name of the database (underlined), the name of the service, the name of the library, and the date of access.

Robnett, Belinda. "African-American Women in the
    Civil Rights Movement, 1954–1965: Gender,
    Leadership, and Micromobilization." <u>American
    Journal of Sociology</u> 101 (1996): 1661–1693
    <u>JSTOR</u>. Loyola U Chicago Lib. 2 March 2003
    <http://www.jstor.org>.

3. Article from an Organization's Web Site

"Not In Our Name: A Statement of Conscience
    against War and Repression." <u>Not In Our Name</u>.
    2002. Not In Our Name. 9 Jan. 2003
    <http://www.nion.us/NION.HTM>.

4. Entire Internet Sites, such as Online Scholarly Projects or Professional Sites

<u>Digital Schomburg African American Women Writers
    of the 19th Century</u>. 1999. The New York Public
    Library. 10 June 2002 <http://149.123.1.8/
    schomburg/writers_aa19/toc.html>.

MLA Form for Non-Print Sources

1. A Film or Video Recording

<u>Africans in America</u>. Prod. Orlando Bagwell. WGBH
    Educational Foundation. Videocasette. PBS
    Video, 1998.

2. A Television or Radio Program

"White House Pressed to Stir Revolt in Iran."
    Narr. Steve Inskeep. <u>All Things Considered</u>.
    Natl Public Radio. WBEZ, Chicago. 31 May 2003.

3. An Interview

Wayani, Shashi. Personal Interview. 17 October
    2002.

4. A Lecture or Speech

Kelly, Kathy. Keynote Address. English Dept.
    Shared-Text Project. Loyola University,
    Chicago. 18 Sept. 2002.

5. A Cartoon or Comic Strip

Follow the cartoonist's name with the title if there is one. Use the label of either *Cartoon* or *Comic Strip* and then give the regular publication information.

Donnelly, Liza. Cartoon. <u>New Yorker</u> 21 and 28
    April 2003: 66.

APA Style

The References page is double-spaced. The entries are typed in the "drop-and-hang" style: the first line of the entry is flush against the left margin; each subsequent line of the entry is indented five spaces.

APA format differs from MLA in a number of important ways: Use only the initial or initials of an author's first and middle names with his or her last name: *Adams, J. Q.* Follow the name of the author with the date of publication in parentheses.

Capitalize only the first word of titles of books and articles and the first word after a colon. Do capitalize the main words of journals and newspapers. Do not put quotation marks around the titles of articles.

Italicize the titles of books and names of journals, newspapers, and magazines. Do not shorten publishers' names, although you may omit unimportant words such as *Publishers, Inc.,* or *Co.*

APA Form for Books

Author. (date of publication). *Title.* City of publication: Publisher.

1. Book by One Author

Kelsay, J. (1993). *Islam and war: A study in comparative ethics.* Louisville: Westminster/John Knox Press.

2. Book by Two or More Authors

APA only uses et al. if there are more than six authors. Use an ampersand to connect the last two authors.

Hammer, M., & Champy, J. (1993). *Reengineering the corporation: A manifesto for business revolution.* New York: HarperBusiness/Harper Collins Publishers.

Perls, F., Hefferline, R. E., & Goodman, P. (1951). *Gestalt therapy: Excitement and growth in the human personality.* New York: Dell Publishing.

3. Book with an Editor or Translator

Jack, H. A. (Ed.). (1956). *The Gandhi reader: A sourcebook of his life and writings.* New York: Grove Press.

Zohn, H., & Ross, K. F. (Trans.). (1967). *What if—? Satirical writings of Kurt Tucholsky.* New York: Funk & Wagnalls.

4. Corporate Author

Central Conference of American Rabbis. (1974). *A Passover haggadah: The new union hagaddah.* H. Bronstein (Ed.). New York: Author.

5. Article or Other Piece in an Anthology

Use the author or title of the article as the beginning of the entry. Put the inclusive page numbers after the title of the book in parentheses.

Chang, E. T. (1994). America's first multiethnic "riots." In K. Aguilar-San Juan (Ed.), *The state of Asian America: Activism and resistance in the 1990s* (pp. 101–117). Boston: South End Press.

Kempton, M., & Ridgeway, J. (1968). Romans. In E. Quinn & P. J. Dolan (Eds.), *The sense of the sixties* (pp. 63–67). New York: Free Press.

6. Article in a Reference Book

Kelly, P.M. (1988). Gaia hypothesis. In A. Bul-
    lock & S. Trombley (Eds.), *The Harper diction-
    ary of modern thought* (p. 341). New York:
    Harper & Row.

Justice. (1997). *The American heritage college
    dictionary* (3rd ed., p. 738). Boston: Houghton
    Mifflin.

APA Form for Articles

Author. (date of publication). Title of article. *Title of publication, volume number,* page numbers.

1. Article in a Scholarly Journal

Windholz, A.M. (1999/2000). An emigrant and a
    gentleman: Imperial masculinity, British maga-
    zines, and the colony that got away. *Victorian
    Studies, 42,* 631-58.

Flanzbaum, H. (1993). Unprecedented liberties: Re-
    reading Phillis Wheatley. *MELUS: The Journal
    of the Society for the Study of Multi-Ethnic
    Literature of the United States, 18*(3), 71-81.

2. Article in a Newspaper

Schmetzer, U. (2003, May 27). Spanish, Italian
    backers of Iraq war survive vote. *Chicago Tri-
    bune,* Sec. 1, p. 6.

3. Article in a Magazine

Schell, J. (2003, March 3). The case against the
    war. *The Nation,* 11-23.

Meyerson, H. (2003, May) The most dangerous presi-
    dent ever. *American Prospect,* 25-28.

APA Form for Electronic Sources

Author. (Date of publication). Title of article. *Journal title, volume number,* issue number, page numbers [if given]. Retrieved date of access,
from where: source URL.

1. Article in a Periodical on the Web

Give the retrieval date and URL only if you believe the electronic version differs from the print version.

Prados, J. (2003). A necessary war? Not according to U.N. monitors—or to U.S. intelligence, which has watched the situation even more carefully. *Bulletin of the Atomic Scientists, 59*(3). Retrieved May 27, 2003, from the World Wide Web: http://www.thebulletin.org/issues/2003/ mj03/mj03prados.html.

2. Article through a Library Subscription Service

Give the date of retrieval and the name of the database service. Follow it with the article number if the database provides one.

Robnett, B. (1996) African-American women in the civil rights movement, 1954–1965: Gender, leadership, and micromobilization. *American Journal of Sociology, 101,* 1661–1693. Retrieved March 2, 2003, from JSTOR database.

3. Article from an Organization's Web Site

Not in Our Name (2002). *Not in our name: A statement of conscience against war and repression.* Retrieved January 9, 2003 from http://www. nion.us/NION.HTM.

4. Entire Internet Sites, such as Online Scholarly Projects or Professional Sites

The New York Public Library. (1999) *Digital Schomburg African American women writers of the 19th* century. Retrieved June 10, 2002, from http://149.123.1.8/schomburg/writers_aa19/ toc.html.

APA Form for Non-Print Sources

1. A Film or Video Recording

Bagwell, O. (Producer). (1998). *Africans in America.* [Videotape]. Boston: WGBH Educational Foundation/PBS Video.

2. A Television or Radio Program

Inskeep, S. (Reporter). (2003, May 31). White House
    pressed to stir revolt in Iran. *All things con-
    sidered* [Radio Program]. Chicago: WBEZ.

3. An Interview

Because interviews cannot be retrieved as a source, APA does not
list them in the References list.

4. A Lecture or Speech

Unless the lecture was recorded, it is also considered a source that
cannot be retrieved and is not listed in the References list.

5. A Cartoon or Comic Strip

Donnelly, L. (2003, April 21 & 28). [Cartoon]. *New
    Yorker,* 66.

IV. Sample Paper in MLA Style

Format

Print or type your paper in an easily readable font type and size, such
as Times New Roman 12 point. Justify the lines of the paper at the
left margin only. Print only on one side, and use white, good quality,
8 1/2 × 11-inch paper. Be sure to keep a backup copy on disk. Use one-
inch margins on the sides and the top and bottom of the paper (except
for page numbers). Double-space your paper, including quotations and
the Works Cited list. Leave only one space after the period unless your
instructor prefers two.

Put your name and the title of the paper on the first page as follows:

Name
Instructor's Name
Course Number
Date

Double-space, and then center the title of your paper on the next line.
Do not underline the title, or put it in quotation marks, or type it in all
capital letters. Capitalize the main words and underline only the words
(such as a book title) you would underline in the text of the paper.
Use the header function of your word-processing program to place
your name and consecutive page numbers in the upper right corner of
your pages.

You can see what a properly formatted research paper looks like in
Emily Fitzgerald's paper that follows.

Emily Fitzgerald

Dr. Evelyn Asch

English 106

April 10, 2003

The Continuing Mistake

The nature of war, like the nature of humans, has inspired art, literature, intellectual pursuit, and insanity throughout the course of history. Despite, or perhaps due to, the power of war, it is a phenomenon that seems beyond understanding. The physical manifestations of war destroy many forms of life, and the mere idea of war can tear people apart from the inside. For those committed to the concepts of morality, the action of war is disturbing. It is confusing, complex, and excruciating. War brings out the worst in people. Nevertheless, it remains a consistent occurrence in the story of humanity. Today war continues to disturb the lives and baffle the minds of individuals, as it has for thousands of years.

Over the last several months, the American public has become consistently more familiar with the idea that the United States is in conflict with Iraq. Phrases such as "weapons of mass destruction," "rogue regime," and "preemption" have become commonplace. Throughout this time period, there has been much discussion regarding the actual plans, intentions, and

activities of the U.S. government and other governments. Debates on live television, at kitchen
tables, and across college campuses have been
continuously rekindled with the development of
the conflict involving the U.S., Iraq, and other
countries. Discussions that had previously
focused on weapons inspections and United
Nations resolutions gradually shifted to highlighting forceful methods of regime change, but
all were based on the idea that the United
States was considering starting another war.

The extended period of time for which this
consideration remained at the forefront of U.S.
news allowed for extensive discussion and argument about what action the United States should
or should not take. The question of whether or
not the United States should wage war on Iraq
seemed to linger for quite a long time. Recently,
however, the context of that question has
changed. No longer is the issue of war hypothetical. A United States military attack on Iraq has
in fact begun. The evils that accompany war are
taking their toll on Iraqis, Americans, and others. Due to this tragic reality, one may be
inclined to focus attention and energy on how to
better the current situation, or how to end the
war. Some may be inclined to cease debating about
whether or not this preemptive strike on Iraq was

Fitzgerald 3

or is just or unjust because the fact of the matter is that the United States is presently at war with Iraq. The decision to wage war has been made and cannot be reversed. But the question of whether or not this action was right in the first place continues to be bothersome, like a sliver residing in the heel of a runner.

Iraqis are being bombed, and the American public is being bombarded with reports of the activities of Operation Iraqi Freedom. Certainly, the attention being paid ·to the conflict these days is deserved due to the severity of the problem. Despite the necessary concern for the safety of American troops and citizens of the world, the notion that this is all a mistake cannot be ignored. <u>The war the United States has launched upon Iraq is unjust and ought not to be waged</u>.

Claim (Thesis)

It is important to consider the moral issues surrounding this war in respect to the Just War tradition. The classic Just War theory is an appropriate model for judgment of the morality of war. This theory has developed as a respected policy throughout history due to the major contributions of thinkers such as St. Augustine, Thomas Aquinas, and Francisco de Vitoria. This theory is not a remedy for war. It does not make the painfully difficult decisions surrounding the concepts and realities of war easy. As John Howard

Warrants (criteria for testing the claim)

Yoder states, "The just-war tradition is not a simple formula ready to be applied in a self-evident and univocal way" (71). It does not give definitive answers, but rather leaves room for debate about when and how war should take place.

Due to varying claims that have used Just War theory for support, David P. Gushee says, "a chorus of dissatisfaction with just war theory is gaining strength in the U.S. . . . .The tradition itself has been split apart." The tradition in reality is only a guide; however, it is a good one at that, and its application is beneficial even today. The tenets of Just War Doctrine include many aspects that should be considered before waging war at any time. This idea is supported by John D. Alexander who wrote, "The just-war tradition teaches us the right questions to ask about a prospective war—but sometimes the answers to those questions are far from obvious and remain open to debate." The tenets of Just War doctrine include just cause, right authority, reasonable hope for success, proportionality, and a last resort. These aspects of a potentially violent situation are quite obviously significant and provide a strong basis for judgment in any violent situation. In referring to Just War tradition, the National Review contends that "its moral criteria are, in the deepest sense of the

Fitzgerald 5

term, reasonable" ("When There Is No Peace"). The tradition of classical Just War doctrine has survived and played a significant role throughout history and ought to continue to be considered today regarding the conflict with Iraq.

Considering the current situation involving the United States and Iraq in light of the guidelines of the Just War tradition reveals that the war the U.S. is waging is not just.

Reason I (subclaim)

First the attacks on Iraq fail to meet the criteria for just cause. The Bush Administration argued prior to the war, and continues to contend, that the attack on Iraq is a necessary means of prevention of future attacks on the United States. Therefore, the proposed cause for this war was the possibility that Saddam Hussein posed a threat to American security. In his National Security Strategy, which was released in September 2002, President Bush stated "'as a matter of common sense and self-defense, America will act against [such] emerging threats before they are fully formed'" (O'Hanlon, Rice, and Steinberg 3). This policy supports preemptive war based on attacks that have not occurred.

Specific Evidence (Data)

The possibility of a threat to security is not just cause for war. Susan Thistlethwaite interprets Bush's reason for war as "because we think maybe, just maybe, Iraq might do something we

really won't like in the next couple of years."
Thistlethwaite argues against the notion that a
preemptive attack is justified. She contends, "We
can see that no part of Just War theory supports
a first-strike option." Thistlethwaite brings up
the idea that in order for a cause to be just,
some damage must have been caused to the nation
that will wage war. The U.S. Catholic Bishops
refer to just cause as existing if harm that is
"lasting, grave, and certain" has been or will be
caused to a nation. When this model is applied to
the situation today, it points to the obvious
facts that Iraq has not attacked the United
States and that the threat of an Iraqi attack was
not evident. Therefore, the cause of the present
war is unjust.

Rebuttal
(Refuta-
tion)

Raises
Objections

There are supporters of the Bush Administration who argue that the cause for war was just,
even within the theory of Just War. These people
interpret a threat of possession of weapons of
mass destruction as a condition grave enough to
wage war in the name of self-defense and protection of the innocent. They support what Gushee
calls the "evolution of the historic tradition in
response to the carnage of the era." Alluding to
the potential violence of terrorism and weapons of
mass destruction, Bush's National Security Strategy states, "'We must adapt the concept of immi-

Fitzgerald 7

nent threat to the capabilities and objectives of today's adversaries'" (O'Hanlon, Rice, and Steinberg 3). Charles Colson argues that preemption would be justified because "if Saddam Hussein were to prepare a missile for launch, the U.S. would certainly be warranted in firing in self defense. Giving a terrorist a dirty bomb is no different." Support for preemption is stated very basically as "the cause of preventing nuclear devastation or its threat is just" ("When There Is No Peace").

Counters
Objections

It is certainly possible that Iraq posed or poses a threat to the national security of the United States, and even more so to countries that neighbor it, if Iraq were prepared to use weapons of mass destruction against these countries. The United States, however, along with a handful of other countries, also possesses weapons of mass destruction and is capable of extensive devastation. Are these countries not a threat to the security of the world? Does the possession of these weapons give cause for attacks on these countries? Will the U.S. wage war on every country that possesses weapons of mass destruction? These are questions that need to be considered in the context of the current situation. The new policy of preemption upon which the Bush Administration has acted is unreasonable considering the realities of and

the possibilities for weapons in the present day
and in the future.

Another problem with extending the doctrine
of Just War to include a preemptive attack on
Iraq is that such a violent action will not in
and of itself prevent nuclear devastation. Going
to war with Iraq will not, as Bush suggests,
"deal effectively with these new threats"
(O'Hanlon, Rice, and Steinberg 3). If the United
States wanted to prevent nuclear devastation,
would it not get rid of its own nuclear weapons
and make efforts to convince other countries to
do the same instead of dropping more bombs? The
decision to wage war is inconsistent with the
goal of preventing violence.

It is possible and hopeful that the Bush
Administration intends to make the world safer for
the citizens of the world. This ideal is certainly
one for which to strive. Good intention, however,
does not constitute just cause to wage war, and
the fact remains that the U.S. has not been the
victim of an Iraqi attack. The war that continues
in Iraq is therefore lacking in a just cause.

Reason 2   Another essential component of Just War tradition is the notion that more good than evil must
result from the use of violence which is evil at
its core. The hope for success and a good outcome
after the war with Iraq is doubtful. Concerns

Fitzgerald 9

Specific
Evidence

highlighted by the U.S. Catholic bishops include

that "war against Iraq could have unpredictable

consequences not only for Iraq but for peace and

stability elsewhere in the Middle East. The use of

force might provoke the very kind of attacks that

it is intended to prevent, could impose terrible

new burdens on an already long-suffering civilian

population. . . ." These results are probable and

raise important issues about the further ramifica-

tions of a war with Iraq. The evils caused by this

war ought to be considered under the tenet of rea-

sonable hope for a good outcome.

Iraq as a country is already hurting. The

people of Iraq face grave dangers without bombs

dropping around them. Nonviolent activist orga-

nization Voices in the Wilderness describes the

conditions in Iraq:

> The sanctions, coupled with pain inflicted by
> U.S. and U.K. military attacks, have reduced
> Iraq's infrastructure to virtual rubble. Oxygen
> factories, water sanitation plants, and hospi-
> tals remain in dilapidated states. Surveys by
> the United Nation's Children's Fund and the
> World Health Organization note a marked decline
> in health and nutrition throughout Iraq. (67)

To this already desperate situation, the

United States is adding complexity and devasta-

tion by dropping bombs and waging war. Over 1,100

civilian deaths have been reported (www.iraqbody-

count.net). Also, tragically CNN has a list of

the names of 132 coalition soldiers whose deaths have been confirmed. This number has risen from 68, which was reported ten days ago ("War Tracker"). This operation is, of course, causing loss of life that affects not only those in the Middle East, but also American and British soldiers and their families. Further destruction of Iraq and attacks that will inevitably cause suffering to its people, along with the casualties of soldiers and civilians, are obvious and significant evils caused by the war with Iraq.

Furthermore, the attacks on Iraq are likely to spark more violence against the United States and throughout the world. This is another negative aspect of the war. It is doubtful that the military force used against Iraq will be helpful in furthering peace. In "The Case Against the War," Jonathan Schell suggests that the use of force by the United States in order to disarm Iraq and change its regime will lead to more violence. He fears that the preemptive strike on Iraq, although intended for disarmament, will actually inspire the use of these weapons instead. In addressing the possibility of waging war with Iraq, Schell contends, "No circumstance is more likely to provoke Iraq to use any forbidden weapons it has." If that did occur, Schell suggests, the U.S might respond with the

Fitzgerald 11

use of its nuclear weapons, potentially creating the most dangerous situation the world has yet faced. These negative consequences, some guaranteed and some speculative, are serious evils that do not make for reasonable hope for the success of the war that the United States is waging. This lack of a good outcome is further evidence of the injustice that is this war.

Reason 3

Ultimately, as is absolutely reasonable, war must be a last resort in order to follow with the Just War tradition. The war with Iraq fails to meet this criterion of Just War doctrine. Prior to the launching of U.S. attacks, the U.S. Bishops urged "that our nation and the world pursue actively alternatives to war in the Middle

Specific Evidence

East." But while attempts at disarming Iraq were in the making within the United Nations, Bush was seeking permission from Congress to use force to initiate disarmament and regime change in Iraq (Kemper and Zuckman). This lends evidence to the case that Bush more actively pursued force than peace. Furthermore, there are arguments that even if Iraq was armed with weapons of mass destruction, this situation could be controlled without violence. "The United States can contain a nuclear Iraq," say Stephen Walt and John Mearsheimer of Harvard and The University of Chicago respectively (qtd. in Schell). Schell

explains that these two analysts believe Saddam
Hussein to be a man who "knows that to engage
again in aggression is to insure his overthrow
and likely his personal extinction . . . He is
65 years old. Time will solve the problem, as it
did with the Soviet Union." It does not make
sense that Saddam Hussein would have used weapons
of mass destruction knowing of the nuclear arse-
nal that could be launched on Iraq as a result of
such an unreasonable action. The deterrence of
Iraq was not impossible before the beginning of
the war. Therefore attacking Iraq was not a last
resort. The fact that despite this possibility,
the United States began a war supports the notion
that the war against Iraq is unjust.

It is understandable that people may be at a
loss as to what to think about the current war
with Iraq. War is, of course, never cut and
dried, but always painful, complex, and confusing. It is not surprising that strong feelings
have ignited fiery debates about the issue of the
U.S. war with Iraq. After all, this situation
deals with issues of life and death, freedom and
oppression. These conditions are at the core of
all of humanity and reveal the complexities of
individuals whose ways of realizing these situations differ greatly. Violence has a history
within humanity. There is a strong case for bene-

ficial results of violent actions, but the woes of war and violence mark this history as a tragic one. An understanding of the tendency for violence has contributed to the continuous development of Just War doctrine, which has come to be a model for judgment of the use of violence. The teachings of this tradition are still appropriate in considering war and ought to be applied to the current state of U.S. affairs. Because the war with Iraq fails to have a just cause, lacks the expectation of a good outcome, and is not a last resort, it is ultimately unjust. It was and is a mistake for the United States to wage the war on Iraq that continues today.

Fitzgerald 14

Works Cited

Alexander, John D. "Be Thoughtful, Not Just Rhetor-
    ical: Use and Abuse of Just War Doctrine."
    The Providence Journal-Bulletin. 30 Jan. 2003.
    LexisNexis. Loyola U Chicago Lib. 6 Jan 2003
    <http://web.lexis-nexis.com/universe>.

Colson, Charles. "Just War In Iraq."
    ChristianityToday.Com. 10 Dec. 2002. 22 Jan.
    2003 <http://www.christianitytoday.com/
    ct/2002/013/41.72.html>.

Gushee, David P. "Just War Divide." Christian Cen-
    tury. 14 Aug 2002. EBSCOhost. Loyola U Chicago
    Lib. 16 Mar 2003 <http://www.ebscohost.com>.

Iraq Body Count (2003). 10 Apr. 2003 <http://
    www.iraqbodycount.net/>.

Kemper, Bob, and Jill Zuckman. "Bush Seeks Broad
    Powers: Congress Asked to Allow Use of Force
    To Oust Hussein, Disarm Iraq; Some Object to
    'Blank Check.'" Chicago Tribune. 20 Sept.
    2002. Newsbank. Loyola U Chicago Lib. 10 Mar.
    2003 <http://infoweb.newsbank.com>.

O'Hanlon, Michael E., Susan E. Rice, and James B.
    Steinberg. "Policy Brief #113: the New
    National Security Strategy and Preemption."
    Dec. 2002. The Brookings Institution. 10 Mar.

Fitzgerald 15

2003 <http://www.brook.edu/comm/
policybriefs/pb113.htm>.

Schell, Jonathan. "The Case Against The War."
The Nation. 3 Mar. 2003. 11 Mar. 2003
<http://www.thenation.com/
doc.mhtml?i=20030303&c=1&s=schell>.

"Statement on Iraq." U.S. Conference of Catholic
Bishops. 13 Nov 2002. 17 Mar. 2003
<http://www.usccb.org/bishops/iraq.htm>.

Thistlethwaite, Susan B. "'Just War' Or Is It
Just a War?" Chicago Tribune. 15 Oct. 2002.
Newsbank. Loyola U Chicago Lib. 22 Jan. 2003
<http://infoweb.newsbank.com/>.

Voices in the Wilderness. "Myths and Realities
Regarding Iraq and Sanctions." Iraq Under
Siege: The Deadly Impact of Sanctions and War.
Ed. Anthony Arnove. Cambridge, MA: South End P,
2000. 67-75.

"War Tracker: Forces: U.S. and Coalition/Casualties."
CNN.com. 31 Mar. 2003 <www.cnn.com>.

"When There Is No Peace." National Review. 10 Mar.
2003. EBSCOhost. Loyola U Chicago Lib. 16 Mar.
2003 <http://www.ebscohost.com>.

Yoder, John Howard. When War is Unjust: Being Honest
in Just War Thinking. Maryknoll, NY: Orbis. 1996.

Index

Credits

Thanks are due to the following authors, publishers, and agents for permission to use the material indicated.

Thomas Aquinas, from *Summa Theologica* 2-2, Q. 40. Trans. Fathers of English Dominican Province, 1920.

Augustine, from "Reply to Faustus the Manichean 22, Nos. 74-75," in *The Nicene and Post-Nicene Fathers*, First Series. Trans. Richard Stothert, 1887.

Laurie Calhoun, "Violence and Hypocrisy," *Dissent*, v. 48, no. 1 (Winter, 2001): 79-85. Reprinted with permission of the Foundation for the Study of Independent Social Ideas.

Charles Colson, "Just War in Iraq," *Christianity Today*, December 10, 2002. Copyright © 2002 by Christianity Today, Inc. All rights reserved.

Confessions of a Faith in a Mennonite Perspective, Article 22, "Peace, Justice, and Nonresistance," 1995. Copyright © 1995 by the General Conference of the Mennonite Church. All rights reserved.

Richard Falk, "Defining a Just War," *The Nation*, Oct. 24, 2001. Copyright © 2001 by *The Nation*. All rights reserved.

Mohandras K. Gandhi, "The Doctrine of Ahimsa," in *The Gandhi Reader*, Rev. ed., Ed. Homer A. Jack, 1994, pp. 138-139. Copyright © 1994 Grove Press. All rights reserved.

Majid Khadduri, *War and Peace in the Law of Islam*, pp. 55-66, 69-70, 71-73. Copyright © 1955 by John Hopkins University Press. All rights reserved.

Douglas P. Lackey, "Varieties of Pacifism," in *Ethics of War and Peace*, 1989. Copyright © 1989 Pearson Education, Inc. Reprinted by permission of Pearson Education, Inc., Upper Saddle River, NJ.

Martin Luther, "Whether Soldiers, Too, Can Be Saved," from *Luther's Works*, Vol. 46, edited by Helmut Lehman. Copyright © 1967 by Fortress Press. Used by permission of Augsburg Fortress.

Michael J. Schuck, "When the Shooting Stops: Missing Elements in Just War Theory," *The Christian Century*, v. 111, no. 30 (October 26, 1994)a, pp. 982-985. Copyright © 1994 by *The Christian Century*. Reprinted with permission from the October 26, 1994, issue of *The Christian Century*.

Stephen R. Shalom, "A 'Just War'? A Critique of Richard Falk," Oct. 21, 2001. Copyright © 2001 by Stephen R. Shalom. Reprinted with permission.

Muhammad ibn al-Hasan al-Shaybani, *Kitah al-Siyar*. Trans. Majid Khadduri, 1966. Copyright © 1966 by Majid Khadduri. All rights reserved.

Susan Thistlethwaite, "'Just War' or Is It Just a War?" *The Chicago Tribune*, October 15, 2002. Copyright © 2002 by Susan Thistlethwaite. All rights reserved.

U.S. Conference of Catholic Bishops, "Two Traditions: Nonviolence and Just War," and "Virtues and a Vision for Peacemaking," in *The Harvest of Justice Is Sown in Peace*, 1993. Copyright © 1993 by U.S. Conference of Catholic Bishops. All rights reserved.

Francisco de Virotia from *De Indiis et de Iure Belli Reflectiones (Of Indians and the Law of War)*, Second reflections. Trans. J.P. Bate in *Classics of International Law*, Ed. J.B. Scott. Copyright © 1944 by the Carnegie Endowment for International Peace. All rights reserved.

Michael Walzer, *Just and Unjust Wars: A Moral Argument with Historical Illustrations*, 2nd. ed., 1992, pp. 76-108 and notes. Copyright © 1992 by the Perseus Books Group. Reprinted with permission.

Arthur Waskow, "Nuclear War or Nuclear Holocaust: How the Biblical Account of the Flood Might Instruct Our Efforts," in *Peace in a Nuclear Age: The Bishops' Pastoral Letter in Perspective*, Ed. Charles J. Reid, Jr., 1986, pp. 241-250. Copyright © 1986 by Catholic University of America Press. Reprinted with permission.

Howard Zinn, "A Just Cause, Not a Just War," from *The Progressive*, December 2001. Copyright © 2001 by *The Progressive*. Reprinted by permission of *The Progressive*, 409 E. Main Street, Madison, WI 53703. www.progressive.org

Cartoon Credits:

Figure 7-1 © www.StrangeCosmos.com

Figure 7-2 © AllHatNoCattle, Inc. All rights reserved.

Figure 7-3 © 2003 Mike Ramirez, reprinted by permission of Copley News Service.

Figure 7-4 © 2002 Kirk Anderson.

Figure 7-5 © 2003 Henry Payne, reprinted by permission of United Feature Syndicate.

Figure 7-6 © 2003 Rob Rogers, reprinted by permission of United Feature Syndicate.